T0330194

THE AGRI-FOOD SYSTEM IN QUESTION

Food and Society

Series Editors: **Michael K. Goodman**, University of Reading and **David Goodman**, University of California, Santa Cruz

---

This series takes an interdisciplinary and integrative approach to food studies. Authors critically assess the key topics, controversies and thematic trends across all aspects of food systems and their diverse geographies, bringing cutting-edge perspectives to the study of food. These accessible research monographs and edited collections are an indispensable library for researchers and food studies courses across the social sciences.

Find out more about the new and forthcoming titles in the series:

bristoluniversitypress.co.uk/
food–and–society

THE AGRI-FOOD SYSTEM IN QUESTION

Innovations, Contestations,
and New Global Players

John Wilkinson

BRISTOL
UNIVERSITY
PRESS

First published in Great Britain in 2024 by

Bristol University Press
University of Bristol
1–9 Old Park Hill
Bristol
BS2 8BB
UK
t: +44 (0)117 374 6645
e: bup-info@bristol.ac.uk

Details of international sales and distribution partners are available at bristoluniversitypress.co.uk

© Bristol University Press 2024

British Library Cataloguing in Publication Data
A catalogue record for this book is available from the British Library

ISBN 978-1-5292-4432-8 hardcover
ISBN 978-1-5292-4434-2 ePub
ISBN 978-1-5292-4435-9 ePdf

The right of John Wilkinson to be identified as author of this work has been asserted by him in accordance with the Copyright, Designs and Patents Act 1988.

Cover design: blu inc
Front cover image: Shutterstock/mervas
Bristol University Press uses environmentally responsible print partners.
Printed and bound in Great Britain by CPI Group (UK) Ltd, Croydon, CR0 4YY

FSC
www.fsc.org
MIX
Paper | Supporting
responsible forestry
FSC® C013604

To Livia, Isadora, and their/my families.
For a life remade in Brazil.

Contents

Acknowledgements

During a long career, I have had the good fortune of being able to research the agri-food system from a large number of angles in collaboration with an equally large number of colleagues, to whom I am deeply grateful. The many references in the text to joint publications testify to the importance of these collaborations for the interpretation offered here of the transformations which the global agri-food system is currently undergoing. To all these colleagues a sincere thank you. In this respect I would particularly like to mention David Goodman, with whom collaboration has been continuous since our first efforts (together with Bernardo Sorj) to understand the implications of the 'gene revolution' in the 1980s. This publication has also benefitted from the considerations of anonymous reviewers, which have helped me sharpen up this final version.

Preface

Over the decades, my colleagues David Goodman and Bernardo Sorj and I have thought several times about resuming the analysis developed in the book we wrote in 1987, *From Farming to Biotechnology: A Theory of Agro-industrial Development* (*FFtB*), which was published in Brazil in 1990 under the title *Da lavoura às biotecnologias*. In research for the OECD and for ActionAid in Brazil, I continued to follow how the big agrochemical groups took control over the advances in genetic engineering by absorbing innovative start-ups both in Northern countries and in Brazil, and weakened the historical role of public research through their control of patents on this technology.

In this research, I aligned the notion of the exceptionality of innovation in agriculture that had guided our analysis in *FFtB* with neo-Schumpeterian contributions on innovation. What emerged as most surprising, however, was the strength of social movements in the countryside and the diverse urban interests mobilized around the rejection of transgenics, which led to restrictive measures by retailers and public policies that limited their use, especially in the European Union. I saw this as the reflection of a fundamental change in the dynamics of the agri-food system expressed in a decline of traditional commodity markets and the emergence of social movements to promote new markets – organic, fair trade, artisanal, natural products.

Our French colleagues understood this to be part of a shift to 'a quality economy' signalling an end to the expansion of the large commodity markets that had characterized what they called 'the 30 glorious years' since the Second World War. In the 1990s and the first decade of the 2000s, I devoted myself to the study of these transformations, including two periods of residence in French institutions. It was in this context that I deepened my studies in economic sociology and the French approach called 'convention theory', focusing on the way markets are porous to the interests and values expressed in society and cannot be analysed only on the basis of their internal dynamics. In the book that I present here, I use this view to identify how changes in values in society can promote transformations and ruptures in the organization of the food industry.

This shift towards quality markets, however, was overtaken by two developments that have renewed global markets for major commodities: the promotion of biofuels to replace fossil sources in transport; and China's extraordinary economic growth, leading it to selectively rely on imports of agricultural commodities for industrial raw materials and feedstock to meet the new demands of a country transitioning to an animal protein diet. The implications of these two trends dominated my studies for a decade, including two visits to China that resulted in several publications. My return to the topic of biotechnologies and the agri-food system came with the invitation to coordinate a study on the food industry under the impact of 'disruptive' technologies in a ten-year perspective, 2017–2027. To prepare this study, I was able to count on the collaboration of Ruth Rama, also an expert on the food industry and biotechnologies. Within the framework of this research, it was possible to appreciate the significance of advances in biotechnologies in the period since the publication of *FFtB*, particularly gene editing techniques and synthetic biology.

What was most striking, however, was the integration of biotechnologies into the digital revolution, with the application of algorithms to track and analyse banks of big data, as well as the technologies of machine learning and artificial intelligence. After this re-encounter with the theme of biotechnologies and innovation in the agri-food system, it was not difficult to accept the invitation of my colleagues at the CPDA from the Federal Rural University of Rio de Janeiro (UFRRJ) in 2021, in the middle of COVID-19, to participate in research promoted by Fiocruz, one of the country's major public health research centres, with an inviting, though somewhat clumsy, title: 'The Global and Brazilian Agri-Food System in the Face of the New Technological, Geopolitical and Demand Dynamics' (!). In the framework of this research, it was possible to appreciate the extent and speed of the ongoing transformations in the global agri-food system and, to my surprise, also in Brazil, where traditional large-scale commodity agribusiness monopolizes so much attention. The stimulus of this research and the positive reaction to the text I wrote from people whose evaluations I hold in high account encouraged me to engage in further research and write this book, enabling me to systematize my vision of the new directions being taken by various actors within and outside the agri-food system, always in dialogue with the original approach elaborated in *From Farming to Biotechnology*.

I wish you all an enjoyable read.

Introduction

This book was written 35 years after the publication of *From Farming to Biotechnology* (*FFTB*), written with David Goodman and Bernardo Sorj (1987, Brazilian edition 1990). That book was conceived under the impact of the entry of genetic engineering into the agri-food system and led to a historical reinterpretation of the industrialization of agriculture based on the concepts of 'appropriationism' (A) and 'substitutionism' (S). In this view, it was not agriculture that became industrialized, but industry that, by leaps and bounds, given the obstacles of nature and biology, transformed the processes and products of agriculture into industrial activities. Today, I return to this theme in the face of the opening of a new and more comprehensive frontier of innovation, in which advances in biotechnology are orchestrated by an even more radical cluster of innovations, now under the baton of digitalization. In this context, the industrial 'appropriation' of agricultural activities, analysed in Chapter 3, gains unprecedented contours in the advance of vertical agriculture and cultivation in controlled environments. The possibilities of industrial 'substitution' of the agricultural product, which we analyse in Chapter 4, were identified in *FFTB* in the first single-cell protein factories and in the production of the 'Quorn' protein from fungi. Today, the entire universe of agricultural and non-agricultural products, in particular animal proteins, has become a target for 'substitution' based on varied technological routes and raw materials.

The book *FFTB* was elaborated from an analytical framework that blended political economy, whose influence on rural sociology was growing at the time, with a neo-Schumpeterian innovation perspective. Thus, even if we captured the autonomy of developments around consumption, especially in our analysis of large retailers, the book focused on the potential for advances in genetics to redefine the relationships between agriculture and food production. For some readers this implied a certain technological determinism. The absence of a chapter on the state, which emerged as a draft but was then then deleted, may have reinforced such a reading. Although informed by a broader analytical focus, *FFTB* focused its attention on theorizing the specific dynamics of innovation in the agri-food system from a historical approach. The book now presented maintains this same ambition, but with its analysis anchored in the sociology of markets literature, and especially the complex interrelations between markets, social movements, and politics, as well as the endogenous and exogenous nature of contestations to dominant markets. The central idea here is the porosity of markets to the varied interests and values of society. Thus, Chapter 1 is dedicated to the decisive role of social and societal movements in the 1970s in setting food agendas for both mainstream business and for public policy. And while it does not have a chapter on the state, policies are shown to be instrumental in imposing new food agendas and priorities, as well as for the approval or rejection of technological trajectories, in terms of public health, natural resources, climate, and food security. These changes in the food system agenda, which redefine what is acceptable in food processes and products, are seen to be as decisive as the existence and degree of economic concentration that attract most of the attention of analyses from the field of political economy. As the processes of 'appropriationism' and 'substitutionism' advance, it is hardly surprising that the economic concentration of the food sector approaches the profile of other leading industries. Nevertheless, as we will point out, food processes and products need to be negotiated with the increasingly organized and institutionalized autonomous forces of civil society and states. It is this permanent clash of conflicting interests that determines how, and whether, the frontier of science and technology is transformed into acceptable processes and products in the food system.

Today, there is broad consensus that the dominant practices of food production and consumption are unsustainable. No matter the perspective – biodiversity, pollution, animal welfare, individual and public health, climate change, social and environmental justice – the various social movements, the scientific community, public health policies and guidelines, global conventions, and national sustainability goals all point to the need for a radical change in food consumption patterns in order to contain the outbreak of non-communicable diseases directly linked to the dominant diet and to curb the contribution of agriculture and livestock production to the destruction of tropical forests and to unacceptable levels of carbon emissions.

For many years, social movements in all their diversity promoted alternative agendas and created markets based on values that today are incorporated into mainstream discourses – organic, fair trade, artisanal products, local circuit markets, whole foods, fresh and natural products, clean labels. The guidelines from international institutions and national public health policies have included these values in their dietary recommendations, favouring fresh products and calling for a radical decrease in the consumption of sugar, sodium, and saturated fats associated with processed foods. Many governments have set binding regulatory targets in this regard, and the leading incumbent companies are being forced to adapt. The first major transformations underway in the agri-food system, therefore, result from this defensive adaptation movement on the part of leading companies trying to reconcile themselves to this new regime of low sugar, sodium, and saturated fat, as well as to the substitution of biological alternatives for the chemical ingredients and additives, all while maintaining the flavours, textures, and functional properties of their products. To do this, they are taking advantage of the scientific and technological frontier – big data, machine learning, artificial intelligence (AI), precision fermentation, and synthetic biology – to track millions, if not billions, of molecules in the search for alternatives. Their investments in these routes, in turn, bring the leading companies closer to a new generation of start-ups that draw on this cluster of technologies, not to adapt existing products but to create substitute products.

Among these substitute products, animal proteins have become a prime target. Meat, fish and seafood, dairy products, and eggs and their derived products have become a central axis of the contestation of the dominant agri-food system, unifying the criticism of their consumption as the main villain of cardiovascular diseases, with the multiple criticisms of their production conditions – cruelty to animals, risks of zoonotic diseases, destruction of tropical forests, and greenhouse emissions. Since Upton Sinclair's novel *The Jungle* in the early 20th century, there has been a line of criticism centred on the industrial methods of breeding and slaughter, renewed earlier this century in the publication of Eric Schlosser's *Fast Food Nation* in 2001, which was made into a film in 2006, and which extends the critique to consumer practices. Today, meat, in its double role with soy in the form of feed, is also seen as a major cause of greenhouse gas emissions and the main threat to the survival of tropical forests, key in the fight against the effects of climate change.

Four main routes are being explored in the search to promote alternatives to conventional meats: combinations of plant proteins to mimic meat; the production of meat via cell culture; precision fermentation of microorganisms and fungi; and the production of food and feed from insects. All these options are now in the commercialization phase, but on a very limited scale in the case of cellular meat.[1] Meats are a central focus of the book because the concern is to evaluate the impact of a repositioning in relation to meat on the dynamics of the global agri-food system, and especially the relations between China and Brazil. However, the milk sector is also centrally involved, and it was estimated that already by 2020 around 15 per cent of the fluid milk market in the United States was composed of alternative proteins. The breadth of the innovations underway is captured by their characterization as a 'second domestication', where it is now a matter of the domestication of microorganisms and their transformation into food, rather than whole plants and animals as in the first domestication, around 12,000 years ago (Tubb and Seba, 2019).

3

While the movements in favour of organics, fair trade, and artisanal products have unified rural and urban interests, the new essentially urban movements around vegetarianism and veganism are viewed with distrust by groups that promote family farming or the peasant economy and those who advocate sustainable farming as an alternative to industrial meats. How this will affect the reception of innovations in the alternative protein category (alt-proteins) is not yet clear, but a line of criticism can already be identified, especially from sectors mobilized around public health, that situate these products as another offshoot of ultra-processed and junk food. Actors more identified with the environment and the climate, on the other hand, adopt more favourable or cautious positions.

The most radical global transformations underway in the food system, unlike the cases of the green revolution or genetically modified organisms (GMOs), have been initiated and are being driven by private and public actors from an urban perspective. Food innovation is being promoted and driven today by venture capital-type financing systems that enable the proliferation of start-ups, accelerating the transformation of science and technology into products on the market and scientists into entrepreneurs. In the case of alternative protein innovations, one notices a widespread sense of 'mission' among start-ups with many of their initiators coming straight out of vegan/ vegetarian or animal welfare environments.

The second major wave of innovations this book deals with is what was initially described as vertical farming but now encompasses the broader category of food production in climate-controlled environments. As the nomenclature implies, these production systems apply nutrients directly through hydroponics or aeroponics, thereby dispensing with the use of land, which allows for production in vertical columns and therefore in much smaller spaces than traditional agriculture. As they are produced in closed environments, all aspects of the 'climate' can be controlled – light, humidity, temperature – and the water resource recycled. This is mostly (but not exclusively, as we will see) dedicated to the production of leafy greens and vegetables that today occupy more and more space in the main meal of the day, and a privileged place in the food guidelines promulgated by governments and international organizations. If the villains are the meats, the heroes of the new diet are the leafy greens and vegetables. Thus, the innovations in these two categories hold the promise of a radical transformation of agriculture, food systems, and rural–city relations. Vertical farming is associated with the work of Despommier (2010), who was motivated by a conviction of the millennial destructive nature of agriculture in relation to the environment. Today, it is being promoted by private and public actors responding to the scarcity of natural resources that are now accentuated by climate change.

Innovation is not imposed by the intrinsic potential of technology and may even lead in the opposite direction. As we have indicated, innovations such as the introduction of organics, the promotion of artisanal products, and to a lesser extent fair trade, supported by urban vegan/vegetarian and slow food movements have transformed food practices and the agenda of the mainstream food industry. Social movements, at the same time, in specific institutional contexts, can block innovations as in the case of GMOs in Europe. In this case, consumer mistrust, courted by retail chains, and the institutionalization of consumer 'voice' in deliberations of the European Union, created a movement sufficient to severely limit the application of genetic engineering in the agri-food sector even against its determined promotion by powerful global chemical companies, which are especially strong in Europe.

Just as important as civil society movements for the dynamics of innovation are the geopolitical and geo-economic relations whose interaction is responsible for the configuration of the global agri-food system. Here, a change is increasingly evident in the axis of trade flows, of investments, and of leading companies, from what is collectively called the Global North, to Asia and more specifically to China. Food security is notoriously a key commitment of the Chinese state and one of its most important bases of legitimacy. The most vulnerable component of that food security is precisely its dependence on imports for the animal protein chain. A series of policies is being put in place to decrease this dependence, among them the promotion of alternative proteins. China is also hit by severe natural resource constraints and extreme weather conditions, aggravated by the speed and extent of its transition to become a predominantly urban country, a process still underway. Thus, China is also investing in vertical farming and climate-controlled food production, even extending this strategy now to pig production.

Brazil, as the second and sometimes the first country supplier of animal feed to the Chinese meat sector, is umbilically linked to the future development of this chain in China. Soybeans, corn, and meat already dominate the new agricultural frontier that extends from the Centre-West of the country and now reaches the Cerrados of Northeast and North Brazil, entering the Amazon region. More than just an agricultural frontier, it is the basis for regional development, which covers large biomes in the interior of Brazil, with strong cultural, political, domestic, and international ramifications. The Brazilian commitments to climate goals depend largely on the performance of this sector, which is causing growing concern among important trading partners, particularly in Europe. For the most part, projections for the coming decades predict a continuation of strong demand for the components of the animal protein diet in China and then in other emerging countries. Our analysis suggests the need for caution in relation to these forecasts with perhaps a less dynamic future for both the soybean model and for cattle ranching, which may exacerbate more predatory competitive strategies or stimulate a reorientation to new markets based on new practices more aligned with climate and sustainability goals.

The intention is to analyse the actors driving or opposing the process and product innovations identified. It is not a question of defending or attacking the tendencies identified, but of better understanding their scope, their geopolitical and economic implications and, above all, the challenges and opportunities that these transformations constitute for the global food system. All these innovations imply, at the same time, a radical redefinition of relations between countryside and city. For meats made from vegetable proteins, the fact of not having to transform vegetable protein into animal protein already drastically reduces the demand for soy, which, being transgenic, is also not welcome for direct human consumption. In this universe, many other sources of vegetable protein compete with soy. The fermentation route uses a variety of carbohydrates, and cellular meat uses a mix of nutrients, again displacing the primacy of soy. Burgers and ground meat products will be most affected by the advances of alt-proteins, leading perhaps to a reorientation of livestock farming toward the production of premium meats in more sustainable systems targeting niche markets.

Throughout the 20th century, slaughterhouses were progressively moved away from the cities as part of the 'de-animalization' of urban life (except for pets). A plant protein factory, however, is indistinguishable from any other food factory. Vertical farming or the production of food in a controlled climate may well become a fully urban activity. So-called agritecture is already a branch of architecture dedicated to integrating agricultural activities into the urban environment, and urban policies increasingly incorporate guidelines for urban agriculture.

The book is divided into seven chapters. In the first chapter, we propose a reinterpretation of the development of the agri-food system from the 1970s onwards, which focuses on the way in which an 'alternative' agenda promoted by social movements daring to create markets based on their demands was defensively embraced by the mainstream, albeit in its own way. These forces on the 'demand' side – a conflicting convergence between more assertive and institutionally recognized consumers, large retailers willing to incorporate the new demands of these consumers, and a public sector concerned with a new generation of diseases associated with processed foods – were able to impose a new imaginary (fresh, natural products) against the 'durable goods' (Friedmann, 2005) of the food industry and, by extension, to frustrate the expectations of the proponents of genetic engineering.

In the second chapter, we situate the innovations that affect the agri-food system within the cluster of innovations under the aegis of digitalization redefining the dynamics of economic and social life globally. We highlight the originality of these innovations when compared to the two great waves of innovations that transformed the agri-food system in the 20th century – the green revolution and the GMO revolution. The current innovations are initiated by actors and interests outside the agribusiness sector motivated by urban and global objectives and seek solutions on the demand side, without considering agricultural supply considerations. The leading companies, the incumbents, are also investing in these technologies to adapt their products to new demands, and to follow, imitate, or even incorporate the innovations of the new generation of start-ups. At the same time, the leading companies are responding to the need to readjust their processes and products to the demands of reducing levels of sugar, sodium, and saturated fats, and to the varying pressures of healthiness, the environment, and animal welfare. Many articles and books already address the efforts of these companies to circumvent these regulations or to lobby to soften their impact or delay deadlines. While acknowledging the adoption of these strategies, most of the leading companies are already investing heavily in the new technological frontier, either in-house, through research and development agreements with research institutions, through acquisitions, or by investing, venture capital-style, in the new companies.

Chapters 3 and 4 deal successively with vertical farming, or the production of food in climate-controlled contexts, and innovations in the alternative protein sectors. The intention is not to evaluate the debates about the technical feasibility of competitive production at scale of either vertical agriculture (where the weak point is energy costs) or of cellular meats (here, technical barriers are at issue in addition to the costs of production at scale). In both sectors, the central role of actors (both innovators and investors) who come from outside not only agriculture but the upstream and downstream sectors of the agri-food system is highlighted.

Regardless of these challenges, or possibly even insurmountable barriers, mission-driven innovators, coming straight out of the academic world and creating start-ups that initially attract the support of 'angel' benefactors and later specialized venture capital firms or investment funds (including sovereign funds), are playing a central role. Globally there are thousands of start-ups, and although the United States still leads both in origin and number, they already constitute a global interdependent ecosystem where collaborations and cross-shareholdings predominate.

In a second moment, the leading grain/meat companies begin to invest heavily in these alt-protein companies, and then acquire them or develop their own production. In the climate-controlled agriculture segment, it is more a question of the entry of new global players from optoelectronics and electro-electronics, and upstream players such as Bayer and Syngenta from the genetics sector. Public policies already exist in the European Union to promote these sectors that also count on the direct involvement of states rich in capital but poor in natural resources, in the Middle East and Asia, and in city-states such as Singapore.[2]

China, as we saw earlier, has already become the new axis of the global agri-food system, whether from the point of view of international trade, the weight of its domestic market, or the growing strength of its leading companies. In Chapter 5, we analyse China's involvement in vertical agriculture and alternative proteins in the light of the centrality of food security goals for the legitimacy of the Chinese state. Its initiatives in the development of climate-controlled production involve one of its largest optoelectronics companies, Fujian Sanan Group, active in China and other Asian countries, in the production of leafy greens. They also include the application of vertical farming to pig production and climate-controlled production systems in inhospitable regions such as the Gobi Desert.

China's involvement in alternative proteins and cellular meats is part of its systemic policy to decrease its foreign dependence in this decisive segment of the urban diet. The range of these policies is analysed in Chapter 5 which shows how the segment of alternative plant proteins is expanding in China, first through North American companies with launches via retail chains also largely dominated by US companies, and then by a generation of Chinese companies with Chinese venture capital. The government is directly involved in promoting this sector through funding for research in alternative proteins and cooperation agreements, especially the agreement with Israeli cellular meat companies, worth US$300 million. The search for soy substitutes as inputs for the meat sectors is included in the same objectives.

Brazil of all countries, the subject of Chapter 6, is the one that has become most integrated into the realignment of the agri-food system around Chinese demand in the latter's gigantic transition to an animal protein diet, starting from around 15 kilograms per capita in 1980 to something on the order of 70 kilograms in 2020, for a population that has increased by about 400 million in the meantime. The grain/meat frontier in Brazil's Centre-West region, opened in the 1970s to respond to Japan's demand for soybeans and its own rapid urbanization and consequent transition to a diet based on animal protein, is now oriented almost exclusively to Chinese demand as from the 2000s. The continued advance of this frontier, now dominated by publicly traded agricultural companies and new forms of financing, motivated by official forecasts of a heated demand extending to the middle of the century, is rapidly advancing over fragile biomes and into the Amazon rainforest. At the same time, the grain/meat sector becomes the centre of national and international targets to reduce greenhouse emissions, which provokes defensive and 'patriotic' reactions in this sector, now aware of its strategic importance and stimulated by the anti-environment policies of the federal government from 2018 to 2022.

Our analysis suggests that China is moving forward on all fronts to decrease its dependence on the global oligopoly soybean and meat markets. This opens the possibility of a shorter horizon for this agrochemical and transgenic, monocultural commodity production model developed on mega-scales, and little aligned with emerging trends in food consumption. Brazil, with its 85 per cent urban population, already shares these trends, as can be appreciated in the indicators of vegetarian and vegan consumers. Brazil has its own plant protein companies that are already conquering international markets. At the same time, the Brazilian domestic market attracts the new generation of plant protein companies emerging in neighbouring countries for which the Brazilian market is the main target. The leading Brazilian meat companies, themselves world leaders, have also launched their own lines of plant proteins, and the Brazilian market has even attracted the global leader of these start-ups, Beyond Meat. Thus, 'rural' Brazil may face not only the cooling of the international grain/meat trade but also urban domestic markets that are contesting the values that bet on the returns of the animal protein economy even at the expense of the long-term sustainability of its biomes and forests.

Our characterization of the actors currently leading food innovation and the new patterns of demand, as well as their role in innovation, points to a growing autonomy of the urban relative to the rural. The two major innovations analysed – alternative proteins and production in climate-controlled environments – radicalize this autonomy and allow us to envisage a shift of food production to the urban environment. Since the deindustrialization that has affected large cities in the Global North from the 1970s and the resulting structural unemployment, combined with the availability of vacant urban land, new social movements have claimed the right to develop urban agriculture. At the same time, concerns about diet and public health and climate impacts on urban life have led to the incorporation of food policies into the urban sphere, while a new generation of urban planners and architects tries to integrate environment and food into the physiognomy of city life. In this light, the final chapter revisits the city–countryside debates in a historical perspective and at the same time identifies indications of a new vision of urban life, where values previously associated with the countryside are incorporated into everyday urban life.

The conclusion discusses the current uncertainties on the future dynamic of the innovations analysed. Since 2022, doubts have deepened both about the ability of plant-based proteins to substitute their traditional meat and fish counterparts, and the technical feasibility of large-scale cell-culture production systems. The future of the Silicon Valley start-ups that became global players in less than a decade is now in question. On the other hand, the innovation ecosystems have become more diverse both geographically and in the technological routes being explored. In addition, new international hubs in the Middle East and Asia have established greater autonomy from the initial Silicon Valley impulse. We also consider in more detail key academic debates referenced at different moments in the body of the text.

While recognizing the quality of the research carried out, we question the predominant conclusions which focus heavily either on discourse analysis or the varied ways in which the incumbent players are seen to be formatting or co-opting the emerging innovation ecosystems. Such conclusions underplay the extraordinary results achieved in less than a decade, and the radical implications of mainstream adoption of alternative proteins, even when promoted by, or in association with, the leading incumbent players. Throughout the book we show how social movements have been decisive in promoting a new agenda for the agri-food system and how they have also blocked the diffusion of unwelcome innovations in the case of transgenics. The future of the current wave of innovations will also depend on the responses of broader societal forces, and while some tendencies are already apparent, market dynamics and regulatory frameworks are still in process of definition.

1

The Agri-Food System in Question since the 1970s

In the book *From Farming to Biotechnology*, mentioned in the Introduction, we identified genetic engineering techniques as the beginning of a process of radical innovation in the agri-food system, in which agriculture would be replaced for the first time by the industrial fermentation bioreactor, whose most advanced references were single-cell proteins, amino acids, and mycoproteins to replace meat and fish protein. This would imply an implosion of the great agricultural commodity chains, all turned into simple biomass in multipurpose refineries, capable of supplying, variously, food, feedstock, and energy (Goodman et al, 1987). Sugar cane was the first chain to suffer its effects with the development of high-fructose corn syrup (HFCS) from corn hydrolysis, and the development of synthetic sweeteners. Attracted by these possibilities, companies outside the agri-food sector – Imperial Chemical Industries (ICI), and British Petroleum (BP) – invested to develop these markets, as also the leading food company of the country whose products most depend on fermentation, Japan's Kyowa Hakko Kogyo. New trading companies arose embracing biotechnologies in a bid to restructure commodity chains – Ferruzzi in Italy being the boldest. Silicon Valley start-ups emerged promoting technologies to revolutionize traditional chains, with Calgene leading the way, promising to eliminate the problems of perishability in the fresh produce chain (Wilkinson, 1993).

Some of these advances have become permanent, particularly in the production and use of genetically modified enzymes and yeasts. On the other hand, the crisis that led to a quadrupling of oil prices in the 1970s and a campaign against the health implications of single-cell proteins based on oil and natural gas undermined the prospects for competitive alternatives in the protein chain. More important, however, was the emergence of social movements in both agriculture and food consumption that opposed the use of genetic engineering in the agri-food system, especially in the European Union, where civil society has strong representation. This in turn reflected the fundamental transformations in the agri-food system itself, in which the economic power of the retail sector was consolidating and imposing itself in relation to the food industry and the trading companies based on its closer articulation with demand. In 1999, in the face of negative publicity, the British supermarkets Sainsbury's and Safeway committed themselves not to sell genetic engineering products (Williamson, 2002).

The double impediment of the evolution of oil prices and strong opposition on the part of social movements backed by retail sectors led to restrictive EU regulations that reduced the 'promises' of the new biotechnologies to transgenic seeds, especially soybean, corn, and cotton. Thus, with genetic engineering markets confined to upstream sectors, agrochemical companies became the main beneficiaries and swallowed up start-ups such as Calgene and Agrigenetics (Bijman, 2001). The adoption and rapid diffusion of transgenic seeds resistant to the use of herbicides and pests allowed for a revolution in agricultural practices by facilitating no-till farming, accelerating mechanization, and decreasing the demand for labour, thus simplifying the management of agricultural activity. As a result, a new pattern of agricultural commodity production emerged in the form of megafarms of thousands and even tens of thousands of hectares, on the expanding agricultural frontiers of the Conesur countries, exacerbating trends towards monoculture, the expulsion of indigenous communities and family farmers, and the emptying of the countryside. The rich biodiversity of these biomes was radically reduced, and deforestation became the main culprit for the increase in carbon emissions (Domingues et al, 2014; Wesz Júnior, 2014).

From the 1980s onwards, two types of analysis of the agri-food system became dominant. On the one hand, there was a focus on processes of economic concentration, largely associated with North American studies, especially of the seed, chemical, and trading sectors, but also in the food industry, resulting from the wave of mergers and hostile takeovers that was part of a more general transition from stake holder to share holder capitalism. Globalization accompanied by the increasing financialization of the economy were seen as accelerators of this oligopoly control of the global agri-food system (ETC Group, 2005; McMichael, 2005). A more recent analysis by IPES, 'Too Big to Feed' (2017), focuses not only on concentration processes, but explores their negative implications for agricultural producers, innovation, the escalation of social and environmental risks and abuses, the control of information, and the ability to set the terms of debates. Our analysis here examines the extent to which leading companies in agri-food, even with levels of concentration comparable to the advanced sectors of the economy (electronics, automobiles), maintain a special relationship with demand that makes them more influenced by social and societal movements. In this sense, the levels of concentration and the economic power that derives from them do not exclude the ability of society to impose substantial transformations in the content of its products and services. The degree to which leading companies are limited to defensive adaptations or are embracing the new food agenda in their own way will be explored throughout these chapters. While acknowledging the growing importance of the Chinese markets, the studies discussed earlier focus mainly on the strengthening of the leading companies in the Global North. Only since the second decade of the 2000s has a new generation of scholars emerged identifying the importance not only of Chinese markets but also the growing economic power of Chinese companies on the world stage (Wesz Júnior, 2014; Oliveira, 2015; Schneider, 2017; Escher, 2020), to which one could add the power of the Chinese state and the centrality of food security as among the fundamental bases of its legitimacy.

A second line of studies, led by European analysts, focused more on the impact of varied transformations in food demand (decline in per capita consumption of basic commodities in Northern countries, population ageing, health, and environmental concerns), and identified a 'shift towards quality' characterized by an effort on the part of the food industry to seek growth via market segmentation and product differentiation. What had driven growth in the post-war period – scale, standardization, unit costs – now yielded to efforts to reactivate demand by appealing to differentiated qualities (Allaire and Boyer, 1995; Valceschini and Nicolas, 1995). While the food industry adopted so-called delayed innovation strategies, in which product differentiation is limited to changes at the end of the production process (ingredients, additives, packaging), the appeal for quality opened a Pandora's box, which led to a questioning of the dominant pattern of the agri-food system (Alfranca et al, 2005).

In both interpretations of the transformations in the agri-food system, the dominant actors are seen to have reinforced their oligopoly power, first on an Atlantic axis and then globally, or maintained this power by adapting to new dynamics of demand. But the success of the movements against genetically modified organisms (GMOs), which mobilized both rural and urban actors in limiting the diffusion of new biotechnologies, pointed to deeper changes in the relation of forces now operating in the agri-food system as a whole. The opposition to GMOs can be interpreted as one component of broader movements that demanded 'a turn to quality' that was not limited to cosmetic changes at the end of the production process but that took into account deeper concerns – of health, justice, the environment, food traditions – directed at the content of food and its conditions of production (Wilkinson, 2002; Goodman et al, 2014).

Thus, instead of looking at the changes from the perspective of dominant actors, we can interpret the 1980s and 1990s as the beginning of a contestation of the agri-food system that took the original form of new social economic movements and alternative markets, and which found an echo in the social and political concerns of other sectors of society around individual and public health, animal rights, and the environment.[1] All this happened in a period when the axis of economic power in the agri-food system was shifting to the large retailers. Unlike the food industry, and even more so the agribusiness sector of trading companies, retail is not reliant on the offer of a specific product or commodity chain and, therefore, is more flexible in its strategies to enhance demand. For this reason, retail sectors could commit themselves against transgenics and see new opportunities in the markets being created by social movements (Wilkinson, 2000).

In their work, *The New Spirit of Capitalism*, Boltanski and Chiapello (1999) identify two lines of social critique of capitalism which have emerged since the 1960s: aesthetic and ethical. According to these authors, the new spirit of capitalism results from efforts to endogenize these criticisms, and the agri-food system clearly exemplifies this process. On the ethical side, the crisis that hit the agricultural commodities trade in the late 1970s led to the promotion of a concept of fair trade, first in the coffee sector, which brings together the largest number of small producers worldwide, and then extended to other chains – bananas, oranges, cocoa – including industrial raw materials (cotton) and the craft products of rural communities. A global articulation of social networks first succeeded in propelling alternative markets by linking peasant organizations in the South with dedicated fair-trade shops in the North, and then entered mainstream consumption with the adhesion of retailers, especially in Switzerland and England. For decades, the food industry, and especially Nestlé, insisted on its promotion of 'quality' as an alternative for the generation of agricultural income, but finally submitted to the pressure to promote fair trade products, an initiative also taken up by Starbucks in the food service sector (Raynolds et al, 2007).

This ethical critique was not limited to the countryside, and a response to the industrial unemployment caused by the global shift of industries to countries of the South, which especially affected Black and Latino populations in the poor neighbourhoods of the United States, was the development of the Food Justice Movement, which claimed the right to develop agriculture in the cities as a response to food insecurity (Gottlieb and Joshi, 2010; Alkon and Agyeman, 2011). In the following years, the importance of urban agriculture would be recognized and integrated into public policies aimed at food and nutrition security in cities, where it has converged with environmental policies to adjust urban life to the times of climate change (Levkoe, 2006; Heynen et al, 2012).

In Brazil, ethical movements, in the context of the end of the military dictatorship and the resurgence of democracy in the 1980s, advanced the demand for land and the recognition of the indigenous and traditional territories geared to food production for own consumption and for domestic markets (de Medeiros, 2015). More than a million families were settled under agrarian reform policies and many territories of indigenous peoples, *quilombolas*[2] and traditional communities were recognized (Souza Martins, 2003). The social movements that have supported these claims have increasingly incorporated aspects of the aesthetic critique in the promotion of organic and ecological products, promoting sustainable practices, and developing direct relations with consumers in local markets. Even when entering mainstream markets, these products claim their own practices of 'quality' control, based on participatory certification systems (Goodman, 2003; Wilkinson, 2011).

The aesthetic critique has assumed key importance in the development of alternative markets (Wilkinson, 2010). One of the most successful expressions of this critique was the contestation of the beer industry that had undergone an extreme process of concentration during the second half of the century leading to the elimination of many local and regional breweries and to the standardization and homogenization of supply around a few types of beer. In England, the campaign around 'real ale' (later the phrase 'real food' would be adopted in the campaigns against ultra-processed food) took the form of an organized urban social movement in 1971. By the second decade of the 2000s, the movement had 160,000 members in Britain in 200 local organizations (Garavaglia and Swinnen, 2017). The movement around craft beer in the United States was very much influenced by Great Britain, but it took off after the legalization of home brewing, in 1978. By the second decade of the 2000s, the United States already had 2,700 craft breweries in operation (and another 1,500 in the planning stage), employing 100,000 people and with annual sales of around US$10 billion (Hindy, 2014).

The movements to promote craft beer (with ramifications for other beverages as well), already present in many other countries, condense the set of characteristics of the new social economic movements based on ethical and aesthetic critiques of capitalism. These are urban movements based on consumption and involve motivated (mission-oriented) activists-turned-entrepreneurs who maintain the spirit of cooperation and open innovation but also face all the challenges of a contestation based on the construction of alternative markets (Henderson, 2020). In a similar fashion to the responses of the agri-food players mentioned earlier, leading beer firms were taken by surprise and reduced to defensive action. There have been timid initiatives to redefine the beer agricultural chain around healthy practices, but the craft beer movement's impact has mainly been in relation to the promotion of community and locality values in cities. Mark Winne, in the book *Food Town USA* (2019), shows the importance of these breweries, along with other small enterprise initiatives, in re-energizing neighbourhoods devastated by deindustrialization. In this process aesthetic and ethical critiques converge.

In agriculture, mobilization around new quality criteria was initially expressed in the organic movement, but also extended to geographical indications, sustainable products and practices of various kinds, and the Slow Food movement, again an eminently urban expression where it is the search for quality in consumption that promotes quality in production. A central component of the aesthetic critique was the counterposing of local markets and artisanal production to the global chains prioritized by the dominant players in the agri-food system (Goodman et al, 2014). This orientation receives strong support today in policies and initiatives that seek to decrease the carbon footprint. The promotion of territorial integrity in rejecting monoculture and the use of pesticides also complements this convergence with concerns related to the environment and biodiversity (May et al, 2005).

From this perspective, the most important elements in the transformations of the agri-food system in the last decades were not the new biotechnologies, to which we can add the diffusion of informatics, a decisive element in the displacement of economic power towards retail. Nor was it the concentration of leading companies into global oligopolies, and the globalization and financialization of their activities. More important has been the mainstreaming of the values propagated by social movements in their aesthetic and ethical critiques of the dominant agri-food system. The major markets today, even though begrudgingly, increasingly reflect these values. The food and drinks policy guidelines in almost all countries express these values in contrast to the still dominant system based on traditional chains and especially animal protein chains.[3] Today, the critique initiated in social movements has become mainstream, whose clearest expression was the publication in 2019 of the results of the collective research in the *Lancet* journal, concluding that the current food system is equally unviable from health, environmental, and climate perspectives (Willet et al, 2019).

The new biotechnologies – in the form of genetic engineering, tissue culture, and innovations in fermentation techniques – promoted from the 1970s onwards, paved the way for radically new processes and products. They led to the absorption of the seed industry by global chemical oligopolies and, while largely limited to the seed sector, enabled new agricultural practices (no-till farming) accelerating mechanization and the emergence of the new model of megafarms in grains production (ETC Group, 2005; Deininger et al, 2013). On the other hand, the social movements and trends that curbed their further diffusion were carriers of stronger forces that affected various aspects of food demand and the actors most articulated with this demand. The new consumer tendencies, which brought together key sectors of the food industry, largescale retail, public health actors (politicians, scientists), and social movements, converged around the valorization of natural, fresh, and healthy products with direct connections to agriculture and farmers, values seen as incompatible with the 'transgenics' being launched by Monsanto and other agrichemical companies (Goodman et al, 2014).

While these social movements have invested in the construction of circuits that were penetrating the mainstream, other movements emerging from the nutrition and food engineering fields attacked ills identified as intrinsic to the food industry model and visible in the exponential increase in non-communicable diseases, cardiovascular ailments, obesity, diabetes, and hypertension (Monteiro and Cannon, 2012). There is an apparent paradox here between a growing reflexivity of the consumer and the effects of everyday practices that favour snacks and ready-made meals. In large part, this also translates into a polarization of diets by income and by patterns of everyday life (Otero et al, 2015). From the 1970s a consensus has emerged in the nutritional field on the harmful effects of the main ingredients used by the food industry both for functional and for taste reasons – sugar, sodium, and saturated oils. International bodies – the Food and Agriculture Organization (FAO) and World Health Organization (WHO) – and nation states from North and South embraced these conclusions and launched dietary guidelines to orient food consumption towards the values advocated by social movements – fresh, natural, organic.[4] And importantly, many countries have established regulations encouraging a reduction in the use of these ingredients – obligatory labelling of nutritional information on products – and have set targets and legal deadlines for their reduction (Mozaffarian et al, 2018).

Large food companies and their trade organizations spend millions of dollars on lobbying activities to influence public nutrition policies (IPES, 2017) but, even if they have had some victories, the content of food guidelines both from international organizations and individual states remains hostile to traditional industry practices. Looking through the websites of leading companies, no matter their place in the global chains, one can grasp the depth of their linguistic repositioning. Agrochemical companies present themselves as 'life science' companies, trading companies as nutritional and health companies, and the retail sector as companies at the service of the consumer. Commitments to sustainability, climate, fresh produce, short chains, clean labels, and decent working conditions permeate all sectors. Carrefour, the second largest global retailer, even presents itself as a leader of the 'food transition':

> [...] because paying attention to what is on our plates, beyond our health and well-being, has a direct impact on the health of our environment, water, air, soil, animals and plants as well. Choosing healthy food produced locally and sustainably, makes it possible both to combat global warming and boost the local economy.[5]

As mentioned, the 'quality turn' of the 1970s by food and beverage companies as a response to the crisis in demand patterns, aimed at the segmentation of markets and product differentiation based on strategies of 'delayed innovation', limited to modifications at the end of the production process. In contrast, the notions of quality promoted by social movements, supported by public regulations and global conventions, included more in-depth modifications in the content of both products and production processes in their economic, social, and environmental aspects along the whole value chain. The Carrefour quote just mentioned shows how the corporate quality agenda has been overwhelmed by the combination of these societal pressures.

For many scholars and civil society organizations, this repositioning is merely a linguistic adaptation with no real effect on the practices of dominant companies. Without minimizing the inertia that the accumulation of organizational market and scientific-technological competences exercises, nor the changes since the 1980s that put many companies under great pressure from shareholders, it is important to evaluate to what extent the verbal acceptance of these values has been translated into new practices that can be identified in the research priorities, in the company's organization chart, in calculable sustainability targets, in the content of established products, and in the launching of new products and services (Henderson, 2020).[6]

On the issue of sustainability and climate, the pressures coming from civil society were reinforced with the setting of successive targets by global conventions – the Kyoto Agreement; the Millennium Development Goals; the Paris, Glasgow, and Dubai COPs – whose fulfilment requires new capacities in the elaboration of studies, evaluations, and the formulation of indicators and monitoring systems. These capacities were to be found mainly in the non-governmental organization (NGO) world. We can see here that the endogenization of ethical and aesthetic values that Boltanski and Chiapello (1999) identify as characteristic of the 'new spirit of capitalism' has led these companies to create sustainability departments and hire staff from NGOs or the 'world' which supports them. Listed companies now need to produce annual sustainability reports, which, for their credibility, require a transition from speeches to targets. The large international NGOs (Greenpeace, World Wild Fund for Nature, Forestry Stewardship Council, Oxfam) are contracted for specific tasks such as the elaboration of indicators, monitoring, and evaluation (Perez-Aleman and Sandilands, 2008). Thus, relations between civil society and the business world, which in previous periods were characterized only by conflict, become more complex, involving even more durable collaborations as in the soy moratorium between the large global trading companies and Greenpeace and Friends of the Earth to control deforestation in the Brazilian soybean chain (Wilkinson, 2011).

Even though they may be fragile components and the first targets for cutbacks in times of contention, the sustainability sectors of companies have progressively ceased to be imposed as appendages. It is possible to identify a colonization process through which sustainability goals gradually permeate the companies' activities. It is, of course, an unequal process, with emphasis on companies listed on the stock exchange and with high visibility in relation to the final consumer. Several global companies are still privately held (Mars, Cargill) and subject to fewer transparency rules, while others, located upstream in the chains, may rely more on the rhetoric of discourse and on their lower visibility. On the other hand, as we have indicated previously, it is notable how leading actors in all links of the chain highlight their sustainability credentials. The key here, perhaps, is the centrality of commitment in the form of targets that require monitoring systems, made possible by increasingly more sophisticated techniques for tracking all links in the chains (Ponte, 2019).

It would be a mistake, therefore, to reduce the position of leading companies to greenwashing responses. Even if each one responds in its own way, it is not simply a matter of speeches nor of social actions disconnected from the company's day-to-day activities. Notions of sustainability shape the practices of companies and their systems of accountability. It is important, on the other hand, to understand that companies are, or were, responding to an imposed agenda. Thus, they adopt mostly defensive positions and always less than the demands coming from different segments of society. There is a tension between the values, objects, and actors that make up a market and those who are excluded from or negatively affected by this market. Conflict, in this sense, is intrinsic to the formation of economic spaces and is central to its dynamics over time, and although truces and agreements may exist, the spaces remain antagonistic, to the benefit of both parties (Callon, 1998; Fligstein, 2001).[7]

Companies do not always position themselves on the defensive and, especially at times of radical advances on the scientific and technological frontiers, agendas are recaptured, as may be happening in the case of innovations that are affecting animal protein chains and climate-controlled agriculture, to be examined in more detail in subsequent chapters. Here, however, we want to focus on the impact of varying societal pressures for the product development and research priorities being adopted by leading companies.

In terms of impacts on their product lines, the initial response of companies has been to launch additional, 'free from' or 'low levels of' labels targeting the three ingredients seen as the principal villains of individual and public health – sugar, sodium, and saturated fats – and more generally, also aiming to promote lower-calorie products. Food allergies have also become a key concern, reinforced by stricter regulations, and the same 'free of'[8] strategy has been extended to gluten in cereals and lactose in the dairy chain. In large part, this food industry response to criticism dovetailed with the more general strategy identified earlier of limiting innovations to the final stages of the production process (Rama, 2008).

The misgivings and criticisms linked to the use of additives include both natural ingredients subject to industrial processes considered harmful (hydrolysis, hydrogenation) and chemical additives (to which chemical residues from agricultural practices that increasingly rely on pesticides, baptized as 'agropoisons' by social movements, are also associated). Even though approved by the WHO, several of these additives are increasingly seen as sources of intestinal diseases and allergies, if not of more serious diseases.

When to these criticisms are added demands around the environment, climate, and the valuing of the 'natural', 'fresh', and 'local', responses limiting innovations to the final stages of the production process became increasingly difficult for leading food companies. In the second decade of the millennium these broader notions were condensed into the ideas of 'clean labels' and 'whole foods' (which became the name of a new retail chain in the United States) and have been adopted by leading companies (Food Manufacturing, 2018).

If initial responses were limited to eliminating or reducing the use of these ingredients, the breadth of criticism and the acceptance of the clean label designation has led companies to search for natural substitutes for ingredients and additives deemed harmful. The big traders, ADM, Bunge, Cargill, Dreyfus, and new companies like Ingredion, are also major suppliers of ingredients to the food industry. This has initiated cooperation in research and in the promotion of joint ventures between food companies and traders, often in partnership with big data, molecular biology, and synthetic biology start-ups, in the search for alternative ingredients and additives. As examples, ADM, Cargill, and Bayer all have partnerships with Ginkgo Bioworks, a newly listed synthetic biology company valued at US$15 billion, specializing in the identification of new molecules and aiming to become a platform for the development of these products (Regalado, 2021).

When we talk generically about the food industry, we include the beverage drinks sector, where 'soft drinks' have been the most targeted. The replacement of sugar with HFCS was the first response. More recently, Coca-Cola has partnered with Cargill and high-tech company Evolva Holding to perfect the use of the natural sweetener Stevia.[9]

Meanwhile, for the first time since the consolidation of the food industry in the first decades of the 20th century, a new generation of companies has begun to emerge contesting niches, such as Ben & Jerry's in the ice cream segment founded in 1978, and Hain Celestial, created in 1993, challenging a whole set of leading brands based on a broad portfolio of organic and 'natural' products. The transformation of the relationship between leading companies and small innovative competitors can be appreciated in a comparison between four generations of companies operating in the ice cream and yoghurt segments: Häagen Dazs, Ben & Jerry's, Chobani, and Snow Monkey.[10]

Häagen Dazs emerged in the Bronx borough of New York in 1959 as a strategy to survive the price war of the big players in the 1950s by a small traditional company, Senator Frozen Products, established by immigrants from Central Europe in the 1920s. It was a 'super premium' product, a dense ice cream with higher use of butter fats but without the use of emulsifiers or stabilizers, with three traditional flavours – vanilla, chocolate, and coffee. The name, invented and meaningless, was chosen because of its exotic evocation of Scandinavia and especially Denmark, the country par excellence of milk. Häagen Dazs conquered its market shop by shop, being sold in a separate gondola at the entrance, and in the 1980s it was bought by Pillsbury.[11]

In the meantime, a new start-up, Ben & Jerry's, created by industry outsiders was competing with Häagen Dazs in the premium category. Launched in a shop of its own, the brand was promoted by publicity stunts, social commitments (against the use of the growth hormone rBGH (recombinant bovine growth hormone), support for war veterans, and for children), and a strong identification with its consumers. Pillsbury had tried to block its entry into large-scale distribution but pulled back in the face of the mobilization of Ben & Jerry's consumer base. In 2000, Ben & Jerry's was bought by Unilever, but with a commitment to maintain its identity through an independent board of directors. General Mills, on the other hand, bought Pillsbury, and then merged its North American operations with Nestlé, which became the owner of Häagen Dazs. For over a decade Häagen Dazs's focus was on product innovation (ice cream bars, dulche de leche flavour, gelato). Increasingly, however, it has incorporated wider issues – bee protection, the phasing out GMOs, the elimination of plastic spoons, as well as its proposed complete recycling by 2025. Unilever retained Ben & Jerry's original profile from the outset – alignment with the world of 'rock', campaigns to vote in elections, creation of political brands, refusal to sell in the occupied Palestinian territories, support for fair trade, and launching 'non-dairy' options.[12] Both Häagen Dazs and Ben & Jerry's were created using their own or family and friends' funds (what we would today call angel funds), and their success was also based on their own efforts, being acquired by leading companies when they had already consolidated their brands. These innovations were introduced by outsiders and involved radically new product designs as well as innovations in marketing, but they were not based on new knowledge and technologies.

Chobani, established in 2005, also by an outsider, Hamdi Ulukay, a Turkish immigrant in the United States, did for the yoghurt segment what Häagen Dazs and Ben & Jerry's had done for ice cream. Based on his knowledge of yoghurt from an Anatolian childhood but now with formal funding from a Small Business Administration loan, Ulukay occupied a closed Kraft factory, incorporated its former employees, and launched his Greek yoghurt with radically new texture and taste. It was a smash hit, and Greek yoghurt went

21

from 1 per cent to 50 per cent of the segment as a whole in the United States between 2007 and 2013. After expanding to Australia and Asia, Chobani secured a US$700 million investment from Texas Pacific Group, a private equity group, to build a new factory, the world's largest, in Idaho. By 2017, Chobani had already overtaken Yoplait, the world's second largest producer of yoghurt.[13]

Chobani stands out for having become a leading global company without being acquired by an established company, a possibility given the new forms of financing. It also stands out, and in this sense follows a trajectory initiated by Ben & Jerry's, for its commitment to social causes – support to war veterans, the distribution of shares to employees, publicity in favour of the gay community – and the development of non-dairy and vegan products.[14]

In 2016, Chobani set up the Chobani Food Incubator, to help new entrants in the food sector with non-equity funding and in 2018 added the Chobani Incubator Food Technology Residence, a program that has already helped several start-ups.[15] Thus, a fourth generation of start-ups was born, but now under the umbrella of a company that has achieved a leadership position on its own. One example is Snow Monkey, the start-up created at Boston University's Entrepreneurial Centre and which was deemed by the CEO of Chobani as having 'the potential to be as disruptive to the ice cream category as Chobani was to [...] yogurt' (Stengel, 2008). Within the university environment, the product was handcrafted by athlete Rachel Geicke to combine indulgence with health and energy and benefited from inputs from food scientists. At the university the start-up won the support of two backers worth US$21,000 and then raised some US$40,000 on a crowdfunding Kickstarter within 24 hours. It was later welcomed by Chobani to join its second incubator programme. In 2017, sales were initiated in ten 'Mamas & Papas'-type shops, which quickly grew to 250. Four years later it was selling in 3,500 sales points at Kroger, Albertsons, and Whole Foods outlets. The future of Snow Monkey is still uncertain and the COVID-19 period made it difficult for the brand to consolidate, but it exemplifies well the evolving innovation ecosystem in food. As with earlier generations, Snow Monkey was created by outsiders to the corporate world of leading companies but was quickly integrated into the new technological and financial infrastructure supporting innovation that includes new leading companies like Chobani (Stengel, 2018).

Thus, in the yoghurt and ice cream segments, new companies, internalizing in several combinations the aesthetic and ethical values we have identified, managed to challenge leaders of the sector and transformed both the profile of products and business behaviour. Other firms have emerged to challenge the dominant players and products both within the dairy sector and in other categories. Many of these have been acquired by the leading firms but now with the recognition that the original brand and its image needed to be maintained. This movement accelerated from the second decade of the 2000s, with the emergence of WhiteWave Foods in the dairy sector in 2013, bought in 2016 by Danone (Watrous, 2017). Other start-ups bought by leading companies include: Bolthouse, which started a new category of fresh packaged products, in addition to Plum Organics, by Campbell famous for its soups; Annie's, an organic and natural products company, along with Food Should Taste Good and Epic Provisions by General Mills; Boulder Brands, a natural food company, by Conagra; Brookside and Krave Jerky, by Hershey; and Enjoy Life, by Mondelez. In all these cases, the innovative proposition of the acquired companies was recognized in the maintenance of separate management and brands (Loria, 2017).

The most emblematic of these firms was Hampton Creek (which remains independent under the new name, Eat Just), which will be discussed more fully in Chapter 4. Founded in 2011 with backing from Khosla Ventures and Founders Fund, its initial goal was to develop plant-based alternatives to foods that used eggs, with the main target being the mayonnaise market dominated by Unilever. Its first products were launched in 2013, Beyond Eggs and Just Mayo, prompting Unilever to challenge in court the use of the word 'Mayo'. Subsequently Unilever dropped the lawsuit and launched its own egg-free mayonnaise product.[16] Later, the company focused on plant-based and cell-cultivated alternatives to meats to be examined in Chapter 4.[17]

Perhaps the most ambitious of all these challenger firms was Hain Celestial, set up in 1993 with the aim of offering a 'natural' and 'organic' alternative to the products of the leading firms. With no competitors, Hain Celestial enjoyed extraordinary growth of 12 per cent per annum based on a strategy of acquiring new companies in each niche. Within a few years it had a portfolio of 60 acquisitions and a turnover of US$2 billion, with 40 per cent of these sales being international. It was in this context that the leading companies started to react by buying start-ups in various niches as indicated earlier. The entry of the leading companies into these 'natural' and 'organic' segments, as well as their strategies, which will be analysed more closely in Chapter 2, of incubating start-ups, has begun to undermine the sales and profitability of Hain Celestial, whose future under new leadership remains uncertain.[18]

The success of the start-ups, and especially Hain Celestial, would not have been possible without the great transformations in retailing in this same period, and the emergence of supermarket chains, such as Whole Foods in the United States, based on the new trends identified by the leading market consultants Neilsen and Euromonitor and a countless number of other surveys in the same vein.

As exemplified in the case of transgenics, the competencies of the retail market lie in its capacity to accompany demand and to articulate the logistics between supply and demand, without any commitment to specific supply chains. At the same time, there is a permanent conflict with the oligopoly power that the leading companies of the food industry exert over supply. The entry of new products that challenge the dominant brands opens an opportunity for retailers to reverse this pressure. In turn, the funding ecosystem allows start-ups to achieve a scale of operations and the financial strength to occupy the shelves of national and global retail chains, making it possible for their brands to become established in mainstream markets. Just Mayo from Hampton Creek in the United States, discussed earlier, and Fazenda Futuro in Brazil, whose vegetable meats and fish were present in 12,000 outlets by 2021 just two years after its creation, are only two of hundreds of other companies whose access to market has been enabled by the emergence of this innovation ecosystem, a theme to be analysed in Chapter 2. Virtual platforms are also allowing start-ups to come into direct contact with consumers in the form of online sales. In this modality, start-ups can avoid negotiations with traditional retail, launch the brand more quickly, calibrate supply, and develop a precise and dynamic monitoring of the evolution of demand with opportunities for feedback and just-in-time adjustments. On the other hand, there are strong financial barriers to ranking high on search engines, a precondition for gaining visibility (Price, 2021).

Analysts correctly point to the high concentration of the agri-food system, which has clearly accelerated with globalization (Howard and Hendrickson, 2020). They also draw attention to the way in which leading companies have adapted to new patterns of demand by superficially modifying their products and aligning their discourses with the demands of healthiness and the environment (IPES, 2022). They point equally to the increase in non-communicable diseases associated with unhealthy diets resulting from the consumption of food industry products (Monteiro and Cannon, 2012). Nevertheless, our analysis suggests that the pressures coming from social movements, NGOs, government regulations and guidelines, and international conventions, as well as the emergence of a new generation of companies based on these same demands, are forcing real transformations in the practices of leading companies. In this sense, we can understand the new strategies of the leading companies, at least initially, as being defensive reactions that lead them to take on these diverse agendas, even begrudgingly. It is also possible that given the opportunities opened by these innovation frontiers, leading companies now glimpse the gains from appropriating this agenda in their own way. One indication of this is the construction of an infrastructure of venture capital and incubators/accelerators on the part of the leading companies, which will be analysed in Chapter 2. On the other hand, we saw how the adoption of transgenics in the 1990s was contested and its appropriation largely limited to the seeds and yeast/enzyme sectors. The future of the current wave of innovations and the degree to which they will be incorporated into the products and services of the food system are uncertain and have not yet been sifted by an increasingly discerning and mobilized demand.

2

A New Pattern of Innovation
in the Agri-Food System

In Chapter 1, we concluded that the new agenda being imposed on the agri-food system was born from a combination of pressures from civil society, the scientific community, government regulations, and new companies entering the food industry. Dominant companies initially limited themselves to small adaptations and to the incorporation of superficial aspects of the agenda's discourse. Today, however these companies are embracing more radical product innovations based on the new scientific and technological advances and appropriating the agri-food agenda in their own way.

We can appreciate the originality of the current wave of innovation if we compare it with the two great innovations that shook the agri-food system in the 20th century. It is important to recognize, however, that there is continuity between the three waves in the increasing control of biological and genetic processes. The first wave involved a combination of plant and animal breeding techniques with the growing influence of the Mendelian approach to identifying individual genes as responsible for specific characteristics. On this basis, the US government, together with the Rockefeller Foundation, developed cooperative programs with Mexico in the 1940s to develop high-yielding varieties of maize and wheat when planted with irrigation, synthetic fertilizer, and chemical pesticides. The same techniques were applied in Asia during the 1960s, now in the Cold War context, making countries like India and Pakistan self-sufficient and even exporters of these grains, in much the same way as Mexico a decade and a half earlier. The results on the African continent were less successful due to poor adaptation of the varieties and the lack of infrastructure and human capacity. It was not until the 1970s that more adapted rice varieties were developed. The diffusion of these innovations requires physical infrastructure (irrigation, roads, electricity), breeders and extension workers, and credit systems for the purchase of inputs. To this end, the International Maize and Wheat Improvement Centre (CIMMYT) was created in Mexico and the International Rice Research Institute (IRRI) in the Philippines. These initiatives were promoted by the public sectors in different countries, led by the United States acting in partnership with the Ford and Rockefeller Foundations. As a by-product, however, a private seed industry emerged based on the industrial secrecy of hybridization techniques – Pioneer in the United States, Limagrain in France, and Agroceres in Brazil – all dedicated to the production and commercialization of hybrid corn (Glaeser, 1987; Briney, 2020).

There is much discussion about the degree to which Mendel's genetic approach replaced or complemented the practices of plant breeders, but in the academic community the genetic approach definitively took hold with the deciphering of DNA in the 1950s and even more so with the identification of the functions of individual genes, as well as the ability in the 1970s to transfer and express genes from one species to another (Charnley and Radick, 2013). The axes of innovation from then on were the universities and start-ups of academics becoming entrepreneurs with the support of venture capital. Patents on genetic engineering processes replaced industrial secrecy, which had prevailed in the case of hybrid seeds and the protection of varieties that was granted to breeders (International Union for the Protection of New Varieties of Plants, UPOV). For a brief period, it looked as if these start-ups might become the stars of a new generation of transgenic seeds and agricultural products, but the problems of scale and the limitations of the new financial ecosystem of venture capital led to their acquisition by the big seed and agrochemical companies. Their mastery of genetic engineering techniques and the fact that the most promising applications, based on the ability to transfer and express only individual genes, were resistance to weeds and pests led to the acquisition also of the independent seed companies, even national leaders such as Pioneer and DeKalb in the United States and Agroceres in Brazil, by the agrochemical giants Monsanto, DuPont, Bayer, and BASF. In contrast to the green revolution led by the public sector, it was these private companies that defined the priorities of the transgenic era (Kenney, 1988; Juma, 1989; Schurman and Kelso, 2003; Fukuda-Parr, 2007).

In the face of the enormous transformations in productivity brought about by the green revolution in Latin America and Asia, initial criticisms focused more on its impacts on the concentration of agricultural production in large monocultures, the consequent agrarian concentration, and the expulsion of small producers. With its consolidation, the negative effects of the integration of agriculture into credit/debt circuits and later the harmful impacts of chemical inputs for agricultural producers and the environment were highlighted. Today the term 'green revolution' has become the hallmark of everything that is objectionable in agricultural modernization. Opposition to the green revolution came from forces linked to rural areas and focused on the impacts for agriculture, in stark contrast to the opposition to transgenics, which, even though it involved 'rural' forces, was and continues to be fundamentally an urban movement focusing on their unacceptability from a consumer point of view (Patel, 2012).

These two waves of innovation had, as protagonists, actors – public in the first case and private in the second – linked to the rural world and committed to transforming the conditions of agricultural supply without questioning the content of this supply. Both waves continue, with the extension of the green revolution to Africa, on the one hand, and on the other, proposals to extend the benefits of genetically modified organisms (GMOs) to food security issues, as in the case of golden rice, which inserts a gene to combat vitamin A deficiency.[1] In the 2000s, in continuity with the tradition of the green revolution, the Bill & Melinda Gates Foundation replaced the Rockefeller Foundation as the major funder of agricultural research (Malkan, 2020). A paper published by Chinese researchers at the Chinese Academy of Sciences proposed extending the green revolution to soybeans based on the new advances in genomics and gene editing (Liu et al, 2020). It should not be overlooked that China's rapid response to Deng Xiaoping's reforms from 1978 onwards was largely enabled by a domestic 'green revolution' promoted by China over the previous decade (Aglietta and Bai, 2013).

The originality of the wave of agri-food innovation that emerges at the turn of the millennium, on the other hand, is its urban perspective. It is not the transformation of agriculture that is in question, but food, whose links with agriculture, including livestock farming, are seen to be the main problem. In the terms of our book, *From Farming to Biotechnology*, we are facing an unprecedented radicalization of both appropriationism (climate-controlled food production) and industrial substitutionism (cellular protein and precision fermentation). The new innovation ecosystem, only embryonic in the 1970s, is now fully institutionalized, composed of academic/entrepreneurial start-ups backed by venture and corporate capital, with capital coming from investment funds, private equity, and sovereign wealth funds worth billions of dollars, capable of taking a start-up through all the stages of funding until it reaches a commercial scale of operations, in record time (Sexton, 2020; Zimberoff, 2021).[2]

Furthermore, this wave of disruptive innovation in the agri-food system is part of a new technological cycle transforming the broader economy, led by the digitalization of big data, machine learning, robotization, and artificial intelligence (Knell, 2021). Since the introduction of GMOs, genetics has become increasingly integrated into big data technology, which has enabled the deciphering of the genome treated, now, as one more code subject to the techniques of digitalization. Thus, new techniques have emerged able to edit the genetic code (CRISPR: clustered regularly interspaced short palindromic repeats) and identify and express specific genetic characteristics with greater precision than the techniques of the 1970s, and without necessarily introducing exogenous genetic material (Isaacson, 2022). At the limit, it opens the perspective of constructing DNA components from synthetic biology. The digitalization of molecular biology allows for the screening of billions of microorganisms and proteins in the search for functional, organoleptic, and nutritional properties for new products that compete with animal and marine protein of all kinds (Tao et al, 2021).

Innovations on this scale, especially when led by digitalization, extend to all aspects of the current agri-food system, and encourage the creation of myriad start-ups that promise to revolutionize agricultural practices, logistics systems, and downstream food services, restaurants, and home deliveries. In the case of agriculture, we are talking about a new generation of instruments and machines (sensors, drones, smart tractors) to capture information of all kinds (prices, yields, weather, weed levels, moisture, and soil conditions) and process it with big data software and artificial intelligence in real time. In this way, the megafarms that have emerged from GMO no-till crop systems can now be managed with the precision and intimacy that was once the competitive advantage of the smallholder. Thus, so-called precision farming is tailor-made for the more efficient management of large farms and offers the immediate prospect of greater efficiency and lower production costs. We can therefore expect a rapid process of adoption depending on the availability of connectivity infrastructure. It is not surprising that most start-ups and, increasingly, large companies in the input and agricultural machinery industry, as well as the big data companies, are dedicated to producing software aimed at those process innovations that tend to reinforce the dominant model (Magnin, 2016; Wolfert et al, 2017; Tantalaki et al, 2019).

Even so, there are major conflicts to be negotiated around the ownership and use of the data. The segment of smart tractors transformed into mobile offices, as well as its leading companies, most notably Deere, now assume a strategic position in the digitalization of agriculture by orchestrating the set of agricultural machines and instruments in a future internet of things (IoT). In England, a sample crop of barley was planted and harvested without the use of labour (Feingold, 2017).

Medium and large farmers who can even accumulate significant capital in times of good prices resent the economic power of the chemical and genetic inputs sector and its ability to reappropriate these gains in price increases. At the same time, many of these farmers are more aware of the harms of agrochemical use. Recent research in Brazil has identified efforts to increase the autonomy of agricultural activity through the development of alternatives in the form of bio-inputs, produced on their own properties or by producer associations (Wilkinson and Pereira, 2018; Salviano, 2021). These initiatives are supported by public rural extension systems, cooperation with public research entities, and start-ups with management software. In response, the leading companies, in addition to producing new generations of transgenics, advance in the production of bio-inputs and software packages to create a viable market for carbon sequestration and sustainable practices (Exame Agro, 2021). Thus, even the large companies upstream of agriculture feel pressured by the environmental mobilizations against the dominant agricultural model and can no longer limit themselves to discourses of efficiency and productivity.

In a wave of innovations as far-reaching as the current one, it is not surprising that all links in the agri-food chain are deeply affected. Where these technologies are in some form already being diffused and where their applications directly affect efficiency, they are quickly adopted by incumbent leaders, as in the incorporation of blockchain systems, into the logistics of marketing and tracking agricultural commodities by all the global traders (Berman, 2018).

We have already characterized the transformations in agri-food as a second domestication where it is no longer the macro-organisms – be they plants or animals – that are the object but microorganisms – genes and molecules – which contain the properties sought by different social groups and are indicated by dietary guidelines. The demand for ingredients and additives, even though also the target of the primary processing industries which in turn are often also the traders, has already led to the emergence of a specialized sector of companies such as International Flavors & Fragrances, Roquette, and Ingredion (Vegconomist, 2021b). Now, molecular screening and prospecting techniques are enabling the creation of a new generation of high-tech start-ups, such as Ginkgo Bioworks and Evolva Holding, already mentioned, specialized in the prospection of molecules, or the dozens of precision fermentation start-ups, or even the synthetic biology start-ups capable of creating proteins and enzymes, all becoming the privileged object of joint ventures and cooperation by the leading players along the different phases of the agri-food chain, from traders to the final food products industry.

The retail sector has been the most revolutionized by the spread of information technology, which, as we have seen, established the large retailers as the new hegemonic actor in the global agri-food system (Lawrence and Dixon, 2015). With the advent of the internet, this sector saw the entry into food distribution of the big online-sales players – Amazon, Alibaba, 3D (Prause et al, 2021). In the most recent period, large retailers have had to face another structural challenge: the increase in the consumption of food away from home, or food consumed but not made at home, and the expansion of the food service sector. COVID-19 hit the restaurant segment hard and accelerated a reorientation towards home delivery, both from individual restaurants and fast-food chains. Inspired by the models of platforms like Uber, a whole new sector of home delivery start-ups has emerged and is rapidly undergoing a process of concentration. At the same time, start-ups and restaurants, often in partnership with well-known chefs, create service modalities involving recipes and semi-ready food kits. The very fragmentation of this sector opens opportunities for the emergence of an entire ecosystem of start-ups (Lee and Ham, 2021; Reardon et al, 2021).

Thus, all segments of the agri-food system are being deeply transformed by the meeting between the social demands pressing for change and the opportunities/threats that the set of new technologies presents. However, what distinguishes the current wave of innovation is the effort to radically modify the content of foods as well as their production conditions. Therefore, we focus our attention on the transformations in the food industry, both in the emergence of a generation of companies dedicated to creating a radically new food base and the efforts of leading companies to take control over this movement.

If in the 1970s and 1980s, the financial support system for the consolidation of start-ups such as Calgene and Agrigenetics was fragile and embryonic, allowing for their rapid incorporation by the sector's leading companies, a mature ecosystem of financing emerged during the second decade of the 2000s in the form of venture capital capable of sustaining a start-up throughout its life cycle until it is launched as a company on the stock exchange or becomes the object of acquisition. Although public policies exist in many countries to support the creation of start-ups or 'small and medium enterprises', there is increasingly a predominance of self-funding, crowdfunding systems, but above all what are called 'angel' investors: individuals dedicated to providing initial financial support, with or without equity consideration (de Bernardi and Azucar, 2020). Forward Fooding, a consultancy that globally tracks this entire innovation ecosystem in agri-food, estimated that at the end of 2019 there were around 980 of these angel investors supporting start-ups in the sector. Another institutional mechanism of this ecosystem that is assuming increasing importance are the entities, often corporate players (calculated by FoodTech at 240) that take on the role of accelerators of start-ups, a specific type of incubator dedicated to the production of a business plan to be presented at subsequent funding stages. Venture capital firms, on the other hand, specialize in identifying promising start-ups, mobilizing the support of investment funds, and subsequently following the successive funding phases. Altogether, there were an estimated 3,260 such companies or funds operating in agri-food. And finally, by the end of 2019 around 260 corporations were identified by Forward Fooding (2021) as investing in this ecosystem, a figure similar to the FoodTech estimate.

All this data is under permanent review on the interactive platform developed by FoodTech and the number of start-ups in agri-food had already reached 8,600 when consulted in February 2022, with similar increases for the other actors. Another platform, Tracxn, which serves over 850 investors (by subscription) and bills itself as one of the largest in the world, had tracked 10,909 start-ups, also as of February 2022. The ecosystem has been dominated by the United States, as is the case with start-ups in general, but today it has become global, with growth particularly in Asia that is certainly underestimated.

The venture capital financing system foresees a life cycle of around seven to eight years from the initial seed money round until the public launch of the company via initial public offering (IPO) or acquisition. The sequence of rounds, each one aiming at clear goals and deadlines, is also conditional on the accomplishment of the targets and deadlines of the previous round, and ties the financing in a way that allows for the quick identification of failures, and guarantees an 'exit', via IPO or acquisition, for the successful ones in the time allotted to remunerate the capital internalized in the form of equity (Lerner and Nanda, 2020).

The food industry is treated in the economic literature as a sector of low technological intensity and only incremental innovation. Even the leading companies spend very little on research and development (R&D) (2 per cent of turnover), and much more on marketing (15 per cent), the reverse being the case for high-tech companies (Rama and Wilkinson, 2019). In 2018, as an example, leading US food companies spent US$6.8 billion on R&D while the average annual investment that food tech start-ups received between 2010 and 2019 was around US$6.5 billion (DigitalFoodLab, 2021). It is estimated that only one third of product launches by leading companies can be considered innovations rather than a simple repositioning of existing products. This explains the emergence of the new generation of companies analysed in Chapter 1 betting on the disruptive power of innovations in a range of food categories. On the other hand, studies by Ruth Rama and colleagues have shown that the food industry is a major user of innovations coming from other sectors – enzymes and yeasts from biotech companies, ingredients and additives from the chemical industry, packaging from petrochemicals, as well as a range of industrial processes (Rama, 2008). Thus, even though it is not a major generator of innovation, the food industry has always been sensitive to the possibilities of innovation and has also become a major user of innovation. It is in this context that we can evaluate continuities and ruptures in the positioning of leading food companies when faced with the new phenomenon of food tech start-ups.

The FoodTech report for the period 2014–2019 (DigitalFoodLab, 2021) divides food techs into various categories discriminated according to the number of firms and the relative percentage of investments. According to the report, the agtech sector that essentially deals with the various precision agriculture components is the most mature segment and began in the United States from the 1980s onwards. Therefore, it is not surprising that they represent the largest number of companies: 1,521. The report highlights the weight of investments from the home-delivery segment where the rapid process of concentration, which follows the Uber-style business model, has led to major funding to bankroll IPOs and acquisitions. But the report draws special attention to the number of companies in the 'next generation food and beverages' category, some 1,210, and the amount of their funding, 10 per cent of the total, also rising rapidly.

Another important source of data and analysis for this ecosystem, AgFunder, plays the dual role of investor in the world of agritechs and, based on its digital platform with 85,000 subscribers, has become an important reference for following developments in the sector. In its annual report published in 2021, AgFunder (2022), presents a summary of the sector during the second decade of the 2000s and a detailed analysis, also broken down by category,[3] of the sector's performance in terms of the number and value of financings, the relative weight of different macro-regions, and the main agritechs involved, as well as their financiers and eventual buyers. In its historical summary of the sector's financing, which comprises the years 2014–2020, the cumulative value reaches US$107 billion, or around US$15 billion per year, far more than double the US$6.8 billion dedicated to R&D by leading US food companies in 2018. The United States remains by far the most important individual country in number and value of deals, but accounts for less than 50 per cent of these deals globally. Table 2.1 presents the leading investor countries for 2020.

Table 2.1: Number and value of investments by country (first 15 countries), 2020

Country	Value (US$ billions)	No. of investments
United States	13.2	815
China	4.8	115
India	1.8	164
United Kingdom	1.1	133
France	0.660	39
Israel	0.482	57
Canada	0.407	130
Colombia	0.359	12
Indonesia	0.339	30
Germany	0.307	38
Holland	0.249	27
Finland	0.225	11
Japan	0.208	62
Ireland	0.196	18
Singapore	0.195	41

Source: AgFunder (2021)

The universe of actors and the values transacted in this agri-food innovation ecosystem (from start-ups, angel investors, venture capital companies, and various investment funds, including sovereign wealth funds) – even if it is only a fraction of this new ecosystem as a whole, where the values under management of venture capital firms in the United States alone have been valued at US$450 billion by 2020 (Lerner and Nander, 2020) – are much larger than the investments from leading agri-food companies. It might be thought, however, that traditional corporations of the sector will be the main beneficiaries of these investments at the moment of 'exit' via stock exchange launches or acquisitions. This may become the case, but for the year 2020 AgFunder presents a selection of the main 'exits', and of the 19 cases analysed only 3 acquisitions were made by the current leading firms – one each by Coca-Cola, PepsiCo, and Nestlé.

However, we have already seen in Chapter 1 that one of the strategies of the leaders is to acquire new start-ups that have already established themselves in the market. Much of the growth of these companies from the 1970s onwards resulted from acquisitions, with the leaders transforming themselves into brand managers (Rastoin et al, 1998). But what is their position in relation to the current innovation ecosystem we have already outlined? It is important in this sense to qualify our discussion of innovation in relation to the food industry. We have seen that it is predominantly characterized by the low in-house generation of innovation, and by a focus on incremental innovations, although, on the other hand, it is a major user and diffuser of innovations (Alfranca et al, 2005). A large part of the food industry was born from the transformation of artisanal into large-scale production for a population in a rapid process of urbanization.

The history of the food industry is also punctuated by radical product innovations that define the profile of the innovative companies. The two leaders for much of the 20th century, Nestlé, and Unilever, were born out of radical product innovations, associated in the first case with powdered and condensed milk and, in the second, the production of margarine (and soap) from fats and oils to compete with butter from milk (Goodman et al, 1987; Wilson, 2022). Kellogg's, with its corn flakes, would be another innovative company at the beginning of the 20th century. Less known, but today with a global reach and revenues around US$4 billion, even though it remains a private family company, is Rich Products, which was born from a radical product innovation: whipped cream made from soy that, unlike the original product derived from milk, could be frozen without altering its properties and, therefore, fitted in with the explosion of frozen products in the 1950s in the United States.[4] Thus, periodically, at times of great transformations, companies arise that have radical innovation on their birth certificates.

By contrast, the current wave of innovation involves thousands of actors, largely independent of the consolidated structures of the agri-food system, all aiming to reconstitute the food system in light of the socio-environmental and geopolitical challenges described in the Introduction and in Chapter 1. This process is, at the same time, conflict-ridden with powerful actors interested in only partial adjustments and determined to maintain their economic power. However, this innovation ecosystem in its entirety tends towards more radical solutions, and the large incumbent companies are aware of this and reposition themselves around the new agendas (Coyne, 2024a; Loria, 2017).

All the four companies we mentioned here – Nestlé, Unilever, Kellogg's, and Rich Products – are already part of the new ecosystem with their own venture capital firms, Nestlé and Unilever since the beginning of the new millennium. Both Kellogg's and Rich Products are investing in alternative proteins, and Rich's has become a strategic investor in China's Dao Foods International venture capital firm, whose goal is to invest in 30 alternative protein start-ups. Food Engineering publishes annually a list of the top 100 food and beverage companies. As we can see from Table 2.2, all the top twelve companies by revenue have their venture capital firms or invest directly in food start-ups.

In a quick search of the remaining companies in this list of the first 100, which includes Unilever (formerly number 2 and today number 17), it was possible to identify 11 more companies that had a direct involvement in the ecosystem.[5] Another survey by Just Food updated to January 2022, which is not limited to these companies, counted 29 companies.[6] All these lists

Table 2.2: The 12 leading food and beverage firms in 2021 and their involvement in the new innovation ecosystem

Company	Year	Venture capital/investment
PepsiCo Inc		Pepsi Cola Ventures Group
Nestlé	2002	Inventages Venture Capital
JBS	2019	Direct Investment
AnHeuser-Busch InBev		ZX Ventures
Tyson Foods		Tyson Ventures
Mars		Seeds of Change Accelerator
ADM		ADM Ventures
The Coca-Cola Company		The Bridge
Cargill		Cargill Ventures
Danone		Danone Manifesto Ventures
Kraft Heinz Company		Evolve Ventures

Source: Costa (2022). Adapted by the author.

are very incomplete. They do not include, for example, Chobani (discussed in Chapter 1), which has set up an incubator with the following mission:

> The Chobani Incubator is a program for companies taking on broken food systems to bring better food to more people. In addition to equity-free investment, we give startups access to our network and expertise in order to scale up their operations and achieve significant growth.[7]

Unlike other companies that create incubators and accelerators or invest in start-ups, Chobani does not take an equity position in these firms.

The involvement of food and beverage companies covers the spectrum of the options previously indicated in the ecosystem. Unilever, which set up its venture capital arm in 2002 and has four different funds, has made 125 investments in start-ups, 13 of these specifically aimed at meeting diversity demands (firms that have women or African Americans as founders). Twenty-three of these firms reached 'exit', and were acquired (not necessarily by Unilever) or launched publicly. In 2014, the Unilever Foundry was created, an incubator aimed at training future collaborators with the company, and Unilever (2022) states that it is in contact with more than 2,500 start-ups.[8]

Most companies created their venture capital arms from 2016, such as Danone, whose motto is 'the idea is to embrace change', and which has already made investments in 14 start-ups. The investment arm of the German Katjes Group, a leader in confectionery, is called Katjesgreenfood and specializes in alternative foods. Kraft Heinz launched its investment fund, Evolve Ventures, in 2018 with the intention, according to Just Food, to 'invest in emerging tech companies that are aiming to transform the food industry' (Coyne, 2024b). Other companies, such as Barilla and Hain Celestial, focus their investments exclusively on start-ups that can be eventually included in their portfolios or that can bring benefits to their core business.

Of the leading meat companies in Brazil, which we will analyse in more detail in Chapters 4 and 6, BRF Brasil Foods participated in an investment round in the Israeli cellular meat company, Aleph Farms; Minerva created a venture capital fund to invest in start-ups directly related to its core business; and JBS acquired the Spanish cellular meat company, BioTech Foods and plans to invest US$100 million in a new plant in Spain and an R&D centre in Brazil for cultured meat (Poinski, 2022). Both BRF and JBS are investing heavily, at the same time, in plant-based meats.

This involvement by leading food and beverage companies is a global phenomenon. We have already mentioned Rich Products' participation in the venture capital fund of China's Dao Foods International. Another example would be Thai Union Group, owner of the John West tuna brand, which set up its fund in 2019 to support 'innovative companies that are developing breakthrough technologies in food-tech', and particularly targets alternative proteins with investments in insect proteins, cellular fish, and meat (Coyne, 2024b).

Thus we can conclude that what were exceptional initiatives in the early 2000s taken by the two leading companies Nestlé and Unilever, strongly identified since their creation with disruptive innovations, by the end of the second decade had become the new normal for the leading food and beverage companies. Some companies, such as Chobani, Kraft Heinz, and Thai Union Group, aim to promote fundamental transformations in the food system by promoting alternative proteins; others like Barilla and Hain Celestial focus on efforts to capture the signals of radical innovation that directly affect their businesses. Even so, we are far from strategies limited to imitating successful innovations by relying on a more powerful structure of distribution, logistics, and marketing, or to acquiring these innovative companies only when their success is confirmed.

Today, leading companies recognize that they face a new global innovation ecosystem encompassing all aspects of the food system and seek alternative solutions rather than efficiency improvements or merely additional new products that can be incorporated into their portfolios. Both in terms of the numbers involved and the amounts of financial resources mobilized, it is not a dynamic that can be controlled by the traditional leaders of the food system. By 2015, what Nestlé and Unilever had realized since the beginning of the new millennium, the industry as a whole came to recognize: the need to participate actively in the prospecting of innovations that might transform the sector and involve itself in the detail of how each specific segment works (Geller, 2017; Coyne, 2024a).

As we have already indicated, agri-food products were late in becoming integrated into this innovation ecosystem. There was a relevant participation in the 1980s in the initial boom of new biotechnologies, but this was limited to the chemical/genetic sector upstream. Venture capital has been associated with successive waves of computing, the internet, and finance since the 1960s, accelerating from the 1980s when changes in the interpretation of legislation allowed pension funds to participate. There is already an extensive literature examining the implications of this model for the dynamics of innovation. In a paper published in 2020, Lerner and Nanda synthesize much of this literature. Citing Puri and Zarutskie (2012), they point out that although only 0.5 per cent of firms in the United States are venture capital beneficiaries, 56 per cent of all firms that went public between 1995 and 2018 and were still active in 2019 had received venture capital. Even if the vocation of venture capital firms is to identify early future champions that might have consolidated anyway, it's hard not to think based on this data that they also influence the performance of the firms in which they invest.

With the globalization of this ecosystem and the greater ease of creating start-ups via crowdfunding, angel investors, or even by the proliferation of public programs of support to innovation and small and medium enterprises, venture capital has evolved from the exclusive search for the start-up that will become a unicorn, worth US$1 billion, to a 'spray and pray' strategy of spreading the word and praying for results, of distributing seed funding more generously in the hope that one or other start-up will come through. For Lerner and Nanda (2020), the priority of venture capital is to concentrate on those sectors where the technology is already known and, therefore, the viability of the business plan can be quickly assessed. Thus, services that are based on software are favoured, but sectors where technical feasibility and possibilities of scale are more uncertain, even if they are sectors of high social return such as alternative energy, may not receive the funding they need. In the case of the agri-food sector, this explains the large resources invested in logistics and home-delivery companies, but it does not explain the heavy investments in still highly speculative technologies such as cellular protein.

In addition to the prospect of high returns over a short period of time that motivates a large part of venture capital, one must take into account the weight of mission-oriented venture capital and 'impact' investment funds, where a commitment to social and environmental objectives characterizes an important part of the funds dedicated to agri-food start-ups. The largest European venture capital firm dedicated to agriculture and food, Astanor Ventures, with a US$325 million fund, has as one of its founders Eric Archambeau,[9] who became involved in agriculture and food through his participation in the Jamie Oliver Food Foundation, the British chef aligned with social, environmental, and health issues relating to food. Astanor Ventures[10] invests in start-ups in vertical farming, insect proteins, and agricultural sensors to monitor plant health to reduce reliance on chemical inputs. Other agri-food funds, among many geared towards transforming the food system in the light of socio-environmental challenges, include Ospraie Ag Science with US$125 million, Agroecology Capital with US$100 million, and Shift Invest (in collaboration with the accelerator StartLife), with EUR70 million.[11] The entry of sovereign wealth funds from countries rich in capital but poor in natural resources (China, Singapore, Middle East) strengthens this orientation towards radical solutions that minimize the use of inputs traditionally associated with agri-food – water and land (Aguilar, 2022).

However, the life cycle of venture capital investments is typically between 7 and 10 years, which does not necessarily coincide with the technological maturity and scale of more radical innovations in, for example, alternative proteins or vertical agriculture whose technical feasibility of production at scale is still in question. The increasing concentration of the venture capital industry and its resources around a few promising companies, trends identified by Lerner and Nanda (2020), could undermine the development of these alternatives if there are a few disappointments along the way.

In the case of alternative proteins, for example, both the long timescales and the magnitude of the challenge cast doubt on the possibilities of a transition without major public investment. On the other hand, the political influence of traditional interests would likely limit public policy engagement in disruptive innovations, especially in countries with an agro-exporting tradition. However, our analysis in this chapter shows that the agri-food innovation ecosystem has become much broader than the world of large corporations, and that these are being induced to participate in this system to maintain their positions in the various agri-food markets and to avoid being overtaken by the ongoing waves of innovation (Coyne, 2024b).

If public policies are playing a modest role in promoting disruptive innovations, their regulations and guidelines on the role of food in public health are already pressuring the sector to review the content of its products. The World Health Organization (WHO) is calling on the food industry to reduce the use of added sugars, sodium, and fats and advocates public regulation as the best way to achieve this (WHO, 2020).

The food industry, for its part, directly via its leading companies or through its numerous associations, lobbies continuously and intensely to prevent regulatory measures – whether around the reduction of targets or transparent labelling systems (red = high levels, orange = medium, green = low), and even against the use of clear terminology, such as added sugars as opposed to the ambiguous notion of total sugars. The operation of this lobby is particularly notable in the European Union, especially in the case of sugar. A study by the Corporate European Observatory (CEO) (2016), identified 61 lobby groups that together spend EUR 21.3 million per year to influence EU policy, and use it against countries that introduce regulatory measures. Their influence was evident in the European Food Standards Authority's (EFSA) conclusion that there was no scientific evidence of a link between sugar consumption levels and obesity (EFSA, 2022). This lobby also uses trade rules to penalize third countries that dare to introduce legislation affecting the use of sweeteners as in the case of Mexico, which had to pay around one hundred million dollars after taxing the import of beverages containing high-fructose corn syrup (ERS/USDA, 1999).

This lobbying, on the other hand, is opposed by non-governmental organizations (NGOs) such as CEO, the European Consumer Organization (BEUC, 2016), and other consumer protection organizations very active in Europe that produce detailed analyses of the food industry's efforts to capture the regulatory process, and finds opposition also in the European Parliament. Soft drinks and snacks, whose consumption particularly threatens children, are strong mobilizers of public opinion and lead to measures to control advertising and ban their sales in school environments (White, 2017).

Leading global companies can influence policies in Europe and the United States, diluting and delaying measures and promoting voluntary public and private partnerships rather than regulation and taxation. Even so, the strength of their lobbying depends on the plausibility of their alternatives. Initially their position was to rebut the WHO by arguing that it was a matter of calories, not sugar; that the problem was the diet as a whole, not individual products; and that obesity could be tackled more effectively through exercise, which led the industry to be a major sponsor of sports.

Subsequently, leading companies recognized the need for a reduction in these ingredients but made this conditional on being able to achieve product reformulations without harming their taste properties. Nestlé accepted the definition of 'added sugars' and set targets to reduce these by 5 per cent, sodium by 10 per cent, and saturated fats by 10 per cent. Between 2017 and 2020, by its own calculations, Nestlé had removed 60,000 tonnes of sugar, a reduction of 4.5 per cent; 10,000 tonnes of sodium, just 3.8 per cent; and had achieved the 10 per cent target for saturated fats.[12]

Obesity, however, is fast becoming a global disease, as are associated diseases such as diabetes and cardiovascular problems, with similar impacts on public health spending in Northern countries. Global companies can target third countries when it comes to international trade, as we have seen in the case of Mexico, but when it comes to the production of their subsidiaries in those markets the situation becomes more difficult. Nestlé, in the same statement, points to its reformulation of a number of products: the McKay Museo biscuits in Chile where sugar has been replaced by natural ingredients, and palm oil with sunflower oil; the 30 per cent reduction of sugar in Nesquick products; the 15 per cent reduction in sodium in the case of Maggi Table Light sold in the Ivory Coast, with the target of similar reductions in all its Maggi products in West and Central Africa (Neo, 2019; Nestlé CWA, 2018).

The case of Thailand is very instructive in this sense. A tax on sugar was introduced in 2017, following the WHO's 'Global action plan for the prevention and control of noncommunicable diseases' (GAP) published in 2013 (WHO, 2013). By 2021, more than 50 countries had introduced excise taxes on sugar, which was rapidly positioning itself as the new tobacco that underwent similar measures quite successfully (Ralph, 2021). In response to the measures introduced in Thailand, Nestlé invested US$6.6 million and mobilized three of its R&D centres to produce the first global sucrose-free version of its chocolate drink, Milo, at the same price as the conventional product. Nestlé subsequently introduced this product in other countries. Suntory PepsiCo responded in the same way by introducing a sugar-reduced version of its Lipton Ice Tea developed exclusively for the Thai market (Drinks Insight Network, 2021).

Unilever, which develops Lipton teas in partnership with PepsiCo, has also embraced the WHO position expressed in the GAP to reduce the use of sugar, sodium, saturated fats, and more generally the number of calories ingested. Under Paul Polman as CEO from 2010, Unilever launched its 'Sustainable Living Plan' and in its 2020 report calculated that 61 per cent of its products were aligned with WHO recommendations (Seymour, 2017). Encouraged by the targets set by the Brazilian government to lower salt consumption from 12 to 5 grams per day per capita, Unilever launched its Knorr brand with zero salt, first in Brazil, to be later extended to other countries. Unilever calculated that in the case of salt, 77 per cent of its products in 2020 already complied with the WHO recommendations, with targets to increase this percentage to 85 per cent by 2022. In the case of added sugar (a characterization that the company also complied with), Unilever had already lowered its percentage in teas by 23 per cent (against a target of 25 per cent) and predicted that by 2025 it would have lowered the presence of these sugars, to 5 grams per 100 millilitres in 85 per cent of its products. The company also committed to reducing the use of trans fat to 2 grams per 100 grams by 2022 but did not specify targets regarding saturated fats. Like Nestlé, Unilever emphasized that substitution or reduction would only be possible through investments in R&D to maintain the taste characteristics of the products (Unilever, 2022).

For the industry it is not simply a question of reducing or eliminating these ingredients, because their taste effects are just as important as their functional qualities. From this perspective, product reformulation is only feasible if other ingredients are found with the same characteristics, especially in terms of taste. Otherwise, there is the risk of losing these markets to competitors. This search for alternatives is bringing the food industry closer to the ingredients sector and to the start-ups specializing in the prospecting of molecules with the support of big data and synthetic biology. In this sense, regulatory policies, as well as the need to react to the wave of innovations coming from new start-ups, are pushing companies to adopt more radical innovation strategies (Unilever, 2022).

The food industry is not only being challenged on the content of its products. Pressures are also coming from the sector's contribution to greenhouse gas emissions, and food companies are being held accountable for the emissions in their respective supply chains. Unilever was one of the first companies to commit to eliminating emissions from deforestation for the supply of palm oil in Indonesia's plantations and was a key player in the creation of the Roundtable for Sustainable Palm Oil (RSPO) in 2004. It was also an instigator of the New York Declaration on Forests in 2014, signed by most of the companies and governments involved in the palm oil chain and which aimed to eliminate deforestation from their chains by 2020 (Seymour, 2017).

The catalyst for this movement was a Greenpeace study, 'Cooking the Climate' (2007), published to coincide with the United Nations Climate Change Conference (COP13) in Bali, Indonesia, showing the responsibility of large food traders and food and consumer product companies in the destruction of forests and peat lands for the opening up of palm oil plantations. In response, most traders, and companies such as Unilever, Kellogg's and Colgate committed to a target of zero deforestation. The Indonesian government introduced a moratorium on new concessions and the Indonesian Chamber of Commerce joined traders to form the Indonesian Palm Oil Pledge (IPOP). In 2015, there was a wave of devastating fires in forests and peat lands with damage estimated at US$16 billion and with an estimated 100,000 premature deaths from respiratory causes. In an atmosphere of recriminations, international NGOs were blamed and the IPOP undone (Poynton, 2016).[13]

In its second study 'Still Cooking the Climate' reassessing this issue in 2017 (p 9), Greenpeace concluded:

> [...] the single greatest threat to rainforests in Southeast Asia comes from small- and medium-sized plantation company and producer groups. This includes producers such as Gama/Ganda, Samling and Salim groups – the latter is the loosely structured parent of Indonesian manufacturer Indofood. These groups often have strong links to the Indonesian and Malaysian governments, or prominent positions in the Roundtable on Sustainable Palm Oil (RSPO), and appear able to use their connections to undermine progressive companies' efforts to reform the industry.

At the same time, Greenpeace found that large traders and final consumer goods firms were still receiving palm oil from newly deforested areas and therefore discontinued its collaboration activities with companies like Unilever, Mondelez and Wilmar to create a monitoring system (Nelson, 2022).

Even so, Unilever is notable for commitments concerning its carbon footprint. The targets include reducing operational emissions in absolute terms by 70 per cent by 2025 when compared to emissions in 2015, to achieve zero emissions in its own operations by 2030, and to reach 'net zero' emissions by 2039. Nestlé, for its part, is committed to halving greenhouse gas emissions by 2030 and to achieve net zero emissions by 2050 (Nestlé, 2022).

The performance of both companies has been subject to severe criticism by the NewClimate Institute (NCI) in its assessment of 25 global companies in various sectors.[14] The study points to the lack of a definition of specific emission reduction targets, criticizes the inclusion in the calculations of gains achieved in the use of its products that may be the result of the decarbonization of other sectors such as energy, and draws attention to Unilever's ambivalence regarding the inclusion of the offsetting mechanism where emissions are compensated by actions or credits in relation to the activities of others, often constituting a form of 'greenwashing'.

It is important to note here that leading food companies, far from acting with impunity or simply relying on their economic power, are permanently challenged by a diverse set of measures and actors that include new entrants into the food sector, government regulations and guidelines, global and local NGOs, stakeholders focusing on the healthiness of their products, and stakeholders concerned with their carbon footprints, as well as the varied reactions of consumers and associated social movements.

As if that were not enough, companies like Unilever need to deal with increasingly activist shareholders. When Paul Polman took over as CEO of Unilever in 2010, he warned shareholders that he would not produce quarterly reports and that the company was committed to a vision of generating long-term value in a sustainable way and recommended that anyone who disagreed with this policy should withdraw their money from the company. On the same day the company's shares fell by 6 per cent, with losses calculated at US$2.2 billion. It was in that same year, as already indicated, that the company launched its 'Sustainable Living Plan' (Henderson, 2021).

Pressure from activist investors can come from opposite perspectives. In the case of Unilever, some have attacked the company precisely for its 'ridiculous' focus on sustainability, others for not making sufficient progress in reducing ingredients such as added sugar, sodium, and fats. The power of shareholders was clear in the rejection in 2019 of Polman's proposal to move Unilever's headquarters to Rotterdam to avoid hostile takeover attempts such as that of Kraft Heinz, controlled by private equity firms focused on short-term profitability, the opposite of Unilever's option (Henderson, 2021).[15]

In this chapter, we have revisited the two main waves of innovation impacting the agri-food system in the 20th century – the green revolution and GMOs – to highlight the originality of the innovations arising from advances in digitalization and its convergence with molecular genetics that gains speed and amplitude from the 2000s and hits the agri-food sector in full, especially in the second decade of the new millennium. Differently from the previous waves, the main focus is no longer agriculture, although this is also targeted, but food, and the main actors as a rule are not part of the agri-food world, or when they are they identify with the consumption side. The concerns driving these innovations are the challenges of feeding a global and urban population, and the starting point is the perception that the current system is broken, either because of its environmental, climate, and health impacts, or because it is a sector that is backward and ripe for the application of disruptive technologies.

This innovation system is made up of thousands of start-ups, centred in the United States and driven by venture capital firms that specialize in guiding the initial steps of these start-ups and leveraging funding from a huge world of investment funds, private equity, and sovereign wealth funds. Leading companies in the agri-food system participate in this vast innovation ecosystem, with their own venture capital entities, incubators, and accelerators, as well as creating investment funds to support start-ups. As powerful as they are, however, these companies are not leading these innovations and are only slowly adjusting proactively, each in its own way, under pressure from the different groups of actors that have been analysed in this chapter.

Chapters 3 and 4 are devoted to two innovation routes that best capture the radical nature of the ongoing transformations in the agri-food system – vertical agriculture (or climate-controlled agriculture), and the alternatives to animal protein. In the first case, by completing the process of appropriation of all rural agricultural activities, including the energy of the sun, it is a question of subjecting agriculture as a whole to typically industrial and urban conditions. In the second case, we are dealing with an equally radical substitution of animal protein by vegetable protein, and vegetable protein by insects, fungi, and cells. There are many different debates and assessments on the economic feasibility of these innovations, as well as the timeframe for these products to become mainstream. The analysis in these chapters takes account of these considerations but focuses primarily on the actors and investments being mobilized, broken down by types of products, actors, and markets, to assess the weight of these ongoing trends. We also analyse the reactions to these innovations, both from affected economic sectors and from consumers of various types. And finally, we will analyse the public policies and regulations that these radical innovations are provoking.

3

Agriculture Reaches for the Skies: Climate-Controlled Agriculture and Vertical Farming

In discussing innovation in Chapter 2, we focused on the two great waves of innovation in the 20th century – the green revolution and genetically modified organisms (GMOs) – to situate the radical transformations underway in the agri-food system. The industrialization of agricultural activities, however, began much earlier in the 19th century, first in Europe and later in the United States. Empirical knowledge about the soil led to the emergence of a proto-fertilizer industry from ground bones (brought even from the cemeteries of the Napoleonic wars on the European continent) and guano (bird droppings) from the Pacific islands of Peru. With the scientific identification of soil nutrients by Liebig (which, according to Karl Marx, was worth more than all the contributions of the economists of the time!), the fertilizer industry emerged in Europe, replacing agricultural fallow practices, where land was periodically left uncultivated or subjected to burning to replenish the soil nutrients. The Haber–Bosch ammonia synthesis was developed to produce nitrogen products, first in Germany by BASF, and then in England by the company ICI, already mentioned in relation to single-cell proteins, which dominated the fertilizer industry for much of the 20th century (Foster, 1999).

On the other side of the Atlantic, it was labour that was most in short supply to clear the agricultural frontier of the American Midwest, and consequently the first phase of industrialization in the United States took the form of mechanization in the industrial appropriation of agricultural labour through the creation of machines and tools for all phases of the agricultural cycle. In 1830 John Deere, a blacksmith by trade, launched a steel plough that became a great success and, in the following century, spearheaded the creation of the tractor industry. J.I. Case (today, New Holland and CNH Industrial) established steam-powered grain threshing machines in the 1860s and later introduced combine harvesters (Goodman et al, 1987). Both companies today lead the development of precision agriculture with their intelligent tractors and machines.

Thus, the fertilizer and agricultural machinery industries developed separately, including geographically, in their transformation of agricultural into industrial activities, leaving the farmer to manage this new combination of costs and practices. For these industries, agriculture simply became a market for their products. From the 1930s onwards, with the spread of hybridization and genetic improvement techniques, a public seed sector emerged together with a new private seed industry, initially almost exclusively for maize seeds. A further branch of industrial products was, therefore, created, appropriating what had been yet another millennia-old activity developed on the farm, increasing even more the costs and decisions that the producer needed to make (Kloppenburg, 1988).

The use of pesticides was practiced by the Sumerians some seven thousand years ago, and over the centuries various substances have been applied: mercury, arsenic, and nicotine. It was only in the 1940s, however, that a pesticides industry emerged based on the products of organic chemistry, arising from the discovery of the now-banned DDT (dichloro-diphenyl-trichloroethane), originally developed to fight malaria in Asian forests during World War II. From there, chemical inputs for agriculture were progressively broken down into various segments – insecticides, herbicides, and fungicides (Brown, 1970).

The industrialization of agriculture, therefore, can be understood as a successive process of transformations of agricultural activities into industrial markets with each segment aiming to increase its sales. Initially, the management of the industrialized farm was primarily the responsibility of the farmer, a responsibility partially mitigated by the development of public rural extension systems or technical assistance from teams of business agronomists who advised on best practices, including the new industrial products. The green revolution marked the first effort to develop agricultural production based on an integrated view of different industrial inputs, which led to its characterization as an 'agricultural package' (Pearse, 1980). With the incorporation of the seed industry into the agrichemical sector from the 1980s onwards it was the private sector that came to offer its own 'package' to farmers (Joly and Ducos, 1993).

In the grains sector (which in this book is of special interest because it is the main source of animal protein feed) a theme that will be a central concern in the following chapters – the introduction of transgenics was accompanied by the adoption of a new system of no-till farming, eliminating the tasks of soil preparation and weed control. This, on the one hand, simplified important aspects of farm management such as the recruitment and supervision of labour. On the other hand, it allowed for very large increases in the scale of production, which made the negotiation of markets and the financing of production more complex, requiring participation in futures markets and hedging (Wilkinson and Pereira, 2018).

This environment favoured the emergence of new players:

1. farmers whose scale of operations now enabled them to act up- and downstream of the chain;
2. agricultural companies listed on the stock exchange or supported by investment funds;
3. companies specialized in the management of all agricultural activities for farmers, who now became simple landowners living off rents.

Where this third option has not been feasible, these companies have bought up the land and moved closer to those in the second category. In Chapter 2, mention was made of this phenomenon involving the creation of megafarms with companies managing hundreds of thousands of hectares, often supported by specialized investment funds (Gras and Hernandez, 2013).

It is in this context, beginning in the 1990s, that the set of new digital technologies converge in the promotion of a 'precision agriculture' based on data-capture instruments (sensors) and software for its processing, often incorporating machine learning and artificial intelligence (OECD, 2016; Monteiro et al, 2021). After a historical process of successive appropriations of all agricultural activities, initially one by one and then in packages, companies are advancing to offer services that effectively appropriate all the information generated by agriculture, outsourcing management itself. This allows for a fine-grained control of farms with tens of thousands of hectares, providing real-time information on both production and market conditions. Control over this information gives enormous economic power to big data firms (Google, IBM) that have entered this market, and has become the object of intense negotiations and conflicts, as well as alternative initiatives that explore the benefits of precision farming for cooperatives and small producers (UNDP, 2021).

Just when it seemed that the uncertainties that have accompanied agriculture since its inception were in the process of being tamed, nature itself has become unpredictable to an unprecedented extent. Meticulous control and management of data and information are powerless in the face of prolonged droughts, heavy rains, and floods aggravated by the silting-up of rivers, and the acceleration of extreme weather events. At the same time, economic and population growth and urbanization have moved to parts of the world where agricultural resources have always been scarce, are becoming scarcer, or are being further punished by the climate crisis. It is in this context that we must place investments and actors promoting climate-controlled agriculture and vertical farming.

Efforts to control the effects of climate on crop production go back a long way. Several accounts begin with the recommendation of the Roman emperor's physician to Tiberius that he should eat a cucumber every day. The challenge of making cucumbers available in winter led to the invention of an apparently successful environmental control system of production according to the account of Pliny, the Roman historian (Paris and Janick, 2008). From the 15th century in Korea, there is a detailed description of controlled-environment heating systems to produce vegetables in winter (Yoon and Woudstra, 2007). In this period, greenhouses started to be built in Italy to produce exotic fruits and medicinal plants. This fashion spread to the Netherlands, England, and other northern European countries from the 17th century onwards, and kings and nobility competed to build their own 'orangeries' or botanical gardens. The Industrial Revolution with its cheaper iron and glass production (and the end of taxes on windows) enabled the construction of large glass buildings and green- or glasshouses became affordable for the middle class. Hydroponic systems were tried from the 1920s onwards and were widely used by the British Army to supply troops in regions of harsh climate (Crumpacker, 2019). They only became a commercial option in the 1960s, however, with the use of polyethylene for plastics, which could replace glass for the installations. Polythene is also used to directly protect the plants, replacing the traditional practice of mulching, where the soil is protected from the sun and weather by various types of dry material – peat, wood chips, or even chicken droppings (Jensen, 2001).

'Plasticulture' was invented in the late 1940s by E.E. Emmert, a horticultural expert of the University of Kentucky, as a cheaper alternative to glass. Today, plastic farming for vegetables, fruit, and flowers already occupies a central place in agriculture in many countries. In the Netherlands, there are 4,000 greenhouses with more than 9,000 hectares of planted area, employing 150,000 workers and with a turnover of EUR7.2 billion. In Almería, Spain, there are 31,000 hectares with a production of 3.5 million tonnes per year exported to almost all the countries of Europe. Morocco has around 25,000 hectares in production and competes with Spain in the European markets. Plasticulture has, in fact, been widely adopted in all the countries of the Mediterranean basin, such as Turkey and Greece (Orzolek, 2017).

Because it is a practice that is less monitored than the production of major commodities and also has short production cycles, data on plastic agriculture vary widely depending on the source. It is clear, however, that plasticulture is already widespread globally on all continents, especially in Asia, and has been growing at annual rates of over 20 per cent. Cuesta Roble, a Californian consulting firm that follows the sector, estimates that in 1980 some 150,000 hectares were devoted to greenhouse-type agriculture and 500,000 hectares to 'protected' agriculture. The same source estimates that in 2019 there were 492,800 hectares of greenhouse-type agriculture and 5,630,000 hectares of 'protected' agriculture (Hickman, 2022).

Unlike the promises of GMOs, whose focus has been on creating genetic 'resistance' traits to the environment and climate (with some success against weeds and some pests but much less so in relation to climatic stresses), here the strategy is that of 'protection' against and control over the environment. Thus, one can trace a path back to antiquity where strategies of protection from and control over the climate evolve in multiple forms in the direction of a 'climate-controlled agriculture', which with the combined technologies of digitalization, big data, automation, and robotization lead today to the phenomenon of 'vertical agriculture', which provides a complete alternative to agriculture by replacing the environment itself. In a similar approach, SharathKumar et al (2020) speak of an evolution from genetic modification to environmental modification. Even so, there are indications that the genetic industry itself, such as Bayer, is adapting to this new reality and developing varieties for climate-controlled agriculture (Bayer, 2023).

In the same way that 'plastic agriculture' was invented by a botanist and was not the result of a strategy by the chemical industry – although it would be transformed into markets that account for over 2 per cent of the world's total plastic use – the notion of vertical farming, in its modern attribution, was imagined by a microbiologist, Dickson Despommier, in the 1990s and put forward as the theme for a final paper in his ecological medicine class.[1] The findings indicated that a 30-floor vertical farm building could feed a population of 50,000 people with 2,000 calories per day for an entire year, and that an area only 20 per cent the size of Central Park in New York City would be sufficient to feed the entire population of the borough of Manhattan.[2] For Despommier (2010), vertical farming represents: 'the next evolutionary leap in humanity's quest for a reliable and sustainable food supply'.

If we place vertical farming in the broader context of climate-controlled agriculture, which, as we have seen, dates to ancient times and may even include 'the hanging gardens of Babylon', it is not surprising that there is a wide variety of types of structure and scale, of location, of product types and of practices.

In their review of vertical farming, Van Gerreway, Boon and Geelen (2022) identify four types:

1. a plant factory with artificial light (PFAL): a vertical farm located in a dedicated building;
2. a container-type farm: a vertical modular farm using shipping containers;

3. a farm inside places of purchase (restaurants, retail) or consumption (canteens);
4. an appliance that can be integrated into the office or the home.

A fifth type could also be included where the verticality is downwards, in underground locations to produce mushrooms and fungi, as originally conceived by Gilbert Ellis Bailey in 1915 (see note 2). In fact, all these four types can use artificial light, and there are factories in custom-built edifices whose design allows the use of solar energy. It is, perhaps, better to think, therefore, of a typology that uses vertical production and artificial light in a controlled climate and then distinguish the types by scale and by sales destination. Thus, in the first type, it is a strategy of scale and cost, targeting mainstream supermarkets. The second, containerized, modular, type, is aimed more at niche markets of microgreens and similar products for direct sale to restaurants. The third type is installed in an already existing building tailored to meet demand and can be an individual shop, a company, or an institution. The fourth type deals with appliances compatible with domestic production and consumption.

Many protected and greenhouse-type farming activities, even though they do not use artificial light or verticality, and are even land-based, can rely on the same companies and big data services as vertical farming. In these cases, we are in the transitional terrain between precision farming and climate-controlled agriculture. Thus, these transformations involve a multitude of processes that naturally lead to the emergence of many hybrid types, typical of an era of disruptive innovation.

Vertical farming, in its 'ideal type' and as idealized by Dickson Despommier (2010), is seen as an urban solution, and in this context the option for production in vertical stacks or tiers corresponds to the need to generate income and occupy spaces compatible with urban reality. Costs and scale also point to the advantages of verticality. However, many companies survive in the urban context by using abandoned buildings, or buildings in abandoned areas resulting from deindustrialization, to reduce the burden of rents.

Companies are also locating their factories outside urban centres and even in areas where land is still calculated in hectares rather than square metres. In the United States, a major incentive for vertical and climate-controlled farming is to decrease quality losses and carbon footprint, a result of the country having developed almost all its vegetable and fresh produce farming on the West Coast, four or five days by truck from the consumption centres on the east coast. The US company AeroFarms, which we will discuss later, envisages the possibility of supplying urban centres in the United States within 24 hours or less with a network of vertical farms located in suburban areas and even in technically rural areas.[3]

Van Gerrewey, Boon and Geelen's typology is based on SharathKumar et al (2020, p 724), whose article we have already mentioned:

> A vertical farm is a multilayer indoor plant production system in which all growth factors, such as light, temperature, humidity, carbon dioxide concentration, water, and nutrients, are precisely controlled to produce high quantities of high-quality fresh produce year-round, completely independent of solar light and other outdoor conditions.

Favourite products of these systems are leafy greens, tomatoes, strawberries, cucumbers, all with low calorie requirements and very short production cycles. When the products are able to charge premium prices or when costs decrease (as, for example, in the adoption of alternative energy sources), the range of products can expand to include a wider variety of vegetables, fruits, medicinal products, and flowers.

China demonstrated new technical possibilities by showcasing giant pumpkins and tubers such as sweet potatoes at the International Conference on Vertical Farming and Urban Agriculture in 2014 (Thorpe, 2014). China is also exceptional in its application of the climate-controlled vertical farm concept to pig production. Chinese pig producer Zhongxin Kaiwei raises and slaughters 1.2 million pigs per year in a 26-storey building, each floor with its own air circulation, connected by a 40-tonne, 65 square metres lift to accommodate 200 pigs. Management is handled by NetEase Weiyang, of the internet sector, which took advantage of the crisis resulting from the outbreak of swine fever and the hike in prices in 2020 to enter this market by applying all the resources of automation, recycling of air, water and waste, facial recognition of pigs, daily temperature measurement, identity cards for each pig and the use of RFIDs (radio frequency identification) to trace the product right through to the consumer (Wakabayashi and Fu, 2023).

In Asia there are other examples of the application of the vertical farming principle to products not contemplated in Northern countries. In 2018, a vertical rice demonstration field was set up in Hanoi Central Square in Vietnam, using dwarf rice varieties with water and nutrient recycling.[4] In the Philippines, on the other hand, we have examples of vertical farming that also adapt the traditional model of terraced farming for rice using a bamboo structure and including rainwater harvesting techniques (Meinhold, 2013).

Similarly, projects that won prizes in the International Tropical Architecture Design competition at the Singapore Green Building Week 2017 event were designed for low-income neighbourhoods. One of the projects aims for a vertical farming complex of 11 storeys divided into 36 m^2 plots targeting the lowest income population (the bottom 10 per cent) to initially produce cabbage, spinach, and tomatoes, and then progress to other types of products. Another project aims to defend urban farmers threatened by the advance of real estate by building houses with roof farms and using solar energy. The houses would be built with stilts and surrounded by bamboo and banana plantations to absorb rainwater. They would also be surrounded by rice fields, imitating the rural traditions of cultivating the backyard.[5]

Even in Northern countries, vertical farming ambitions go beyond niche markets. In England, Jones Foods Company's goal is to supply 70 per cent of English demand for fresh produce within ten years, and Denmark's Nordic Harvest estimates that 20 vertical farming plants alone could meet the country's entire demand.

Arama Kukutai, the CEO of Plenty, one of the largest vertical farming companies in the United States, which has received a total of US$900 million in funding, commented in relation to the support it received from Walmart in 2022:

> It creates the opportunity to actually get to scale, not just being a niche provider of expensive greens, as the category has been somewhat accused of in the past. This isn't just about high-quality, organic leafy greens. This is about getting to consumers on a more democratic and broad basis. (Repko, 2022)

Similarly, Jamie Burrows, CEO of Vertical Future, a leading firm in the technology for vertical farming, states:

> Unlike others in the vertical farming sector whose technologies and ambitions are restricted to growing only premium-priced salad and microgreens for a premium domestic and restaurant market, we are aiming to feed everyday working families with fairly priced, higher-quality produce. (Ridler, 2022)

Fischer Farms, which operates one of the largest vertical farms in the UK:

> over the next 10 to 15 years [...] plans to scale its operations and reduce its cost base to enable it to ultimately grow soya beans, rice, and wheat in significant volumes and at price points that compare favourably to global commodity prices.[6] (Flynn, 2021)

Aquaculture, or fish farming, accounts globally for more than half of fish, seafood, and shellfish consumption, and China alone accounts for more than half of this. In the diversification of traditional global commodity chains in the 1980s, shrimp farming, together with horticulture, became one of the most important non-traditional export markets for developing countries. This is the fish farming counterpart of climate-controlled agriculture. In many traditional systems there is a combination of fish and food cultivation, where the fish waste is used as plant nutrients. Vertical farming also includes systems that combine plants and fish. In the same way that vertical farming is seen as a strategy to reduce long circuits and food miles, companies such as Upward Farms already identify the local production of fish and shellfish in vertical systems as a major opportunity to replace imports, which supply up to 90 per cent of domestic consumption in the United States[7] (Peters, 2021).

This brief description of different types of vertical farming seeks to demonstrate the variety of their structures and scales, location options, and types of products and producers, in addition to identifying the way that precision farming in the form of high-tech greenhouses converges with the principles of vertical farming in a broader concept of agriculture – or rather of food production – in controlled climates.

By 2020, the global vertical farm market was estimated at US$5.5 billion and forecast to reach US$19.86 billion by 2026. The investments of the financial ecosystem were calculated at US$1.3 billion in an assessment by AgFunder, or 5 per cent of the total for the agfood tech sector in the same year, while PitchBook's calculation came to US$1.9 billion.

The major concern of consulting firms tracking the sector is with the first type of vertical agriculture identified by Van Gerreway, Boon and Geelen (2022) and reformulated here: farms installed in custom-redesigned buildings based on LED (light-emitting diode) artificial lighting systems, also known as plant factories with artificial lighting (PFALs). In this segment, the priorities are scale and cost, and the focus is on leafy greens, microgreens, tomatoes, strawberries, cucumbers, peppers, and spinach. In the United States, the leafy vegetable market is valued at US$22 billion and the global market at US$100 billion, while the global market for the whole of the fresh produce category reaches up to US$1.3 trillion, close to the size of the global meat market.[8]

This is still a phase of much experimentation with different technological routes involving new competencies and players. There are very different systems of land replacement – hydroponics, aquaponics, aeroponics – as well as a wide range of components – irrigation, lighting, sensors/automation/ robotization, and climate control systems using big data. Companies specializing in each component coexist with firms that offer turnkey solutions (Allied Market Research, 2023).

The central challenge of vertical farming stems from its stubborn desire to replace the sun's role in photosynthesis. It is not surprising, then, that this challenge attracts the global electrical power companies. General Electric acts through its subsidiary, Current; Philips with its company, Signify; and other global companies (Everlight Electronics Company, NTT, Osram GmbH, Dell, and Nokia) invest in the sector, all committed to increasing the efficiency of their energy use and LED lighting, adjusted to each type of plant and time of year. It is estimated that between 2010 and 2017 the prices of LED systems fell by 10 times, fulfilling 'Haitz's law' formulated in

2000 predicting that LED prices would fall ten-fold and their power would increase 20 times every 10 years.[9]

The sector also attracts the big electronics, computer, internet, and telecommunications companies – Samsung, LG, Panasonic, Mitsubishi, Tencent, Huawei, Alibaba, JD.com – which cooperate intensively among themselves, especially in the Asian region. New companies are emerging that specialize in delivering entire systems, such as Tsunagu Community Farm in Japan, Infinite Acres in the United States/Europe axis, YesHealth Group in Taiwan, Sky Greens in Singapore, and Sananbio in China.[10]

Urban Crop Solutions from Belgium, which also offers turnkey solutions, presents itself as the 'front runner in indoor plant biology research'.[11] Tom Debusschere, its CEO, states that:

> the true step-change will be plant biology. Many seed manufacturers are taking notice and are now investing in developing the right seed genetics and improving yield. Here is the good news: with improving yields, we are just a few years away from the real breakthroughs of the vertical farming industry. (Boekhout, 2021)

An indication of this is the partnership between Bayer and the investment fund Temasek (Singapore) in setting up the company Unfold specifically to provide vegetable and fruit germplasm suitable for vertical farming (Hall, 2020). In 2021, a major vertical farming company in the United States, Kalera, which specializes in supplying large consumer centres such as airports and theme parks and is already a leader in plant sciences, acquired the seed company Vindara Inc., the first to produce non-GMO seeds specifically for climate-controlled environments. Its breeding technology, which includes machine learning, allows for a reduction in the development time of a new variety from 5–7 years to 12–18 months (Antos, 2021). Other companies are starting to enter this sector, such as Kasveista from Germany, which specializes in developing open-source cultivars that can broaden the product base of vertical farming, as well as cultivars adapted to climate-controlled environments.

With the emergence of transgenic seed markets in the 1980s, patenting strategies were adopted by the leading companies as a substitute for the protection system of genetic breeders that had hitherto ensured a type of open innovation. The protection of innovations by patents has now become widespread in the case of vertical farming systems. China's Sananbio had 416 patents by 2020; Singapore's Sky Greens' modular tower system is patented; BrightFarms in the United States is dedicated to 'patented growing solutions'; and Plenty, another US company in the sector, which in its last two funding rounds received US$140 million and US$400 million respectively, is described as having, 'a robust intellectual property portfolio'.

Patents and 'trademarks' also characterize the strategy of AeroFarms, the US vertical farming pioneer whose breadth can be appreciated from its notice on the company's website:

> AeroFarms processes, equipment, and components such as soilless growth media, methods of growing plants using soilless growth media, cleaning soilless growth media, and marking plant tissue may be covered under one or more of the following patents assigned to New AeroFarms Inc. DBA AeroFarms ('AeroFarms').[12]

Until 2007, the number of patents granted annually for the vertical sector was below 50, a number that had risen to around 900 in 2020, dominated by companies such as Panasonic and LG (Newell, 2021).

Van Gerreway, Boon and Geelen's (2022) typology, which prioritizes distinctions in terms of facilities and equipment, is useful as it simultaneously points to the different environments where they are used, which opens the possibility for specializations within the sector. On the other hand, there is a common technological base across all types which includes: dispensing with the use of soil, resorting to artificial light, and management by computerized control systems. Companies that supply technologies and systems can operate in all categories. It would be better, therefore, to broaden the application of this typology by interpreting the different environments as different relations between production and consumption. In this way, different conceptions of what the fundamental problems of the dominant food system are and how they should be faced, as well as different conceptions of the relations between city and countryside, can be highlighted.

In a surprising catchphrase, the owner of Sky Greens (a company that combines the supply of large modular tower systems with the franchising of containerized microfarms) described Singapore as 'a microcosm of the rest of the world' (Tan, 2021). Many visions of the future of vertical agriculture restrict its applicability to high-income regions that suffer from extreme lack of natural resources. Singapore, in this sense, would be suitable for vertical agriculture precisely because of its conditions of extreme dependence on food imports, which account for up to 90 per cent of its needs.

However, vertical agriculture is characterized by its rapid globalization, and has already spread unevenly throughout the world. The growth of the global population and its simultaneous urbanization against a backdrop of the energy crisis and climate change means that a scarcity of natural resources, masked in many cases by the integration of agri-food markets into long global chains, is becoming a reality for most countries in the world. The Middle East, like Singapore, lacks water and land to supply itself with food, but northern Europe depends on fruit and vegetable imports from southern Europe and Africa, and the eastern United States depends on the same fruits and vegetables from the West Coast and Mexico. The Nordic countries suffer from a lack of natural light and inhospitable conditions for agriculture for much of the year. China loses huge amounts of agricultural land to urbanization and the network of highways and railways, and suffers from regions of extreme conditions such as the Gobi Desert. Even regions of exuberant agriculture are threatened by prolonged droughts, increasingly violent fire, or devastating rainfall against which not even the 'protected' agriculture of Almería in Spain has been immune (Alonso, 2021).

Panasonic, which invests heavily in vertical farming in China, Singapore, and Japan, specializes in food production in extreme environments and carries out research on Ishigaki Island on vertical farming that can withstand tornadoes and hurricanes (Panasonic Group, 2021).

The motivations behind the promotion of vertical farming are varied. In the case of Dickson Despommier, agriculture represents the greatest historical assault on the environment, a view shared by the CEO of Nordic Harvest in Denmark, who sees the internalization of agriculture in the city as an opportunity for returning the countryside to nature, a notion known as 'rewilding' (Monbiot, 2022). Most of the promoters of vertical farming in the United States, however, point to the anomaly of a food system where the place of greatest consumption, the East Coast, is four or five days by truck from the production regions of the leafy vegetables and fruits they consume. This is increasingly unacceptable as the values of healthiness prioritize fresh and local produce. In this sense, leaders in the vertical farming sector characterize the dominant agri-food system as 'broken'.

This same perspective is shared by the CEO of Nordic Harvest in Denmark, who complains that an apple arriving by air from New Zealand benefits from the premium prices of an organic certification denied to his company's local, pesticide-free production. In northern Europe, the bigger motivation, however, is to replace dependence on products from southern Europe and northern Africa, with similar consequences as in the United States for the climate and the healthiness of products (Persson, 2021).

The category that dominates the sector corresponds to the first type described in the typology presented previously. It is vertical farming developed in high-tech buildings almost exclusively based on artificial light with high degrees of automation and even robotization where all aspects of the environment are controlled by big data systems. The largest cluster is in the United States – AeroFarms, Plenty, BrightFarms, AppHarvest, 80 Acres Farms, Bowery Farming – but Japan's Spread was the first company to produce on a large scale as of 2008, and there are big players, almost all claiming to be the biggest, also in Europe and Asia – Sananbio in China, Sky Greens in Singapore, YesHealth in Thailand, the Jones Food Company in England, Intelligent Growth Solutions in Scotland, Nordic Harvest in Denmark, and Crop One and Badia Farms in Dubai (Nex, 2018).

AppHarvest is the only one of these companies to complete an exit or go public (IPO), and this experience was quite negative with a sharp fall in the value of its shares soon after launch and a further reduction in 2022 after declaring major losses in 2021. AeroFarms also prepared for an IPO in 2021 but then desisted. However, these companies continue to receive tens and even hundreds of millions of dollars in successive funding rounds. AeroFarms itself has received US$238 million since its inception in 2004. In 2022, in 'series E' of its funding, Plenty received US$400 million, after having already received US$140 million in the previous round. Bowery Farming, for its part, has already received US$300 million, BrightFarms received US$112 million, and 80 Acres Farms raised US$160 million, with Siemens among the investors (SustainFi, 2022).

The scale of operations is a key feature, and while there is no single best practice, areas vary between 5,000 and 35,000 m^2, productivity per cultivated area can be up to 300 times greater than in conventional agriculture, and harvesting time can be reduced to less than a month. With these dimensions, daily production reaches tens of thousands of units per day, with continuous production, day and night, for 365 days. In the case of lettuces, the most popular of the leafy varieties, production, depending on the plant, can reach 20,000 or even 30,000 lettuces per day.

This scale of production is only viable through long-term contracts with the large retailers, and all these vertical agriculture companies are characterized by these ties. In the case of the Plenty company, the last round had the participation of Walmart, which, in return, has a seat on the board of directors. Walmart chose this partnership with Plenty for being a company that in addition to leafy greens also produces vegetables and fruit. AeroFarms has partnerships with Whole Foods, ShopRite, Amazon Fresh, and Amazon Direct; Bowery Farming with Whole Foods and Foragers; BrightFarms with Walmart, Giant, and Metro Market; 80 Acres Farms with Kroger; and AppHarvest with Kroger, Publix, Walmart, Food City, and Meijer (Repko, 2022).

The same relationship prevails in Europe, where England's Jones Food Company Ltd is funded by Ocado, a leading online retailer that in turn created Infinite Acres, a vertical farming technology solutions company in partnership with 80 Acres Farms and Priva BV of the Netherlands, which specializes in climate-controlled buildings. Ocado has also established partnerships with other retail sectors in England, Marks & Spencer; and in the United States with Kroger (Mattinson and Nott, 2020).

AeroFarms illustrates most clearly the strategies of this large-scale vertical farming. Founded in 2004 in New Jersey and considered an industry leader in the United States, AeroFarms produces around one million kilos of leafy vegetables per year in this plant and plans another larger plant in Virginia. The company's goal is to establish hubs in every region of the country in partnership with major retailers so that they can be only 24 hours away from any retailer. On their websites, these companies justify the option for vertical agriculture, citing the energy costs for the climate and for the quality of food of a system based on long – even global – food supply chains. They also cite water savings and the non-use of pesticides. On the other hand, by promoting an unprecedented concentration of production, vertical-scale agriculture needs to integrate with large-scale retailing and thus reinforces the current distribution system. It may be local production, but it implies the promotion of local markets for sale to supermarkets and not to the consumer (Klein, 2021).

Dickson Despommier (2010) had already highlighted the concentration of production in vertical farming by arguing that a 30-storey building would be able to provide food all year round for 50,000 people, or that the entire consumption of Manhattan could be supplied in an area only 20 per cent the size of Central Park. Arthur Nelson, the CEO of Nordic Harvest, captured the implications of this for market dynamics by claiming that just 20 vertical farming plants could supply the whole of Denmark with salads. Jones Food Company, whose plans include a new plant capable of producing 1,000 tonnes of leafy vegetables a year, has already translated this insight into a business strategy by setting a target of supplying 70 per cent of UK demand for fresh produce within 10 years. For some analysts, the vertical farming sector in Manhattan is already suffering from overcrowding.

Most of the literature critical of the agri-food system focuses on concentration processes in agricultural production with the emergence of megafarms, which indeed represents a qualitative transformation in agricultural dynamics. However, in Brazilian grain production where the phenomenon of megafarms is perhaps most in evidence, there are still more than 240,000 soybean/corn producers. The horticultural sector in the United States, where vertical farming is beginning to come into its own, has just over 23,000 producers (2014 data), a third of whom are defined as corporations. More than 80 per cent of production goes to the wholesale sector, while small producers sell primarily to retailers. In contrast, the production of vertical farming is sold directly to retailers, and a dozen or so companies alone can supply the entire market (Letterman and White, 2020).

This new dynamic of competition, typically industrial, is leading to rapid growth strategies and early globalization, enabled by the high levels of funding for these companies. AeroFarms has already established a research centre in Dubai targeting the Middle East market, and Jones Food Company is looking to produce a plant there as well. Taiwan's YesHealth Group provides technology to Nordic Harvest in Denmark and builds plants in China. The Japanese Panasonic invests in China. Singapore's Sky Greens trades its technology in Thailand, China, Malaysia, India, and Canada. Japan's Spread prospects markets in Europe, the United States, and the Middle East.[13]

It is not easy at this stage of market development to distinguish between companies dedicated to production ('growers') and providers of technology services, either in the form of entire turnkey, off-the-shelf systems, or specialized segments. Producers may develop plants as 'proofs of concept' or may have strategies to occupy and dominate this new market like AeroFarms, Nordic Harvest, Jones Food Company, and others, but they tend also to develop an intellectual property portfolio to sell technology services. On the other hand, there are companies that specialize in offering these services for which the market is global from the outset.

Rob Laing is the CEO and founder of Farm.One, which provides complete installations controlled by smartphones to be installed in sophisticated restaurants, initially in Manhattan and then in various states across the United States. According to Laing, despite the hundreds of millions of dollars invested and the scale of its operations, vertical farming has not yet proved profitable and simply reinforces the power of the big supermarkets without introducing innovations to the food system and he foresees an increase in retailers' contractual control over agriculture (Laing, 2021).

While these aspects of economic power may be confirmed with the consolidation of vertical farming, important innovations accompany this process. There are significant gains in reduced transport costs, carbon footprint, and the non-use of pesticides. AeroFarms has developed an aggregate nutritional density index, which measures the nutritional superiority of its products. Jones Food Company, as well as other companies such as Spread in Japan, adopts systems of automation and robotization that ensure products do not come into human contact in a 'no touch' system and do not need to be washed before consumption. Large-scale vertical farming can indeed lead to a strengthening of economic power, both through contractual controls and by marginalizing the wholesale sector of this chain. On the other hand, it also brings a new normal of quality levels, both in terms of healthiness and in relation to the environment. In Asia and the United States, its production can be certified as organic, while in Europe and in the understanding of the International Federation of Organic Agriculture Movements (IFOAM) the management of the soil and its nutrients is a precondition for this certification. Alternative certifications, generated by the companies themselves or by class associations, specifying the characteristics of vertical farming systems, including the non-use of pesticides, may eventually replace organic certification and ensure premium prices (Neslen, 2021).

On a macro structural level, large-scale vertical farming, while appealing to the virtues of 'local' production, does not imply a questioning of traditional agri-food relations or the place of food in urban life. AeroFarms' strategy of creating a network of vertical farming hubs to supply all the major US cities within 24 hours is indicative in this sense. It is, as before, a supply system that links production to consumption through large-scale retailing. Nordic Harvest has the same vision of production on a country-wide scale but sees this as a means of internalizing food production in cities and freeing up rural areas for the recuperation of nature.

The typology presented earlier identified several other systems and types of equipment for vertical farming, each pointing, in our reinterpretation of the typology, to different relations between production and consumption and, at the limit, to radically different conceptions of the position of food in urban life and its implications for the planning and design of cities.

Several of the companies that operate on a large scale also develop a line of small container-like equipment. Bowery Farming from the United States supplies systems for restaurants; Singapore's Sky Greens sells a microfarming system that integrates the production of fish, vegetables, and leafy greens. Many companies specialize in the delivery of automated systems and operate globally. Freight Farms in the United States claims the position as the world's leading producer of turnkey container systems whose operations are controlled by smartphones. The target audiences are small business owners and community institutions, and its website shows operations in various regions of the world (Marston, 2023).

Infarm from Germany, established in 2013, has raised EUR254 million in funding which includes EUR169 million during the COVID-19 pandemic. It already operates its small facilities in 30 cities and 10 countries and produces more than 500,000 plants per month. The idea is to produce at the places of purchase or consumption. All these facilities are controlled from a cloud-based, centralized 'farm brain' that collects 50,000 items of data over the life of a plant, using all the power of digitalization to learn, adapt, and improve plant performance. According to co-founder Erez Galonska:

> The coronavirus pandemic has put a global spotlight on the urgent agricultural and ecological challenges of our time. At Infarm, we believe there's a better, healthier way to feed our cities: increasing access to fresh, pure, sustainable produce, grown as close as possible to people. As we scale to 5,000,000 sq ft in farming facilities across Europe, North America and Asia by 2025, this investment will help us make a truly global impact through our network, preserving thousands of acres of land, millions of liters of water and ultimately change the way people grow, eat and think about food. (Tucker, 2020)[14]

Infarm has partnerships with 17 of the top 50 global supermarket chains, which points to an interest on the part of retailers to combine their contractual relationships with large vertical farming companies with the on-site production of fresh produce, particularly in their smaller facilities. In Tokyo, seven supermarkets have contracted with Infarm to install their small-scale indoor farms motivated by the goal of decreasing the energy costs, gas emissions, and food waste that characterize conventional products.

The beginnings of vertical farming are often associated with the United States, but the first vertical farming company at scale was Spread in Japan, which was established in 2007 and by 2021 was supplying 2,500 supermarkets under its Vegetus brand. The ageing rural population was an initial stimulus, but the earthquake and tsunami in Fukushima in 2011, which damaged the nuclear power plant in the region, provided a more urgent stimulus, and the city government there subsidizes the A+ vertical farm company, which produces 20,000 lettuces per day.

Spread became profitable as early as 2013, a feat that many companies have yet to achieve, and established a second factory in 2018 with a capacity of 30,000 lettuces per day based on what it calls its second-generation production system, Techno Farm, which involves automation, artificial intelligence, and the internet of things (IoT). In 2021, Spread partnered with the Eneos Group, one of Japan's largest corporations, to develop a third plant, this time located in Greater Tokyo, that incorporates all of Techno Farm's technology, will have 28 levels of cultivation and will use solar energy. The company aims to have some 10 plants in operation by 2025 and a production capacity of one hundred tonnes per day by 2030. Based on its new partnerships, Spread aims to expand into Europe, the United States, and the Middle East (Harding, 2020).

The decriminalization of cannabis for recreational purposes in 14 states and for medicinal purposes in 36 states in the United States, as well as its decriminalization in some countries in Europe, has been a major stimulus for small-scale vertical farming using the latest technology, especially LED lighting. In the United States, the legalized market was estimated at US$17.5 billion in 2021 with the forecast to reach up to US$41 billion in 2026 according to BDSA, a cannabis data platform. At the same time, the illicit market is estimated at US$100 billion, indicating the growth potential of this market. Several companies specialize in systems and equipment for this market: Illuminex Technologies, AEssenseGrows, Heliospectra. Surna, based in Colorado, one of the first states to decriminalize this market, provides indoor solutions for over 800 customers (Yakowicz, 2021).

A quick search on the internet reveals many types of equipment for sale to set up vertical farming options in houses, garages, and flats. The German company Agrilution, created in 2013, whose founder fits into the new generation of engaged or 'mission driven' entrepreneurs, and was motivated by his experience as a child in rural China and then as a member of Greenpeace to find sustainable solutions to the global food system, manufactures 'a personal farm ecosystem'. The fully automated Plantcube measures 120 × 62.5 × 46 centimetres. The system is controlled by a company app, and the seeds, called seedbars, can be bought from the company's website. The company's motto is 'No plastics, no supply chains, just greens' (Albrecht, 2019).[15]

Vertical scale farming adapts to the profitability demands of the economy by verticalizing its production or occupying and converting abandoned or low-value buildings. It can also, as in the case of AeroFarms, be located in rural areas close to large consumer centres. In any of these options, these are autonomous buildings designed to optimize costs and profitability by supplying food for supermarket chains. Very different are those strategies whose aim is to meet the food demands of city dwellers in their daily lives and, therefore, develop appropriate units for different urban environments – schools, workplaces, community centres, houses, and condominiums. Companies can, however, combine both strategies like Sky Greens in Singapore. We have already seen the strategy of Infarm, the German company with Dickson Despommier as consultant, of providing small modules inside supermarkets. Here we are talking about a local production that does not require packaging, in line with Agrilution's motto: 'no plastics'.

One goal of these companies is to embrace the concept of the circular economy in the reuse of water, the adoption of renewable energy, and the elimination of waste or leftovers. These goals are being supported by vertical agriculture research centres. Technische Universiteit Delft in the Netherlands:

> [explores the integration of vertical farming] in buildings and cities to capture, share, and reuse resources such as carbon dioxide, heat, rainwater, food, and nutrients. This includes integrating vertical farms with a building's electricity, heat, and resource systems as well as the broader integration with urban heat grids and micro electricity grids, making them a constituent component of future circular resource systems in cities. It is hoped that by leveraging symbiotic relationships between vertical farming and the built environment, the reduction in energy use of vertical farms can be fast-tracked, without relying solely on the technical advancements of equipment within the farm. (Jenkins, 2022)

The notion of establishing a symbiotic relationship between vertical farming and its built environment is stimulating a new generation of architects to rethink the urban environment where vertical farming is integrated into everyday urban life. The Réinventer Paris project launched by the City of Paris included a competition for urban renewal projects that resulted in the design of a series of hybrid buildings and complexes combining work, housing, and food production that were presented at the conference of the same name in 2017 (Rosenfield, 2015).

In Singapore and Shanghai, vertical farming is being integrated into urban planning and policies. The Singapore Food Agency encourages the cultivation of food in living areas and workplaces, promotes rooftop gardens on car parks being built by Citiponics, and a programme of retrofitting commercial and office buildings with vertical farms initiated by the company Sustenis. At the same it has designated two industrial areas, Lim Chu Kang and Sungei Tengah, for large-scale urban agriculture and aquaculture.[16]

In the case of Shanghai, the Sunqiao Urban Agricultural District has been created, designed by Sasaki Associates from the United States – an area of 100 hectares dedicated to vertical farming, teaching, and research to produce the leafy vegetables that are so important in the city's consumption. Shanghai, like other cities in China, has a long tradition of food production within the urban perimeter that is being threatened by the advance of urban equipment and land valuation (Grove, 2022).

We return to this theme in Chapter 5 in the context of a broader analysis of the way in which China is addressing food security challenges and the role that the government attaches to the waves of innovation transforming the agri-food system. In the final chapter of this book, we analyse the impact of these transformations on the historical relations between countryside and city and the emergence of new policies and conceptions of planning on the place of food production in the urban environment.

Leading vertical agriculture companies are valued in the billions and are the targets of venture capital, the retail sector, and large high-tech companies. At the same time, many of them are surviving on funding without showing operational returns. The ecosystem we have outlined in previous chapters favours fast growth but with equally fast returns. By 2021, the shares of AppHarvest, the only vertical farming company to go public, plummeted; and AeroFarms, touted as the largest company in the United States, gave up its stock market launch at the last minute after partnering with a special purpose acquisition company (SPAC) for that purpose.

In the light of these developments, Henry Gordon-Smith, CEO of consultancy Agritecture, asks where vertical farming stands in the famous 'hype cycle' elaborated by Gartner.[17] According to Gartner, the cycle starts with an innovation trigger that leads to a spike in inflated expectations, followed by a low of disillusionment. But from there, the cycle can resume an upward slope of 'enlightenment' until it reaches a plateau of productivity. Gordon-Smith identifies the current situation as that of the beginning of disillusionment but bets on a recovery if the sector can move beyond the hype (Gordon-Smith, 2021). In our analysis, in addition to the amounts of venture capital that favour large investments and fast returns, we emphasize the presence of sovereign wealth funds, of public policies in rich developing countries with scarce natural resources, and the diverse range of global high-technology companies investing in the sector. If we add to this the exponential decline in the costs of LED electricity, and the increasing use of renewable energy sources, we can conclude that while certain types of venture capital may hesitate in the face of negative IPO results, vertical farming already relies on strong segments of the real economy and on public authorities for which traditional agriculture, in light of the uncertainties and costs of long supply chains, no longer guarantees their food security.

As central components of this real economy, we have seen that large-scale global retail has already inserted vertical farming into its supply chains. In this segment of horticulture, climate-controlled forms of agriculture account for half of all production, and their share only increases. For retailers, therefore, the transition to fully controlled agricultural systems that are not only protected but entirely 'indoors' can be assimilated as a natural evolution. At the limit, this implies the elimination of the agricultural chain and a concentration of production at industrial levels. At the same time, it implies a 'domestication' of this type of vertical agriculture into the already established supply circuits of large retailers. A more radical view of the potential for redefining food supply systems in cities emerges when we deal with the other types of vertical farming that can be inserted into any building and into all the contexts of everyday life in cities. The disruptive impact of vertical farming in cities is most evident in urban design projects that propose hybrid buildings and neighbourhoods that integrate the cultivation of food in the daily life of city dwellers.

4

Animal Protein Chains
under the Spotlight

We have just looked at the emergence of a system of food production that no longer requires the use of land, light, and sun, and creates its own environment, all perfectly suited to urban life. In this chapter, we will examine transformations in food products that point to radical changes in the human diet through the supply of equally nutritious and tasty substitutes for the whole range of animal protein products: meats from all kinds of animals, milk and dairy products (butter, cheeses, whipped cream, yoghurts, ice cream, and even human milk),[1] eggs and egg products (mayonnaise, egg white), together with fish and shellfish of all kinds.

It is not only a question of increasing the number of vegetarian and vegan options, millenary traditions in human history and strongly represented in the founders of the modern food industry, as indicated in previous chapters. Nor are the motives limited to spiritual or mental and physical health issues but include the valuing of animal welfare in the face of the cruelty of industrial systems of rearing and slaughter. Added to this is the perceived impossibility of generalizing an animal protein diet to the increasingly urban global population, given the example of the extraordinary growth of Chinese demand for meat in the last two decades. Above all, however, are the costs of the various animal protein chains, in terms of fossil fuel use, destruction of forests and biodiversity, and their strong contribution to greenhouse gases.

This set of factors is driving the extraordinary wave of product innovations whose stated aim is to replace the conventional global animal protein food chains. Climate-controlled agriculture and vertical farming promise to displace much of 'protected' agriculture and integrate horticulture into urban life. Alternative proteins based on plants, algae, fungi, and insects promise a drastic reduction of land devoted to livestock and feed production. Half of the world's habitable land is devoted to agriculture and 70–80 per cent of this to livestock (Ritchie and Roser, 2024). The release of this land for rewilding of various kinds, especially in the form of reforestation, extends beyond the recovery of cattle-raising areas, because the direct consumption of vegetable protein also avoids the costs of converting this protein into animal protein, which in the case of beef demands eight to ten kilograms of feed for one kilogram of meat. Cellular or cultivated protein, on the other hand, in which meats are produced from the multiplication of animal cells, reduces even more drastically the reliance on agriculture by replacing feed with culture media, including algae. These are innovations whose objectives involve nothing less than a redefinition of country–city relations, consolidated during the last 12,000 years.

As we have already indicated, vegetarianism and veganism have been part of dietary choices from time immemorial.[2] Because of the difficulty of hunting, it is estimated that plants, fruits, nuts, and fungi were the mainstay of our ancestors' diet. However, studies also suggest that the energy derived from meat was decisive for human evolution (Zink and Lieberman, 2016). There is evidence that the Egyptians had a 'plant-based' diet four thousand years ago, probably for religious reasons, this being also the case with the ancient Greeks and Romans, led by Pythagoras and followed by Aristotle, the poet Ovid, and the philosopher Seneca.[3] Vegetarianism has been identified with self-control, abstinence, and even pacifism, on the understanding that the refusal to kill animals would also lead to valuing human life. Several streams of Christianity embraced vegetarianism where the Garden of Eden provided the reference to a time of innocence and coexistence with animals and a diet based on fruits and plants. Contact with the Indian subcontinent revealed a millenary culture, uninfluenced by Christian traditions, associated with vegetarianism. The 19th century saw the creation of vegetarian societies in England in 1847, and the USA in 1850. Famous figures identified themselves as vegetarians, such as Benjamin Franklin, Tolstoy, Louisa May Alcott, and George Bernard Shaw. In the second half of the 19th century, vegetarianism suffered from its association with eugenics, which would show its monstrous face in the following century (Stuart, 2008; Spencer, 2016).

Marta Zaraska (2016) argues that the hardships of the two world wars and the abundant supply of meat, especially poultry and pork (also beneficiaries of new hybrid genetics from the wave of innovations associated with the green revolution) in the post-war period, marginalized vegetarianism. From the 1970s on, however, there was a renewal of vegetarianism on new bases. In 1971, Frances Moore Lappé published the book *Diet for a Small Planet*, defending vegetarianism from the point of view of its necessity to preserve the environment. In 1975, Peter Singer published *Animal Liberation*, which also defended vegetarianism but from the perspective of animal welfare, repeating Pythagoras's ethical criticism in the context, now, of industrial mass slaughter in the horrendous conditions described by Upton Sinclair and later by Eric Schlosser, to whom we referred at the beginning of this book. Thus, vegetarianism leaves the niche of people more motivated by spiritual reasons and converges with movements mobilized around the environment and animal rights, reinforced also by the growing association of meat consumption with cardiovascular diseases.[4]

In the first two decades of the new millennium, both vegetarianism and veganism (an indicator of the growing weight of animal welfare considerations) increased in popularity. The Vegan Society in the UK commissioned market research by Ipsos Mori, which interviewed 10,000 people and calculated that the number of vegans had increased from 150,000 in 2006 to 542,000 in 2016 (Finnerty, 2020).

Famous figures (Beyoncé, Natalie Portman, Gisele Bündchen, Serena Williams, Brad Pitt) have taken up vegan diets, and a series of documentaries – *Earthlings*, *Cowspiracy*, *Seaspiracy*, *Forks Over Knives* – has reproduced for a new generation the impact *Fast Food Nation* had in the early 2000s by revealing the guts of the industrial system of large-scale meat and fish production and slaughter. The Veganuary campaign, the commitment to try a vegan diet during the month of January, the traditional month of new resolutions, was launched in 2014 with 3,300 sign-ups and exploded to 250,000 subscribers in 2019. In Europe and the United States, calculations indicate vegans as being something around 2 per cent to 3 per cent of the population, and vegetarians around 7 per cent to 8 per cent, and may even reach 10 per cent in the case of Germany, where Berlin, which has a population of 3 million, has 80,000 vegans (Wunsch, 2022).

For some analysts, veganism has already become mainstream, although it retains the characteristics of a social movement. Indications of this are the weight of the coverage of vegetarianism and veganism in culinary magazines, television shows, and social media. More important is the migration of vegan dishes to the big supermarkets and fast-food chains: Marks & Spencer, Pret A Manger, Pizza Hut. For others, the adoption of vegetarian and vegan dishes by leading companies is not aimed only, nor principally, at those committed to these diets but rather bets on the growth of what are called 'flexitarians', people who want to reduce their meat consumption and are willing to incorporate vegetarian and vegan dishes in their daily lives (Fi Global Insights, 2019).

Although flexitarians are a social category that can be captured in statistics, there are as yet no flexitarian products. Thus, identification is based on the willingness to consume vegan or vegetarian dishes. The current period is one in which social movements that promote new markets provoke and converge with broader changes in consumer preferences. Estimates of the number of flexitarians vary widely. The consultancy Packaged Facts calculated that they represented 36 per cent of the North American population in 2020, while YouGov estimated these at 12 per cent in the United States and 13 per cent in England (Dabhade, 2021). Even at the lowest calculations, the sum of this potential market amounts to 25 per cent of the population of these countries.

However radical in its transformation from rural/agricultural to urban/ industrial activities, vertical and climate-controlled agriculture fits into the ongoing changes in dietary practices that are leading to the increased consumption of fresh, 'green' produce. In contrast, the shift away from meat in favour of alternative proteins, clashes head-on with consumption patterns rooted for centuries, particularly in countries where meat also carries strong social and gender symbolism (O'Doherty Jensen and Holm, 1999). Many studies, on the other hand, identify an increasing mistrust of meat, influenced by all the reasons that animate social movements, but conclude that changes in consumption practices are more ambivalent and that the statistical data do not point to a decline in consumption in these countries, although they do suggest that in Europe consumption has stopped increasing since 2020 (Holm and Møhl, 2000; Sijtsema et al, 2021). A review of research conducted in Australia, USA, Canada, New Zealand, Denmark, Portugal, Switzerland, Germany, UK, France, Netherlands, and Belgium concludes: 'In most cases in the midst of a majority of dedicated carnivores, these surveys offer growing evidence for the presence of a distinct category of flexitarians' (Dagevos, 2021, p 535).

The percentages of flexitarians identified in each study vary hugely, but in the median they converge with the figures indicated by Packaged Facts and YouGov. It is, at the same time, an internally heterogeneous category. Firstly, a distinction is made between 'reducetarians', who as the name suggests simply reduce their meat consumption, and those who actively replace meat with alternative proteins (Kateman, 2017). This distinction is crucially important for the new generation of alternative protein start-ups, and the leading companies that follow them, who want to occupy and expand this emerging space of a replacement market.

The surveys also adopt several categories to indicate the degree of commitment: semi-light, medium, heavy, potential, unconscious/conscious flexitarian – all of which point to a dynamic situation in a state of flux. The proliferation of studies on these changes in consumer behaviour reflects a consensus on their central role in responding to the challenges that current and projected levels of meat consumption present for public health and their ability to contain the effects of climate change (Raphaely and Marinova, 2014).[5]

The consensus becoming established in the academic and scientific world and being disseminated in the various media is reinforced by the convergence of national and international public directives guiding food priorities. We saw in Chapter 2 how stronger measures are being taken in the case of sugar, where more than 50 countries have already implemented a tax on this product. In the case of meat, Denmark, Sweden, Germany, the Netherlands, and New Zealand are studying the feasibility of imposing a meat tax, and the UK government has already commissioned a study in this direction (Charlton, 2019).

On the other hand, subsidies for the meat and dairy sectors in the US have reached US$30 billion in 2020 (Ho, 2021a), and in the European Union direct payments for these sectors reached between EUR28 and EUR32 billion. Moreover, the European Union spent EUR259 million, or 32 per cent of its advertising budget between 2016 and 2020 to promote the meat and dairy sector (Greenpeace European Unit, 2019). At the same time, the sector benefits from a strong lobbying system on the part of its numerous organizations that tries to soften the impact of the World Health Organization's clear position – that consumption of red meat and processed meat is associated with cardiovascular disease and cancer – in national guidelines for a healthy diet. In the United States, for example, the recommendation to eat less meat was replaced by encouraging the consumption of lean meat in the guidelines updated in 2015 (USDHHS and USDA, 2016). In addition to funding and publicizing research that questions negative conclusions in relation to meat, the industry contests the impacts on greenhouse emissions with the argument that the 'nutrient density' of meat is higher than in the case of vegetable protein, which would lead to exaggerated conclusions in studies based on a kilo-by-kilo equivalence (Fleischhacker, 2007).

In contrast, the financial sector is becoming an important factor in monitoring leading global companies with respect to their economic, social, and governance (ESG) commitments. Farm Animal Investment Risk and Return (FAIRR), a network of investors whose combined equity is valued at US$70 trillion, focuses its attention on the animal protein sector and monitors leading companies annually through its Protein Producer Index. In 2017, FAIRR published a Livestock Levy White Paper advising companies to prepare for the application of a 'behavioural' tax (known more popularly as a 'sin tax') by anticipating the adoption of a 'shadow price' on their balance sheets that would reflect its likely impact. At the same, it is working closely with leading companies such as Kraft Heinz, Nestlé, Unilever, Tesco, and Walmart to develop alternative plant-based protein sources (FAIRR, 2022).

It is in this troubled environment that a new generation of start-ups has emerged to attack the meat and animal protein sectors head-on and which enjoys strong support in the world of venture capital and new investment funds. As we saw in the first chapter, in the examples of companies that have launched substitutes for mayonnaise, ice cream, and yoghurt, this is part of a more general contestation of the dominant products in the food industry that began with the dairy chain. In this chapter, we present an overview of the initiatives to supplant the range of conventional animal protein-based products (including fish and shellfish).

A vegan or vegetarian seeks the nutritional equivalent of animal protein, without being interested in reproducing the visual and gustatory qualities of meat, fish, milk, or eggs and their various derived products. Thus, a traditional substitute for meat has been tofu made from soy, which is closer in appearance and taste to cheese. A wide range of vegetable milks replaced animal milk, each with its own distinctive flavour. The new generation of start-ups is not aimed at this public, but at the carnivores willing to decrease their consumption of animal protein: the 'flexitarian'. Thus, the main objective is to reproduce the organoleptic characteristics of animal protein via plants, algae, fungi, insects, or cell culture, even if nutritional qualities are eventually impaired, leading some critics to characterize these alternative proteins as junk food (IPES, 2022). As we will see later, successive versions of these products have been reformulated in the light of these criticisms.

The category of alternative proteins includes a range of different strategies and technological routes. The vegetarian/vegan niche experienced strong growth in the first two decades of the 2000s. In this case, it is a matter of promoting the traditional ingredients of these movements with efforts to develop more appetizing recipes by chefs and celebrities that are widely disseminated in the media. Although flexitarians may be tempted by these options, we focus here on efforts to win their market, perceived as habitual meat eaters, with products that taste and look as good as, or even better than, the animal protein they intend to replace. In this sense, we are facing the continuation and expansion of the strategy initiated by Rich Products Corporation when it launched its whip-topping in 1945 made from soy rather than milk, described in Chapter 2.

This general strategy can be broken down into four components based on the raw material prioritized and the technology adopted, although individual companies and products themselves may combine one or more routes:

1. the 'plant-based alternatives to animal protein' segment;
2. animal protein produced from cell culture;
3. protein fermentation from fungi and precision fermentation;
4. protein production using insects.

The 'alternative plant-based meats and proteins' segment has more products on the market, more start-ups involved, more funding from venture capital and investment funds, and more direct investments by leading food companies. Within this segment the meat and dairy alternatives dominate the market, although as Asian companies and the Asian market become more relevant, fish options will multiply. Many companies, in the case of meat alternatives, mainly use soy as an ingredient because of its high protein content. In the case of direct consumption, however, the association of this grain with transgenics throws doubt on its acceptability to consumers and has led to a search for non-GMO soy sources and for other products such as peas, beans, and lentils. Companies are also turning to a variety of legumes because they have the advantage of fixing nitrogen in the soil and therefore increase the sustainability of the whole supply chain (Magrini et al, 2018).

To reproduce the texture and taste of meat, companies also explore combinations of ingredients that become 'industrial secrets' or are protected by patents.[6] The search for ingredients leads to the adoption of screening and the tracing of molecules with the use of big data techniques, machine learning, and artificial intelligence. Companies specializing in the identification of such molecules are emerging among start-ups to provide new flavours, textures, and functional properties, such as Shiru in the case of proteins and Yali Bio for fat characteristics, both from California. The global food ingredients market is estimated at US$400 billion and is seen as poised for transformation. In the words of Chuck Templeton, director of investment fund S2G Ventures, whose focus is on healthy eating and sustainable agriculture and who is also a board member of Shiru:

> The global food sector is on the cusp of an innovation explosion. Shiru is at the vanguard of a new generation of startups that will transform the agriculture sector paving the way for a livable planet and increased quality of life for all of us. (Essick, 2021)

The burger is the leading product in this segment of meat alternatives, followed by other types of unstructured meats, such as nuggets, sausages, meatballs, and ground meats. Some companies incorporate 3D printing technology to produce meats with structure, such as steak. Many combinations try to reproduce the sensation of blood and the smell of meat, with emphasis on the heme molecule extracted from soy roots, which is the hallmark of the Impossible Burger from Impossible Foods, and is protected by trademark and patents.

Historically, meat, dairy, and fish have generated very distinct production chains with only occasional points of convergence (feed, slaughter). Companies as a rule specialized in one or another chain: JBS or Tyson in meat, Danone and Nestlé for dairy products, Asian and Nordic companies for fish. In the new dynamic of 'animal protein' based on plants (including algae), it is indifferent which alternatives are produced from the perspective of the firm, whether different types of meat, milk, or eggs and their associated products, or fish. Everything comes down to the right combination of molecules and the right ingredients. Tyson, for example, the global leader in meat, has acquired the following start-ups: New Wave Foods, which produces alternatives to fish[7]; MycoTechnology, which uses precision fermentation based on fungi; and Believer Meats (previously known as Future Meat

Technologies), which produces cellular meat; in addition to launching its own brand, Raised & Rooted, a blend of meat and vegetable protein.

We saw in the first chapter how dairy products have become the prime segments of a new generation of companies (Rich Foods, Chobani, and Snow Monkey), challenging the established leading companies (the incumbents). Milk itself has also become a target for substitutes in the West since the early 20th century, particularly after waves of immigration from China where soy milk has been known for 2,000 years. Rice milk and soy milk factories sprang up in the United States and Europe in the 1920s, with the involvement even of the leading breakfast foods company, Kellogg's, and the first patent for soy milk was approved in this period. These milks became the target of legal action by organizations representing the traditional industry that challenged the right to use the word milk, and alternatives such 'soylac' and 'soygal' were occasionally adopted (Charvatova, 2018).

In Asian countries and the Middle East, without the European tradition of 'dairy farming', alternative milks date back to time immemorial – almond milk is mentioned in a Baghdad cookbook from the 13th century and in a text in England in the same century and became very popular in Europe as an alternative during fasting days. 'Horchata' milk came from the Middle East in the 8th century to Spain, and from there would later go to the 'New World' (Henesy, 2021).

Two companies have been responsible for the boom in alternative milks. The start-up WhiteWave Foods in the United States launched its Silk brand of alternative milks in 1996, initially from non-GMO and organic soy and in 2010 from almonds. Sales exploded and the company was bought first by Dean Foods and then by Danone, and in this transition the commitment to organic and non-GMO was dropped. Almond milk, incorporated into the Starbucks chain, came to overtake soy milk as the best-selling alternative milk in the United States as of 2020, even with all the criticism in relation to its low protein content and the compensatory use of additives (IstoÉ Dinheiro, 2016).[8]

The second company is Oatly, with its oat milk, created by Swedes in 1996 to meet the demand from lactose-intolerant consumers. For almost two decades it remained a niche option in the Nordic countries but in 2014 adopted a strategy to enter the North American market. Oatly emphasized its environmental profile compared to animal milk and targeted the coffee-shop sector in a joint venture with Verlinvest, a Belgian private equity firm, and the state-owned China Resources took a majority stake in Oatly in 2016. Other investors include Oprah Winfrey and former Starbucks CEO Howard Schultz. By the end of 2020, products from Oatly were sold in 8,500 retail shops and 10,000 coffee shops in the United States, making oat milk the second choice among plant-based milks behind almond milk. In 2021 Oatly went public, raised US$1.4 billion and was valued at US$10 billion. Oatly holds six patents on its products and processes with more pending, which increases its competitiveness against other entrants in the oatmeal segment such as Chobani and the Silk brand (Lu, 2021).

In the wake of WhiteWave and Oatly, new start-ups have entered, such as Ripple Foods, which debuted in the US market in 2016 with its pea-based milk reaching 20,000 points of sale (Watson, 2021). Chile's NotCo, which launched NotMilk in South American markets based on plant ingredients identified using 'Giuseppe', a proprietary artificial intelligence technology, then entered the North American market in 2021 and quickly reached 3,000 sales outlets. Perfect Day, a start-up that has already received US$750 million in several investment rounds and is valued at US$1.5 billion, sells bioidentical 'dairy' proteins and ingredients for cheeses, cakes, breads, and confectionery, based on precision fermentation that accurately reproduces whey and casein proteins (Starostinetskaya, 2021).

In 2020, two leading US dairy companies filed for bankruptcy: Dean Foods and Borden Dairy Company. Certainly, the advance of alternative milks was a factor in this decision, but the decline in consumption of milk as a beverage in the United States (and other countries) has been continuous since the 1940s, due to changes in eating habits (less breakfast at home) and competition from other beverages (water, orange juice, and soft drinks). We saw in Chapter 1 that plant-based options were already entering the segments of creamers, yoghurts, and ice cream. A deeper challenge is yet to come with the more decisive entry of plant-based and precision fermentation alternatives into the cheese segment (Terán and Cessna, 2021). San Francisco start-up New Culture is developing a mozzarella cheese said to be identical in composition to a milk-based mozzarella with precision fermentation, targeting the pizza market (Axworthy, 2022). The French leader Bel is producing cheese for the US market under the Nurishh brand label, using Perfect Day's proteins (Poinski, 2022).

According to Nielsen, four companies controlled 80 per cent of the alternative milks market, which by 2021 already occupied 15 per cent of the fluid milk retail market in the United States. All alternative dairy lines since Rich Foods just after World War II have been launched by new companies and start-ups, and these initiatives have been met with continued opposition to the use of the name 'milk' by the leading incumbent companies. Seeing these markets consolidate, the traditional leading companies such as Danone have opted for acquisition strategies. Even so, the price of this partial regaining of control has been the acceptance and promotion of a milk agenda promoted by social movements and public health policies whose expression in the market has taken the form of challenger start-ups and new companies. By the end of the second decade of the 2000s, the dairy sector (milk and dairy products) dominated retail sales of plant-based foods, as can be seen in Table 4.1 based on data from the North American market.[9]

Table 4.1: Sales of plant-based foods in the United States (retail)

Category	Sales 2020 US$	Per cent growth 2019
Milk	2.5 b	20.4
Meats	1.4 b	45.3
Frozen foods	520 m	28.5
Ice cream, etc.	435 m	20.4
Creams	394 m	32.5
Yoghurt	343 m	20.2
Proteins in powder	292 m	9.6
Butter	275 m	35.5
Cheese	270 m	42.5
Tofu and tempeh	175 m	40.8
Bakery	152 m	1.2
Ready-made drinks	137 m	12.0
Seasonings and mayonnaise	81 m	23.4
Pasta	61 m	83.4
Eggs	27 m	167.8
Total	**7.0 b**	**27.1**

Source: Plant Based Foods Association (2022)

In the second decade of the 2000s, it was the turn of beef cattle to feel the threat of products, both plant-based and cultured from cells removed from the animal by a simple biopsy. Initially, five companies dominated this scenario, all start-ups led by 'mission-based' academics or innovators. The imagination of the media and of investors was sparked by the launch in London of a burger grown from animal stem cells by Dutch academic Mark Post in 2013. At a cost of US$300,000, that burger's road to the supermarket shelf seemed long and uncertain. However, it was enough to trigger contributions from venture capital and to encourage the scientific world (Shapiro, 2018).

In the middle of that decade, two start-ups of plant-based alternatives to meats, Beyond Meat and Impossible Foods, launched their first burgers. Unlike the veggie burgers that occupied niche markets for vegans, these burgers aimed to replace meat burgers by reproducing their organoleptic characteristics without incurring their environmental and health costs. To do this, they used big data analysis of hundreds of thousands of molecules.

Created in 2009, Beyond Meat launched a line of 'chicken strips' in 2012 (discontinued in 2019 for not achieving the desired quality), but it was with its burger that it firmly entered the mainstream in 2014. From there it received continuous rounds of funding reaching a cumulative value of over

US$2 billion, allowing for an explosive expansion of its production not only in the United States but in Europe and China, both via restaurant chains and large retail (Reese, 2018).

In the same year Beyond Meat was established, the future founder of Impossible Foods, Patrick O. Brown, took a sabbatical to research how best to eliminate intensive livestock farming, perceived as the most important environmental problem. A year later, Brown organized an academic conference to raise awareness of the issue. Seeing that the impact of the conference was minimal, he decided it would be better to create a product that would replace animal meat and in 2011 founded Impossible Foods. Unlike Beyond Meat, which uses beetroot to reproduce the blood effect, Impossible Foods has opted for heme, a molecule found in all living things, responsible for the specific meat flavour and produced by precision fermentation where yeast or fungi are genetically altered to produce the heme extracted from the roots of soy (Shapiro, 2018).

In the second decade of the 2000s, these two companies launched their burgers and experienced vigorous growth in restaurant chains and large retail, first in the North American market and then in Europe and Asia, especially China.[10] The two received successive funding injections, which led Beyond Meat, valued at US$1.48 billion, to launch itself on the New York Stock Exchange in 2019 (Bonani, 2019). Impossible Foods, which received a total of US$2 billion in funding, and was valued at between US$7–10 billion, prepared an IPO for 2022, but as of 2024 the company is still private.

The initial focus of the trade press was almost exclusively on these two start-ups, but attention quickly shifted to the large number of companies entering the sector, both other start-ups and leading companies in the meat sector and the food industry in general. Consultancies such as Bloomberg, drawing on the evolution of alternative products in the dairy sector, projected a market of around 10 per cent of the global meat sector, or US$140 billion, to be reached by 2035 with annual growth rates in double digits (Henze and Boyd, 2021). The taps of financial capital were turned on full blast, pouring US$2.1 billion into plant-based alternatives by 2020 (GFI, 2021). Start-ups sprang up in all countries targeting all kinds of meat, dairy, fish, and seafood alternatives. What had been centred on Europe and the US now became a global phenomenon, with independent venture capital ecosystems, investment funds, incubators, and accelerators emerging in many countries. Singapore, Israel, Australia, the United Arab Emirates, China, and India have all become autonomous hubs promoting alternative proteins with strong support from public policies.

The Golden website that maps companies globally in real time recorded a total of 497 plant-based alternative companies by May 2024.[11] Included in this number are the leading meat companies: JBS, BRF, Marfrig, Cargill, ADM, Tyson, Smithfield Foods/WH Group from China, and Charoen Pokphand

Foods from Thailand, together with food industry leaders (Unilever, Nestlé, Conagra), retail (Tesco, Marks & Spencer), and fast food (McDonalds, KFC, Dicos from China). In addition to launching their own products, almost all these companies, as we saw in Chapter 3, promote start-ups in this segment through direct investments, incubators, and accelerators.

Not surprisingly, by 2022 the specialized press identified a saturation, an 'overcrowding' of the market for plant-based alternatives. Even more so, doubts arose about their durability, interpreting the 2020 boom as a combined effect of greater consumption at home as a result of COVID-19 and the novelty factor, not necessarily leading to a permanent shift in favour of plant-based products. This interpretation was reinforced by articles pointing to a sharp downturn in the sales of Beyond Meat and Impossible Foods in 2021 (Terazono and Evans, 2022).

Other observers highlighted the negative identification of plant-based alternatives with processed foods, even branding them as junk food (IPES, 2022). The dominant extrusion techniques favour the production of ground-meat alternatives, and the most targeted products for replacement have been burgers, which reinforces this image. A comparative analysis of plant-based alternatives and meat burgers carried out by FAIRR found higher sodium and saturated fats, but lower cholesterol and fewer calories. In 2019, Impossible Foods reported:

> we created Impossible Burger 2.0 with significant nutritional improvements. We lowered sodium by 36%, decreased saturated fats by 43%, added more fiber, improved the protein quality, and increased the amount of several essential micronutrients, including folate, calcium, potassium, and zinc. (Klapholz, 2019)[12]

The tracking of molecules using big data, machine learning, and artificial intelligence is the hallmark of these companies in their quest to reconcile nutritional and organoleptic values, which guarantees the continuous evolution of their products.

By working at the level of molecules, the entire universe of animal protein becomes the object of plant alternatives (and of microorganisms and insects, as we will see later in this chapter), composed of markets with a combined value of around US$2.5 trillion.[13] From fish fingers to salmon and foie gras, from burgers to steaks and Wagyu beef, from fluid milk to cheeses and dairy ingredients for baking and cooking, all are targets for start-ups with funding to progress from proof of concept to a business plan and from there to production at scale and a marketing strategy. Advances in extrusion techniques are now complemented with innovations of shear cell technology (cutting cells) and 3D printers to produce more structured 'meat' and 'fish', which enormously expand the possibilities of substitution. Thus, the universe is infinitely larger than the world of burgers and, even if COVID-19 has shifted the mix of in-home and out-of-home consumption with important implications for business strategies, the medium- and long-term determinants – climate change, public health, and animal welfare, and the global demand for animal protein – have not changed. COVID-19 and the escalation of geopolitical conflicts have only accentuated the unsustainability of a food system dependent on global sources of supply.

Emerging country demand for animal protein, particularly in Asia and the Middle East, has been the backdrop stimulating innovation and investment in alternative proteins, and companies that monitor these markets highlight their increasing importance in the third decade of the 2000s. It is not just a matter of individual companies but of entire ecosystems of start-ups, venture capital, investment funds, incubators, and accelerators. In contrast to the United States and to a lesser extent Europe, these regions stand out for the importance of the support from states and public policies where the stimulation of alternative proteins fits into comprehensive food security strategies. Even though in some Asian countries the adoption of Western-style meat consumption has been notable, meat is incorporated much more as an ingredient in their culinary traditions, which facilitates the promotion of alternatives that reproduce its olfactory and flavour characteristics without involving the same concerns around the structure of steak-type meats.

The interchangeability of final products is the hallmark of a food industry whose raw materials are molecules, but different technological routes still maintain their specificities. As we saw at the beginning of this section, an alternative to the efforts to reproduce the characteristics of animal proteins by means of plants, microorganisms, or insects, is to produce the meat itself, but in another way, without slaughtering, from the cultivation of cells taken from a living animal in the form of a biopsy.

Following Post's demonstration in 2013, two start-ups have dominated attention in this segment: Hampton Creek/Eat Just and Memphis Meats/ Upside Foods. We've already met Hampton Creek, established in 2011 as a producer of plant-based mayonnaise and whose radical innovation was, ironically, challenged in court by Unilever, a company also created from a radical product innovation, margarine, but now in these markets an illustrious incumbent. Hampton Creek, renamed Eat Just, is a company that is doubly hybrid as it combines its plant-based egg substitutes with the production, as of 2017, of cultivated chicken, whose final product is 70 per cent cellular and 30 per cent plant-based. Eat Just, like other similar start-ups has established itself in the California environment and consolidated itself based on the US market, but its recent expansion is geared towards Asian and Middle Eastern markets. Singapore, a global vanguard of both the promotion and regulation of cultivated meats was the first country, in 2017, to authorize their marketing, and the product that received the green light was Eat Just's chicken, from its subsidiary, Good Meat (Steffen, 2021).

Hampton Creek/Eat Just raised more than US$650 million in funding during its first decade, reaching 'unicorn' status (being worth more than US$1 billion) as early as 2016. By 2021, Eat Just had begun construction of a plant in Singapore worth US$120 million with the support of Proterra Investment Partners Asia, both for 'eggs' and for cellular meat, and another plant in Qatar, estimated at US$200 million, with funding from Doha Venture Capital, for cellular meat. In addition, it markets its egg replacers in China through the Dicos retail network (Gilchrist, 2021).

MemphisMeat/Upside Foods was set up in 2015 by an Indian resident of the United States, Uma Valeti, who became a vegetarian when confronted with the level of animal suffering in the meat chain. As a cardiologist, Valeti was amazed to see heart muscles regenerate after injection with stem cells and wondered whether it was not possible to grow meat muscles in the same way. Convinced of this possibility, Valeti set out on the production of cellular meat, creating a typically science-technological company, Crevi, which was later renamed Memphis Meats in the search for funding for the scale-up phase (Shapiro, 2018). The timing was very favourable because, in addition to the media success of Post's burger in 2013, several entities dedicated exclusively to the promotion of alternative proteins emerged in this period, such as New Harvest by Matheny and Datar, the Good Food Institute (GFI), as well as the Alliance for Meat, Poultry and Seafood Innovation (AMPSI).

In this environment, Valeti organized a tasting of its 'dumplings' – meatballs – in 2016, now costing just US$1,200, which garnered huge media attention, leading to a US$17 million contribution with the participation of Bill Gates, Richard Branson, Jack and Suzy Welch, and – most significantly – Cargill. In 2020, there was further funding worth US$160 million. This initiative was backed by an infusion of capital from Singapore-based Temasek Holdings, which had already funded Eat Just, along with several investment funds, as well as Tyson Foods (Shapiro, 2018). With this backing Memphis Meats built the largest cellular meat plant capable of producing 400,000 lbs of meat per year, and planned to go into operation as soon as it received regulatory approval. The plant, called the Engineering, Production, and Innovation Center (EPIC), hosts virtual tours on YouTube where a tasting restaurant is located right at the entrance allowing for a view of the entire production process separated only by glass walls. The video emphasizes the compatibility of the plant with the urban environment and highlights its similarity to a brewery. Memphis Meats changed its name again in 2021, to Upside Foods, with the justification that: 'the future of food is all about activating the upside' (Feedstuffs, 2021). In 2023 the US Department of Agriculture (USDA) gave Upside and Eat Just the green light to market their cellular chicken.

Although Mosa Meat, Eat Just, and Upside Foods have dominated the media coverage, there is a whole global ecosystem of start-ups involved with cellular meat. Quartz had identified 30 such companies by early 2020 (Purdy, 2020), while *New Scientist*, in May of the same year, estimated their total at 60, including companies targeting cell culture media, the construction of scaffolds to give structure to meat and the development of bioreactors to scale up production. In its 2020 report, GFI increased this number to 'over 70', with a further 40 companies in life sciences stating that they were developing a line of business in support of this sector. In a YouTube video from 2021, an Upside spokesperson estimated that there were more than 100 companies operating in the sector.

Quartz and GFI put the support received in 2020 from foundations and venture capital for the development of cellular meat at US$500 million. The estimates from Crunchbase News are much higher (Table 4.2).

The announcement in December 2021 of a US$347 million financing for the Israeli company Future Meat (now Believer Meats), in a round led by ADM, a major global player in grain trading and processing and now also in the provision of ingredients for plant-based alternatives, does not appear to have been included in the 2021 data.

Of the 70 companies identified by GFI, 23 are in the US with a further 15 in northern European countries. More than 30 companies, on the other hand, are spread across 19 of the most varied countries, most notably Singapore, Israel, and China/Hong Kong. Although timid, public funding also began to support the sector from 2020, examples being the National Science Foundation in the United States, the Horizon 2020 funding of the European Union, in addition to initiatives by the governments of Singapore, the United Arab Emirates, China, Japan, and Australia (GFI, 2023).

Unlike plant-based products, cellular protein products in 2023 are still in the tasting phase or that of limited offerings in exclusive restaurants, and the possibility of achieving full-scale production has been met with scepticism – either for strictly technical or cost-focused reasons. Upside Food's already completed EPIC factory, Eat Just's two factories under construction in

Table 4.2: Investments in cellular meat (US$)

2017	152 million
2018	191 million
2019	604 million
2020	1.238 billion
2021	913 million up to 31 October

Source: Turi (2021)

Singapore and Qatar, as well as Believer Meats' plant in Israel, suggest that the issue of scale is being addressed.

At EPIC, Upside intends to start with 25 tonnes per year but with the possibility of producing 180 tonnes per year, and Believer Meats, for its part, also intends to produce around 180 tonnes per year. In relation to costs, Believer Meats estimated that it would have a production cost of US$22 per kilo in 2022, dropping from US$330 per kilo in 2019, and with a forecast to continuously lower these costs. A study conducted by CE Delft with 16 cell protein companies in 2021 concluded that within a decade cellular meat would be cost competitive with some types of conventional meat (Gursel et al, 2022).

Foetal bovine serum (FBS) has been the preferred culture medium to produce cellular meat in the laboratory and was used in Mark Post's demonstration in 2013 and also in the chicken marketed in Singapore. However, the companies understand that its use is unacceptable in terms of cost and from an animal welfare point of view, being a by-product of the slaughter of dairy cows. A research priority for the whole industry is to develop alternative culture mediums. Believer Meats' cost calculations are based on not using FBS, and Upside Foods has stated that it will not use animal-derived culture media (Bond, 2021).

We have just seen how alternative protein companies combine in practice different technological routes and raw materials. Impossible Foods uses precision fermentation to achieve the distinctive flavour of its plant-based burger. Eat Just combines in the same company the plant-based production of egg-based products with cellular meat production, and its famous cellular chicken on the menu at restaurant 1880 in Singapore is 30 per cent plant-based protein.

At the same time, we can identify firms taking an alternative route, occupying animal protein markets with microorganism- and fungi-based products using biomass fermentation and precision fermentation techniques. We provided an example of this third segment in our discussion of the wave of biotech innovations in Chapter 2 and the production of the myco protein, Quorn, which results from a natural fermentation process of a fungus in a wheat-based glucose syrup medium that turns carbohydrate into protein. This fungus family, *Fusarium venenatum*, was discovered after screening more than 3,000 soil samples. Quorn, which can be produced quickly at scale, is competitive in price with meats, has a low carbon footprint, simulates the texture of chicken or 'fishless fingers', and serves as the protein base for many foods. It was approved as a safe food in the 1980s and has been marketed ever since. Previously producing 22,000 tonnes per year in England, Quorn Foods doubled this production in 2022 and has already established a niche market in many countries. Quorn Foods, initially a joint venture between Rank Hovis McDougall and ICI, after passing through several companies was acquired by Monde Nissin, a noodle company launched on the Philippine stock exchange in 2021 that is investing heavily in promoting the Quorn product in the United States where it has already had a presence since 2002 (Quorn, 2019).

Quorn was for a long time the only company that produced and marketed meat analogues on a large-scale by fermenting fungi, but the advantages of this route are stimulating the entry of several start-ups, such as Nature's Fynd (Watson, 2022), which produces sausage patties and creamy cheeses (showing the lack of differentiation between meat and dairy for these firms that we mentioned earlier), and Meati, which has raised US$50 million and aims to produce 7,000 tonnes of chicken in 2022 from the fermentation of the roots of a mushroom (Peters, 2019).

The Good Food Institute, a global organization that promotes alternatives to animal protein, has identified 51 companies working with fermentation to produce 'animal-free' dairy products, meats, and eggs. Of these companies, 28 were set up between 2019 and 2020. Thus, this is the newest segment in the alternative protein ecosystem but with indications of an already rapidly accelerating growth. In 2020, US$587 million was raised by these companies, double the previous year, and more than half of the funding for this segment in the entire period (GFI, 2021). Fermentation factories can be located in urban centres, reversing the expulsion of slaughterhouses during the 20th century, and reproducing the trend identified in the case of vertical farming of integration into the urban environment.

The specialized literature (Suescan Pozas, 2020) identifies three types or routes of fermentation plants in the urban environment:

1. traditional fermentation which uses microorganisms to modify plant-based ingredients, one example being tempeh, a product of soybean fermentation.
2. biomass fermentation, which produces protein on a large scale from selected microorganisms that feed on carbohydrates and sugars.
3. precision fermentation that turns microorganisms into factories to produce desired ingredients.

Quorn and other similar products are produced from biomass fermentation, which consists of identifying and selecting fast-growing microorganisms with high protein content. Biomass fermentation products are cost competitive and can stimulate the making of hybrid products combining plant-based and fermentation ingredients to achieve competitive prices. Of the 51 companies identified by the GFI, 22 work with biomass fermentation.

Microalgae produced from biomass fermentation are becoming a preferred option particularly in Asia for producing plant-based meat, fish, and dairy products. There are more than a million species of microalgae on the planet, a treasure trove in the search for proteins with specific characteristics. Sophie's Bionutrients of Singapore produces a high-protein meal from a proprietary strain of algae in a fermentation process that utilizes the by-products of the city's industries. At the same time, this firm is already producing a burger and a dairy alternative on a small scale. The Temasek Foundation, so important in funding the alternative protein sector, has provided a US$1 million grant to help build a production facility in Singapore (Green Queen Team, 2021).

The same number of companies, 22, are turning to precision fermentation techniques where the microorganism itself is modified to produce the required properties more accurately. Of the start-ups in this category, 18 have been created since 2018. Impossible Foods, as we mentioned, is the most notable example of the potential of this route by using precision fermentation to produce the heme molecule, key in the differentiation of its burger.

Of the 51 fermentation start-ups, 23 are based in the United States and 9 in Israel, with 14 countries responsible for the remaining 19. Except for Singapore, India, and Argentina, this route is dominated by companies from Northern countries. Asia, however, is seen as a key market given its tradition of consuming fermented products and the more favourable regulatory framework in several countries on that continent. Perfect Day, a California company that has benefitted most from funding in this segment, with around US$300 million, produces proteins bioidentical with milk, and has set up a research and development centre in Singapore in partnership with the Singapore government's Agency for Science, Technology and Research (A*STAR). At the same time, Perfect Day has partnered with Igloo Dessert Bar and Horizon Ventures to launch Asia's first 'animal-free' ice cream in Hong Kong. Change Foods, another precision fermentation start-up, is also targeting the Asian market for its 'bioidentical' cheeses that are still at the prototype stage. Cheeses are second only to red meat in the level of greenhouse gas emissions, and as well as saving water, land, and energy, producing cheese via fermentation takes only a few days and doesn't need to wait two or three years for the raw material, the time to raise a dairy cow to then make the cheese (GFI, 2021).

In mapping out a new generation of companies radically contesting the dominant products of the food industry in Chapter 1, we mentioned Hampton Creek's production of an eggless mayonnaise, Just Mayo, made from mung beans. Clara Foods (now Every Company), which has the second largest funding in this segment of around US$70 million, produces egg-white proteins based on precision fermentation. Unlike plant-based protein alternatives, the protein is fully soluble and neutral in taste. Thus, it targets products that aim to offer higher protein content without modifying texture or taste. Every Company aims to achieve global scale through its partnership with Ingredion for distribution and BioBrew and AB InBev for fermentation (Southey, 2021).

Novozymes, a Danish company and global leader in enzymes, microorganisms, and biotechnology products, is building a US$320 million plant to produce plant-based proteins in Nebraska in the United States in partnership with major players in the food industry and retail. At the same time, it has launched Mycoprotein Innovation Call to identify partners who can participate in a global platform in the search for 'advanced protein solutions'. In the words of Amy Louise Byrick, executive vice president:

> Novozymes is launching this global platform to help transform the future of food through the power of fungi and mycelium. Transforming our global food systems at scale will require radical new ways of working, bringing together the most cutting-edge scientific and business expertise from across industries and sectors – and that is what the Myco-protein Innovation Call is all about. (Danstrup, 2021)

The Plenitude project captures very well the combination of distinct routes and an openness to hybrid solutions. Led by the Scottish-based mycoprotein company 3F Bio (now branded as Enough) and with funding from the European Union's Horizon 2020 initiative, it brings together the cellular meat start-up Mosa Meat made famous by Mark Post, the meat producer ABP Food Group, plant-based meat producer Vivera, bioplastics start-up Lactips, and the biofuels group Alcogroup. The project aims at the sustainable production of protein with zero waste to be incorporated into hybrid meat products which are seen by 3F Bio CEO, Jim Laird, as the best way to reduce global demand for meat. At the beginning of this chapter, we stated that there was no such thing as a flexitarian product, but this strategy of mixing meat and microprotein or, as in the case of Eat Just, mixing cellular meat and plant-based protein, can become the hallmark of a flexitarian product.[14]

The publication 'Edible insects: Future prospects for food and feed security' by the Food and Agriculture Organization (FAO) of the United Nations in partnership with the Department of Plant Science at Wageningen University in 2013, placed insects – our fourth alternative protein segment – on the agenda of debates on food security. According to this report, more than two billion people traditionally incorporate insects into their diets, and of the estimated 4–30 million species of insects on the planet, only a million have been described and only 2,000 incorporated into our diets. Even then, only bees, cochineal, and the silkworm have been regularly domesticated.

Countries on the African continent are the largest consumers of insects, although they have also traditionally been part of diets in Asia. In Latin America, the Aztec empire, with no domesticated large mammals, incorporated insects into its diet, and perhaps it is this tradition that explains the large number of insect companies in Mexico (Diamond, 2005). Of the 161 insect companies identified globally by the Bugburger website, 16 are in Mexico (Engström, 2023). It is speculated that their absence from diets in Europe and the cultural antipathy to their consumption resulted from Europe's monopolization of 13 of the 14 species of large mammals that have been domesticated out of a total of 148 recorded species, and which became the main sources of protein in the West (FAO, 2013). In addition, with the adoption of agriculture, insects began to be seen as pests.[15]

Surprisingly, it was precisely in Europe that the FAO publication had the most impact, and the emergence of dozens of companies can be identified here in the second decade of the 2000s. In their review of the edible insect industry, Pippinato et al (2020) identify 59 European firms producing three product lines for human consumption – whole insects accounting for 50 per cent of the market, flour for 20 per cent, and protein bars, snacks, and pastas for 30 per cent. The first two lines use traditional technologies and are composed almost entirely of insects (>90 per cent), while protein bars snacks and pastas contain less than 10 per cent.

Crickets and earthworms (not technically insects) are the most commonly used, along with the black soldier fly and the grasshopper, and are generally not produced by these companies but are supplied by insect farms. Legislation on the marketing and importing of insects is in flux in the European Union, with differences also between European countries, but the transitional measures concerning 'novel foods' allow the importation of insects from some countries outside the region. A study by the consultancy Meticulous Research (2022) predicts that the global edible insect market will reach US$17.9 billion by 2033 with a volume of 4.7 million tonnes.

Cultural resistance to insect consumption in the West leads to efforts to disguise their origin and distort their organoleptic characteristics as in the case of protein bars, in stark contrast to the strategies to reproduce the characteristics of meat in the case of plant-based alternatives. Another strategy is to rename insects, like the suggestion of naming grasshoppers, for example, as 'sky prawns' (FAO, 2013, p 36).

In the light of these factors, most investments in the West are directed towards the markets for livestock feed, for aquaculture, and for fertilizers. It is estimated that 20 per cent of the world's meat production is consumed by domestic animals and that 25 per cent of farmed fish is used as feed in aquaculture. Thus, their replacement with insect protein would be an important contribution to food security. Several studies have highlighted the virtues of using insects, both for their nutritional qualities and for the reduction of the carbon footprint (Dossey et al, 2016; Henchion et al, 2017). By 2020, eight out of the ten European insect start-ups identified as the most promising by the website Silicon Canals, targeted these feed and fertilizer markets (Silicon Canals, 2020).

Of the 59 start-ups identified by Pippinato et al (2020), the UK emerges clearly in first place with 14 companies. When it comes to these new insect markets for feed and fertilizers, however, it is France that stands out in Europe. In contrast to Silicon Valley's private initiative model, France is promoting an innovation ecosystem based on a set of public policies to promote a favourable environment for the emergence of start-ups. This support includes funding, incubators (Station F and Next40), and a fund to prevent the acquisition of these start-ups by foreign companies (Jackson, 2021). The sector also benefits from the International Platform of Insects for Food and Feed (IPIFF), which acts in the field of regulation of these activities.

In France, two firms are of particular note: Innovafeed and Ynsect. Innovafeed was created in 2016 and develops feed (ProtiNova and NovaGain) for aquaculture, poultry, and pigs. In 2020, it opened a factory with the capacity to produce 15,000 metric tonnes of protein and 5,000 metric tonnes of oil, which can replace 400,000 metric tonnes of feed per year. This plant, which Innovafeed's co-founder calls a 'vertical farm', uses large-scale automation and artificial intelligence. The company plans to have 20 plants in operation in various locations around the world by 2030. Ambitions are not limited to these initiatives and in 2021 Innovafeed partnered with ADM, one of the big four global traders that is also a leader in the ingredients segment, to build a plant in the United States four times larger than its factory in France.

Ynsect, meanwhile, was created in 2011 with the mission of responding to 'some of the biggest issues of our time: feeding the world while protecting the environment, ecosystems, biodiversity, and combatting climate change' (Jackson, 2021). Based on extensive patent protection, Ynsect produces worms in vertical farms for feed and for fertilizer. By 2021 it had received US$425 million in various rounds of funding, a sum greater than the total investments in the sector to date. In 2021, Ynsect started construction of what it claims to be the world's largest insect farm with a capacity of 200,000 metric tonnes to be managed through the digital collection and processing of a billion items of information per day. By 2030, Ynsect plans to have a total of ten vertical farms distributed around the world.

In stark contrast to the situation in Europe and the United States, in Asia, Africa, and regions of Latin America, insect consumption is part of traditional diets, often based on collecting non-domesticated species. At the same time, thousands of small farms cultivate and process insects for food, cosmetics, and medicinal purposes. The FAO report in 2013 and its work to promote insect farming on these continents as core strategies aimed at food security has been a strong stimulus. The International Centre of Insect Physiology and Ecology (INCIPE) in Nairobi, Kenya, together with the Rockefeller Foundation's Alliance for a Green Revolution in Africa, have been equally important in promoting the cultivation of the black soldier fly (BSF) as a protein feed and have trained 11,600 farmers, 40 per cent of whom are women.

The World Bank has reinforced this campaign with its report, *Insect and Hydroponic Farming in Africa: The New Circular Food Economy* (2021). The report cites South Korea, which in less than a decade has consolidated more than 2,500 insect farms. It could also have cited Thailand, which has registered more than 25,000 of these farms. In China, insect farms are part of rural life, producing insects for food and for medicinal purposes. In addition, there are around 100 large farms growing billions of cockroaches that feed on the food waste of the cities. It is estimated that a farm of one billion cockroaches consumes 50 tonnes per day of urban food waste. The World Bank estimates that in Africa there are already around 1,000 insect farms and argues that the activity requires little land, few natural resources, and little capital. The report concludes that:

> Within a year, African insect farming can generate crude protein worth up to US$2.6 billion and biofertilizers worth up to US$19.4 billion. That is enough protein meal to meet up to 14 percent of the crude protein needed to rear all the pigs, goats, fish, and chickens in Africa [...]. (World Bank Group, 2021, p xxvi)

At the same time, there are high-tech start-ups in this insect segment in most countries in Asia (Thailand, Malaysia, Indonesia, Vietnam, Cambodia, China), with a regional hub in Singapore, where its food agency has approved the use of BSF as fish feed, and a major start-up accelerator, Bits x Bites, in Shanghai. A leading start-up investor in Singapore, Enterprise Singapore, together with Seeds Capital, is funding Nutritional Technologies whose plan is to produce 18,000 tonnes per year of feed and fertilizer from BSF. As we noted in the case of vertical farming in Chapter 3, there has also been rapid globalization in this segment. We have already seen the global ambitions of the French start-ups Innovafeed and Ynsect; two farms in Vietnam are owned by British and Singapore companies respectively; the British investor Future Protein Group owns the grasshopper farm Cricket Lab in Thailand that exports flour to Sens in the Czech Republic, also owned by the same investor, which then exports protein bars and other products to the German market.

In Africa, we have seen that there is a long tradition of growing insects for human consumption, but it is the potential of the feed market that attracts most start-ups. AgriProtein Technologies from South Africa was the first to come in with big funding (US$135 million) and global ambitions to build 100 factories around the world in a partnership with the conglomerate Christof Industries. After four years, however, the South African plant was sold and the company went into liquidation. The then CEO now operates a smaller BSF company in Cape Town and questions the validity of adopting state-of-the-art technologies that require large scales to achieve profitability (Driver, 2021). Despite this setback, new companies InsectiPro, Ecodudu, and Victory Farms are emerging mainly in East Africa around INCIPE in Nairobi, which aims to become a new hub for BSF production targeting the feed market (Tanga et al, 2021).

In this chapter, we have shown the breadth of actors and technological routes mobilized to develop alternatives to the industrial system of raising, fattening, and slaughtering animals to supply protein. Leading incumbent companies are increasingly engaged in developing and dominating these new alternative protein markets but they have not initiated this movement. Even so, from an initially defensive position, the companies traditionally identified with the meat and dairy chains are beginning to call themselves protein companies, making their relations with the primary sector more flexible.

In the initial chapters of this book, we described the way in which the agendas of social movements have been incorporated into public policies and have occupied an increasing space in the business world to the extent that the principles of sustainability and social justice are institutionalized into the everyday practices of companies. In the same way, the various frontiers of science and technology have been mobilized in the search for solutions for a food system that needs to adapt to the demographic, environmental, and health challenges of an increasingly urban global population. The protein alternatives examined in this chapter have been driven by committed scientists and engaged entrepreneurs who, supported by a global ecosystem of funding, were able to see the rapid transformation of their ideas into commercial propositions. Dominated initially by the United States and northern Europe, this world of start-ups driven by venture capital and investment funds has, in less than a decade, become a global phenomenon with hubs on every continent.

We have identified four major technological and associated raw material routes: molecule screening to identify plant/algae proteins; growing meat from animal cells; precision fermentation using microorganisms and fungi; and insect farming in climate-controlled systems. In some contexts these are complementary routes, in others competitive, but there is a growing pragmatism in efforts to engage not the staunch vegetarian or vegan but the flexitarian, which results in a willingness to combine technologies and raw materials into hybrid products that may blend plant protein with cellular meat or with protein from microorganisms and fungi.

In the introduction and the first chapter we showed how the critiques of the dominant agri-food system became consolidated from the 1980s onwards, but it was only in the first decade of the 2000s that the impact of China's explosive growth was felt in global agri-food markets, sparking these waves of radical innovation aimed at making Chinese demand, and that of other emerging countries and continents, compatible with the sustainability of the planet's natural resources and climate. In Chapter 5, we analyse the impact of Chinese demand on the (re)organization of the global agri-food system and China's food security strategies, including its policies and initiatives in relation to climate-controlled agriculture and alternative proteins.

China: The Pivot of the Global Agri-Food System Restructuring

What is the significance of China for the future of the agri-food system? We have shown throughout the previous chapters that the agendas contesting the dominant agri-food system developed since the 1980s by social movements, both rural and urban, and successively incorporated into global policies and conventions, also embracing the academic and scientific world, have begun to invade the mainstream with the creation of sustainability departments, the adoption of socio-economic and environmental criteria of accountability, and adherence to climate targets. These agendas mainly addressed a global agri-food system dominated by 'Northern' players and markets (including Japan), where changes in consumption patterns in these countries (lower per capita consumption of staple foods, concerns with health and wellbeing, including animal welfare, and environmental preservation) could be, at least partially, accommodated in corporate quality product strategies.

China's explosive economic growth since the reforms of Deng Xiaoping in 1978, with its population larger than that of the 'Northern' countries combined, only began to have an impact on the global agri-food system with China's entry into the World Trade Organization (WTO), and its definition of soy – a key component of animal feed for its rapidly expanding meat industry – as an industrial input whose supply could therefore depend on world markets. For China, from time immemorial and reinforced by memories of the famine of the 1960s, food security understood as self-sufficiency in staple foods has been seen as central to the legitimacy of the state. The definition of soy (and later corn) as industrial products alongside cotton, tobacco, cellulose, and other non-food raw materials, allowed the state to maintain the discourse of food security understood as self-sufficiency, but quickly transformed the dynamics of world trade in agricultural products, particularly the food chains linked to the transition to a diet of animal protein resulting from China's industrialization and urbanization.

Thus, from the 2000s onwards, the world agri-food system was once again dominated by the dynamics of commodity markets, now no longer meeting the demands of Europe and Japan as in the post-war period but those of China and other 'emerging' countries. In China, as an authoritarian country, civil society agendas hardly influence the policies or strategies of companies, many of which are state-owned in the agri-food sector. In this context, the future of socio-environmental agendas partially incorporated into the global agri-food system has been called into question with the decline in importance of the European market in world trade and with its leading companies generating more income in the Chinese market itself and other emerging countries than in Europe and the United States. At the same time, the socio-economic and environmental costs of this huge transition to an animal protein diet consequent on the economic growth and urbanization of large emerging countries have become a central concern. It is the search for answers to this question that drives the waves of innovation we analysed in Chapter 4, and also extends to the promotion of climate-controlled food production that we addressed in Chapter 3. In this chapter we examine the impact of this shift for the advance of the socio-environmental agenda in the global agri-food system, together with the way China is positioning itself in the face of new waves of product innovation that may radically change global markets and historical rural–urban relations.

Based on Deng Xiaoping's reforms in 1978 until the beginning of the new millennium, China grew at almost 10 per cent a year (and continued to grow at that speed for another decade) without resorting to structural food imports, and this in a period also of massive population transfer to urban areas. The dominant explanation for this is based on an assessment of the positive impact of the 1978 reforms, especially the promotion of the Township and Village Enterprises strategy, as well as direct access to markets for peasants (Naughton, 2006; Huang, 2008). Aglietta and Bai explore this issue in *China's Development: Capitalism as Empire* (2013) to understand how it was possible to sustain food security for a population already in the midst of an urban transition and demographic growth before 1978. In the historical debates on this theme in the cases of Holland and especially England, the identification of a 'second agricultural revolution' (Thompson, 1968) of 'high farming' in the 18th century (when the discovery of nitrogen fixation by legumes boosted large increases in productivity) explained the possibility of an urban-industrial transition before these countries resorted to the colonial supplies of their respective empires. Aglietta and Bai, in turn, identify 'a silent green revolution' from the 1950s to the 1960s onwards (despite the disasters of the Great Leap Forward and the ensuing famine that killed around 20 million people), which was delivering significant productivity results well before the reforms. As early as the 1950s, China developed a national system of agricultural research and development

(R&D) coordinated by the Chinese Academy of Agricultural Sciences. In 1964, a high-yielding dwarf variety of rice was created and in 1961 hybrid maize was also developed. In the early 1970s, China imported 13 ammonia and urea factories creating the basis for a fertilizer industry, and its irrigation systems were reformed. Thus, well before the 1978 reforms, China had already achieved a new level of agricultural productivity to sustain the transition to an urban-industrial society.

As we have already indicated, the impact of China's food demand on global markets and agricultures was only to be felt after its entry into the WTO and its redefinition of soy as an industrial product and therefore not subject to the rules of self-sufficiency. In the following two decades Chinese demand for agricultural raw materials dominated the dynamics of global markets raising the spectre of a return to the world of basic agricultural commodities that characterized the first six decades of the 20th century and an undermining of the turn to quality identified from the 1980s onwards.

Chinese demand for food and non-food raw materials from the 2000s onwards could only be met by an unprecedented expansion of the agricultural frontiers of Latin America and Asia that entailed the extensive logging of tropical forests threatening indigenous peoples, eroding biodiversity, and exacerbating climate problems and carbon emissions (Escher, 2020).

Suddenly China became a player in world trade for non-food agricultural products such as cotton, pulp, and tobacco, and then for soybeans, the key product in animal protein chains, reflecting the impacts of the accelerated urbanization of the population and the consequent transition to an animal protein diet (Zhang, 2018). Chinese imports exploded in the first decade of the 2000s, increasing from between 5 and 10 million tonnes at the beginning of the decade to around 60 million tonnes in 2010. In that same year, Brazil's soybean harvest reached a record 68 million tonnes, only a little more than the demand for Chinese imports. Even with a very efficient agriculture, in the face of processes of urbanization and an ageing of the rural population, and given the amount of rural land absorbed in the expansion of cities and its network of highways and railways, China depends increasingly on imports, exposing the limitations of world trade. Even low percentages of China's dependence on world markets create unprecedented demands for imports (Wilkinson et al, 2022).

In 2019, China suffered a swine fever outbreak that decimated its herd, lowering production from 54 million tonnes in 2018 to 41 million tonnes in 2020 with a consequent domestic shortage and a sharp rise in prices. Immediately, China doubled its imports to more than 2 million tonnes creating an international price explosion in a global market that amounts to only 10 million tonnes and which was also severely affected by COVID-19 (Shahbandeh, 2022). Foreseeing this vulnerability, China, through the Shuanghui Group (now the WH Group), had already acquired Smithfield

Foods, the largest pork company in the United States in 2013. It was clear that world trade was not scaled to meet the pace and size of Chinese demand to ensure its food security so central to the legitimacy of the Chinese state.

Fortunately, in the case of soybeans, a huge new grain frontier had been opened in Brazil as the result from the 1970s onwards of a long-term programme of cooperation with Japan, which at that time was also experiencing difficulties in grain supplies in its transition towards a meat diet and feared the implications of dependence on only one supplier country, the United States. In 1997, world soybean trade was worth about US$10 billion, the United States accounted for two-thirds of exports and China imported only 5.5 per cent. Twenty years later, that trade had grown to more than US$60 billion, with China responsible for 63 per cent of imports, and Brazil had become the largest exporter (De Maria et al, 2020). Unlike Japan, China faces a duopoly where the expansion of its demand to 100 million tonnes in 2021 was only feasible with the extraordinary expansion of the new soybean frontier in Brazil. Thus, especially in troubled diplomatic times, which in the Brazilian case may be short-lived but promise to be long-lasting in the case of the United States, this dependence provokes an unease in China similar to that which Japan felt in the 1970s. In this perspective, one can identify strategic efforts on the part of China to decrease its dependence that are analysed later (Schneider, 2017).

China's entry into world markets causes a double shift: from a Europe where food demand is strongly guided by a vibrant and politically legitimized civil society, to an authoritarian regime where this has little expressiveness; and to a demand now measured in terms of quantity and price and no longer by the differentiated qualities that had redefined the profile of the agri-food system. Even more seriously, this shift occurred at a time when criticism focused above all on the threats to the environment, as well as their implications for global sustainability and climate change goals.

In other publications (Wilkinson, Wesz Júnior and Lopane, 2016; Wilkinson et al, 2022), we have identified a set of initiatives taken by China to circumvent the vulnerabilities of international trade in agricultural commodities, seen either as a chronological evolution or as complementary measures. Firstly, and as a reflection of this 'return to commodities' (which included the promotion of biomass for renewable energy to replace gasoline, HLPE, 2013), China, like many other countries and global companies, with the entry also of financial funds, invested directly in the purchase of land in Asia, Africa, and Latin America. Several countries, including Brazil, responded by hindering or limiting foreign land purchases, targeting (in the Brazilian case) China specifically (McKay et al, 2018). As an alternative, especially in the Conesur countries (Brazil, Uruguay, Paraguay, and Argentina) but with the same strategy in Ukraine for wheat contracts, China tried to close long-term contracts with cooperatives and state governments, again without success. At the same time, in a strategy like that of Japan in the 1970s, China oriented to investments in infrastructure and logistics for soybeans (and related commodities, especially corn): roads, railways, and ports, especially to expedite Brazilian exports through the north of the country from the Centre-West frontier now advancing towards the Amazon region.

During this period, China also launched its strategy for the 'going out' or the internationalization of its leading companies (Sharma, 2014; Schneider, 2017). At the beginning of China's opening of its soybean markets, its domestic production was seriously damaged, and after a debt crisis in 2006 much of the Chinese grain-crushing sector was acquired by global traders: Archer-Daniels-Midland (ADM), Bunge, Cargill, and Dreyfus (called the 'ABCD'), and by Asian traders such as Wilmar International (Solidaridad, 2017). By following this going out strategy, the Chinese companies – COFCO, Sinograin, Chinachem, and to a lesser extent the Shanghai Pengxin Group – began to challenge ABCD's global control of the grain/meat chain. Fiagril, a major regional player in soybean expansion across the Midwest frontier in Brazil, was acquired by the Shanghai Pengxin Group. Chinachem, a state-owned company, bought Syngenta, a world leader in agrichemicals and seeds, which now markets the Conesur soybeans it receives through bartering arrangements directly with the Chinese state company, Sinograin. COFCO, another Chinese state-owned company, has directly entered the soybean market through the purchase of Nidera and Noble Agri and now challenges the leadership of the 'ABCD' group in soybean origination in the region (Wesz et al, 2023).

Throughout the 2000s, China experimented with various strategies to deal with the challenges to its food security while relaxing its policy of self-sufficiency. Underlying all of these, however, has been a determination to establish a level of control over grain supply and stocks so as not to become a simple price-taker and hostage to the ABCD group. Its policies of stockpiling and preferential treatment for grain and not meal imports complement this strategy, in addition to the creation of the Asia Pacific Futures Exchange dedicated, for the moment, to palm oil.[1]

China's ambitions have proved much bolder since the launch of the Belt and Road Initiative in 2013 that aims at nothing less than redesigning trade flows by land and sea around its own market. 138 countries are affected by the initiative and 60 countries have already committed to declarations of intent and projects. According to Morgan Stanley, China had already spent US$200 billion by 2020 and predicted investments reaching a total value of US$1.2–1.3 trillion by 2027. This initiative opens up new sources of agricultural supply with great potential in central Asia, where climate change may even increase the land suitable for agriculture (McBride et al, 2020). In 2019, China and Russia signed a cooperation agreement that includes all stages of the soybean chain and foresees an increase in exports to 3.7 million tonnes by 2024 (Donley, 2020).

In the global value chain literature, this shift in trade flows from Europe to China and from higher value-added products to simple raw materials (in this case, grains rather than meal and other derived products) has been seen as a process of downgrading by undermining the strategies and policies of internalizing higher value added in the initial stages of these chains by exporting countries (Kaplinski et al, 2010). In research coordinated by Barrientos, Gereffit and Rossi, these notions of 'upgrading' and 'downgrading' were expanded to capture contradictory processes and to focus on social and environmental impacts and not only their economic implications (Barrientos et al, 2010). With the advance of the soybean frontier from the Cerrado towards the Amazon region in Brazil and, to a lesser extent, into the Chaco forests in Argentina, and in the context also of the pressure from global conventions (UN Sustainable Development Goals and climate change Conferences of the Parties [COPs]) to adopt quantifiable and monitorable targets for sustainability and carbon emissions reduction, the implications of the change in the axis of world trade for China has become central.

In another publication (Wilkinson et al, 2022), we have provided a detailed analysis of China's position in relation to sustainable development goals and the reduction of carbon emissions. Conrad (2012) and other authors (Xiaosheng, 2018), have drawn attention to the mismatch between domestic policy developments and the positions adopted by China in international forums, especially at the Copenhagen COP in 2009. China has a long tradition of participation in international movements around sustainability and participated in the first meeting in Stockholm in the 1970s, even though it rejected any commitment that could hold back its economic development. Since then, environmental policies have acquired an institutional and legal status, and in the context of the United Nations Rio de Janeiro conference in 1992 China drew up its Agenda 21. According to Mol and Carter (2006) the Chinese Environmental Agency had 160 thousand employees in 2004. Even so, in international forums, China maintained its identification with the position of developing countries of 'common but differentiated responsibilities', by demanding that Northern countries assume the burden of emissions reductions. This position was adopted by both the Group of 77 and the BRICS countries, which includes Brazil, and at the COP in Copenhagen in 2009 China refused to accept any reduction targets for its emissions.

In its twelfth Five Year Plan (2011–2015), however, China formally committed to changing its fossil fuel-based energy model and set a goal to reduce emissions that was transformed into quantifiable targets in the following Five Year Plan. In 2015, in the absence of the United States, China took the lead at the Paris COP by committing to peak carbon emissions by

2030 and a per capita reduction of emissions to 60–65 per cent of its 2005 levels, also by 2030 (CCICED, 2016).

As China adopts quantifiable targets, it has turned to international environmental NGOs – Greenpeace, WWF, FSC – and to Friends of Nature, a local organization and the oldest NGO in China (founded in Beijing in 1993), to draw up the metrics to measure and monitor the targets adopted, even though it has a history of repressing civil society organizations. At the same time, its leading companies in the soy chain have aligned themselves with a series of environmental commitments developed within the business world and social movements of the North. Sinograin became the first Chinese company to receive a certification by the Roundtable on Responsible Soy. COFCO, for its part, integrated itself into the Conesur agribusiness associations, adhered to the moratorium excluding the purchase of soy from recently deforested areas of the Amazon region, and assumed the commitment to have all its supply chains 'cleared' of deforestation by 2023 (Wilkinson et al, 2022).

Thus, even if the debate around downgrading remains relevant in terms of added value and income generation, the fear that there would also be a downgrading in relation to the environment does not seem to proceed. In 2016 the Chinese Council for International Cooperation on Environment and Development published a report, 'China's role in the greening of global value chains' where it specifically refers to the soybean chain in these terms:

> Joining global efforts on soy would strengthen China's reputation on the international stage, its relations with producing countries, and the competitiveness of Chinese companies in the global market. It would also reduce China's contribution to climate change – deforestation from the expansion of soy and other major commodities accounts for more than 10% of global emissions. (CCICED, 2016, p 9)

Thus, even in the context of an authoritarian country where social pressures are stifled, China is showing itself to be increasingly aligned with global conventions on the environment and climate. At the same time, in the two decades before it turned to international markets, a middle class of hundreds of millions was emerging in China and continued to expand in the following decades of the new millennium, reaching 400 million by 2020 according to the National Bureau of Statistics of China. A new level of concern about the basic quality of food accompanied this rise, and the scandal surrounding baby food and the adulteration of milk in 2008 led to an appreciation of imported products with a focus on quality assurance, marking a turning point in this regard (Sun et al, 2020).

The second expression of this consolidation of a middle class was the adoption of a Chinese turn to quality. An indicator of this is the World

Integrated Trade Solution (WITS) import data from the World Bank 'food products' category in 2018. The top ten exporters to China in this category add up to a value of US$20 billion, led now not by Brazil or the United States, but by France, followed by Australia, the Netherlands, New Zealand, Peru, Thailand, Brazil, Germany, Japan, South Korea, and Canada. Differently from the duopoly in the case of soy, the amounts are fairly evenly distributed among the ten leaders.[2] Examples of this shift towards lifestyles that imply new food qualities would include the increase in the consumption of cheese, wine, and coffee. In the case of cheeses, we can intuit their importance from France's leadership in exports, but data from the United States is no less impressive. The United States exported 2,000 metric tonnes at the start of the new millennium, and by 2017 these exports had increased to 108,000 tonnes. China has already become the world's second largest market for wine, aggressively buys vineyards in France, develops its domestic production, and is already considered the world's largest market for the 'top end' wine segment (SCMP Style, 2018).

China is the country par excellence for tea, and per capita consumption of coffee is still very low when compared to Northern countries. Even so, consumption tripled between 2012 and 2016, a year in which Starbucks already had 2,000 shops with plans for 500 new ones per year in the following years (Meyers, 2016). Dunkin' Donuts, a major coffee consumer, also had 1,400 shops in the country by 2020. The biggest demand, however, continues to be for Nestlé's instant coffee. Production of the coffee, concentrated in the Yunnan region has increased rapidly since the early 2000s and China has risen from thirtieth place to become the world's fifteenth producer by 2020, exporting 70 per cent of its output. Traditionally identified as low-quality coffee, the production targets in 2021 are sustainability, organic production, and quality tracking via blockchain (Grant, 2021).

Thus, China's centrality in redirecting the global agri-food system does not imply a simple return to a world dominated by large commodities. Environmental and climate concerns are very much present in China and, since the Paris COP in 2015, it took the lead in setting carbon reduction targets and aligned itself through its leading companies with movements against deforestation. Food security, at the same time, is a sine qua non of the legitimacy of the state. Thus, to ensure that its goals on sustainability and climate are compatible with both food security and its economic development commitment, China is adopting a systemic strategy that, in addition to increasing its control over global trade and incorporating 'the quality turn', includes policies to reduce waste along its supply chains, stimulate changes in consumption patterns, and invest in innovations at the new technological frontier (Wilkinson et al, 2022).

In a position very much in tune with the Lancet research findings mentioned in the Introduction of this book, Xi Jinping has set a target, incorporated into the country's food guidelines in 2016, to reduce meat consumption by 50 per cent (Conexão Planeta, 2016), and the Ministry of Health has adopted the design of 'a pagoda' to provide dietary guidelines, similar to the pyramid used in WHO, Brazil and many other countries.[3] In a further comparison with the United States, China now has a large incidence of obesity that has also become the object of public policies.

Its policies against waste began in 2013 with the campaign, 'Operation Empty Plate', directed against extravagant feasts especially from the public sector. WWF China estimated that in 2015 China wasted between 17 and 18 million tonnes of food. Other calculations have estimated that the amount of food wasted would be enough to feed between 30 and 50 million people throughout the year. In 2019, Shanghai introduced strict regulations on food recycling for both individuals and businesses, a policy that has been adopted in other cities across the country.

Following another statement from Xi Jinping in 2020, there was the launch of the 'Clean Plate' campaign, which penalizes those who order more than they can eat. Wuhan's catering industry, meanwhile, has adopted a policy of 'one plate less', or 'N−1', in relation to the number ordering a meal together in restaurants. In April 2021 a law against food waste was enacted that made it illegal to show videos of eating competitions. Restaurants were allowed to charge extra for dishes ordered but not consumed, and fines were set for oversupply of food by the food service industry. In this document it was estimated that the catering industry wasted 18 billion kilograms a year (BBC News, 2020).

The combination of its green revolution and allowing peasants to sell their produce directly to markets made possible the first stage of an agricultural revolution to sustain China's rapid development after the 1978 reforms. From the 2000s onwards, a combination of factors – the opening to world markets, the loss of land to urbanization, the degree of soil contamination, the ageing of peasants, food scandals, swine fever, as well as the policy of promoting urbanization and welcoming the wave of new technologies – led the Chinese state to move towards the promotion of large-scale agriculture. To enable this development the government modified land rights in 2016 by distinguishing between land ownership (still state-owned) and rights to 'operate', which can be transferred for a period of up to 30 years (Zhan, 2019). Based on this and a policy of subsidies, large 'dragon heads' and agribusiness companies have entered agricultural production, and it is estimated that 30 per cent of China's arable land has already been transferred under this 'operators' rights' system (Glenn and Yao, 2016).

In his chapter, 'Agriculture 5.0 in China: New technology frontiers and the challenges to increase productivity' in the book *China-Brazil*, edited by Jank, Guo and Miranda (2020), Jianjun Lyu shows in detail the degree to which China invests not only in digitalization technologies for agriculture

(25 per cent of farms had broadband access in 2018), but also in the integration of big data with the internet of things (IoT), artificial intelligence (AI), and robotics. The article also shows how at the same time these technologies are being used to enable the entire production/marketing cycle of small producers and cooperatives. The purchase of Syngenta, the world leader in agricultural inputs, by the state firm Chinachem, while increasing its influence among global agribusiness players, is aimed especially at improving the productivity of its domestic agriculture (Lyu, 2020).

Vertical integration from production to consumption is seen as key to what Huang (2008) calls 'China's new age small farms', but the question for this author is whether this integration goes through producer cooperatives or will be dominated by what he characterizes as the aggressive advance of agribusinesses in adopting this model. The Chinese government seems to favour the model of horizontal and vertical integration by promoting large-scale agriculture, responding either to agribusiness pressures, including global agribusinesses, or to more macroeconomic considerations that prioritize a model of urban development and rural exodus, and may also point, as a justification, to the aging of the rural population where the average age exceeds 50 years and some 25 per cent are over 60.

This advance of large-scale agriculture goes beyond the major commodities but especially affects the pork sector, a market that has been hit hard by swine fever domestically and which has caused unprecedented turbulence in the international pork trade. The collapse in herd size was on the order of 50 per cent, creating an extra demand of somewhere around the size of the global pork trade. The response to the crisis was an acceleration in the concentration of production, which had been underway since the early 2000s, accompanied by the adoption of frontier technologies. According to the China Animal Husbandry Handbook cited by consultant Richard Brown on the website Pig Progress, 70 per cent of pork production came from farms with up to 50 animals in 2003, dropping to a forecast of only 3 per cent by 2022 (ter Beek, 2020).

Large companies, including companies from outside the industry, most notably NetEase Weiyang of the internet sector (mentioned in Chapter 3), have taken advantage of the rising price of pork and the collapse of traditional production systems to invest heavily in the sector. These investments use cutting-edge technology: automation; recycling of air, water, and waste; facial recognition of pigs; daily temperature measurement; identity cards for each animal; and the use of RFIDs (radio frequency identification) to trace the chain back from the consumer. Muyuan Foodstuff, the sector leader, is investing in a plant that will slaughter 2.1 million pigs per year, incorporating all these technological resources (Patton, 2020).

With its exclusive breed of small black pigs, NetEase Weiyang targets the new middle-class market, invests heavily in building a brand, focuses on online sales (although it also sells through 16 supermarket channels), and, in addition to the technologies indicated earlier, manages to train the pigs to use a reserved area for defecation, which allows for the recycling of waste. Moreover, it has adopted a music atmosphere for the pigs and has created a playlist that was successfully launched on the internet (Borak, 2018).

Even with these new investments, the concentration of the sector is still very low, and the top ten companies account for only 12 per cent compared with 30 per cent in the United States. On the other hand, the new Chinese breeding and slaughtering models are up to ten times the average size of plants in the United States. Developed during the swine fever outbreak, these investments are high-risk but rely on new technologies to ensure safety. In the United States, in the context of COVID-19, there was a movement to limit the size of slaughter plants, which if successful could create restrictions on world trade. Chinese investments, however, are still aimed at their own domestic market.

Although China is an authoritarian country where social movements that mediate interests and values between civil society, the market, and the state are strictly controlled, from the second decade of the 2000s onwards it has embraced the environmental agenda that had invaded the global agri-food system since the 1980s. China took a leading role in the 2015 Paris COP and its companies have aligned themselves with commitments on deforestation, decarbonization, and the certification of their supply chains. At the same time, its middle class, larger than the entire population of the European Union, shows the same concerns for individual and environmental wellbeing that reinforces demand for the quality products typical of Northern countries.

On the other hand, the reformulation of food security, that had always prioritized self-sufficiency, to accommodate the need for structural imports led to efforts to control global markets that face increasing geopolitical obstacles. To the tensions over the two principal feed suppliers, Brazil and the United States, were added the disarticulations of global chains resulting from COVID-19 and the invasion of Ukraine by Russia in 2022, which weakens two other key sources of grain supply. It is in this context that we must appraise the modernization measures of China's agri-food production systems and the efforts to influence consumption patterns, particularly for animal protein. In concluding this chapter, we point to the growing importance of initiatives and policies to promote climate-controlled agriculture as well as alternative proteins.

In Chapter 3, we noted that while in the United States and Europe vertical agriculture products are essentially limited to the 'salad' sector and often even to 'leafy greens', China is more adventurous in experimenting with giant zucchini and tubers (sweet potatoes) (Thorpe, 2014). Even more radical is the new investment by the Zhongxin Kaiwei company that adopts vertical breeding in the construction of a 26-storey fully digitalized building (each floor with its own air circulation system) for the fattening and slaughtering of 1.2 million pigs when in full operation under the management of NetEase Weiyang. The internet/telecommunications sector – Huawei Technologies Co., JD.com, and Alibaba Group Holding – is starting to invest heavily in this new type of high-tech farming (Olho No Araguaia, 2021).

Analysis of China's urban agriculture and, within that, its vertical agriculture needs to take into account the specificity of the administrative responsibilities of the municipal cities that traditionally encompass the surrounding agricultural regions (Natrajan, 2021). Historically, local and regional authorities have been responsible for ensuring food security, a practice that lasted until the 1990s. Research conducted in this period in Shanghai by Cai and Zhang (2000) estimated that 41 per cent of the workforce was engaged in agriculture, 80 per cent of which was part-time. 100 per cent of poultry, eggs, and milk, and 80 per cent of vegetables and freshwater fisheries were produced within 10 kilometres of the city centre.

Natrajan[4] identifies four types of urban agriculture, two informal: in private gardens, and in unoccupied areas of cities (with a certain tolerance by local authorities); and two formal ones: peri-urban agriculture, and high-tech vertical agriculture. Public policies from the 1990s onwards have favoured the modernization of peri-urban agriculture and been inspired by Japan's adoption of high-tech vertical farming but with small-scale applications for small farms and housing. The first initiative took the model of urban agricultural parks that combined technological, educational, recreational, and environmental policies. In Beijing there are 33 such parks and the model has been replicated in other cities. With China adhering to the United Nations Sustainable Development Goals (SDGs), the 'National Agricultural Sustainable Development Plan (2015–2030)' was launched, which focused on the use of new technologies for the purpose of combining efficiency and sustainability. The Chinese Academy of Agricultural Sciences (CAAS) took on more importance and in 2013 initiated the Agricultural Science and Technology Innovation Programme, which included a special programme for 'indoor' and vertical farming.[5] The Research Centre for Protected Agriculture and Environmental Engineering (CPAEE) manages 40 institutes in all regions of China responsible for the engineering development of greenhouses, vertical farming factories, as well as efficient hydroponics and energy-use systems. As early as 2013, China had 75 vertical farms, 25 of which operated using artificial light (Thorpe, 2014).

The leading company in this segment in China is Sananbio, which emerged from a joint venture of the Institute of Botany and the Fujian Sanan Group, the optoelectronics giant and the largest producer of LED chips. It owns or manages 50 vertical farms in ten countries in Asia, Europe, and the United States and produces more than 300 varieties of vegetables, leafy vegetables, fruits, herbs, medicinal plants, and edible flowers. Through a subsidiary, Uplift, it has developed a fully automated farm and, at the same time, produces a container-type model, the Sananbio Ark, which can be used in any environment and requires minimal prior knowledge to operate. The company also has a model for home use (Sananbio, 2020). In 2020, Sananbio had 416 patents and predicted that the costs of vertical farming would be competitive by 2025.

The Japanese multinational Panasonic has two vertical farms in operation in China and invests heavily in developing this sector in the region (Singapore, Japan). Its speciality is to guarantee production in extreme environments and for this it is researching on Ishigaki Island in Japan. The goal is to produce sensitive foodstuffs – tomatoes and strawberries – year-round under any climatic conditions. To this end, it has already developed its passive greenhouse model that can withstand tornadoes, and a robotic system to harvest tomatoes (Panasonic Group, 2021). In Shanghai in an aquaculture system that uses shrimp and crabs to produce fertilizer, a 30-acre farm is producing bananas of many different varieties (iJinshan, 2021). China has to cope with extreme climatic conditions in various parts of the country, most notably the Gobi Desert where with a combination of state-of-the-art technology from Israel and capital and technology from wealthy regions of China such as Fujian province, tens of thousands of hectares are now cultivated with horticultural crops and vineyards under climate-controlled conditions (Xie et al, 2018).

In the Introduction and Chapter 2 of this book we described the wave of unprecedented innovation in the agri-food system enabled by the opening of new frontiers in digitalization and in biotechnology at the end of the 20th century, driven by global considerations (population, urbanization, energy, natural resources, health/welfare, and climate) where animal protein chains occupy a central place. In Northern countries, the issue is the need to reduce per capita consumption of animal protein, especially red meat, while in developing countries the challenge would be to ease the transition from a diet of vegetable to animal protein, the result of urbanization and income improvements. Measures to contain consumption are being put into practice for these purposes, but the central focus is on the introduction of radical innovations that are reconceptualizing the world of meat.

The implications of China's continuous growth at double-digit rates over the past four decades, with its mega population, has provided the wake-up call. In the 1980s China had a per capita meat consumption of around 14 kilograms, increasing to 45 kilograms in the second decade of the 2000s. In 2022, China accounts for 18.5 per cent of the world population and consumes 28 per cent of the world's meat supply and 50 per cent of its pork (Milman and Leavenworth, 2016). If animal protein consumption in the North is seen as one of the greatest threats to individual and public health, the pace of its demand in emerging countries is perceived as a threat also to the health of the planet. We will see its implications in greater detail when considering the case of Brazil in Chapter 6.

As we analysed in Chapter 4, the first companies, the first investors, the first markets for alternative protein, and the whole ecosystem of support, emerged in the countries of the North and especially in the United States, led in the case of meat by Beyond Meat and Impossible Foods, followed by a proliferation of start-ups and also by established leaders such as Cargill, Tyson, ADM, DuPont, Nestlé, and Unilever contesting different slices of these new markets. Four years after the launch of the first burgers in 2016, the globalization of investments and markets was already evident with Beyond Meat's presence in 80 countries and over 100,000 points of sale. Impossible Foods followed the same strategy, but its entry into many markets – Europe, UK, China – depended as recently as 2023 on the regulation of the ingredient heme, a product of precision fermentation used to simulate the effect of blood in its burger (Dunn, 2021).

As of 2019, while remaining the most important market, North America lost its near monopoly on investments, with Europe, the Middle East, Latin America, and Asia coming to account for 30 per cent of new financing (GFI, 2021). Bloomberg projections, followed by Global Market Insight, suggest that the global market for alternative proteins would reach over US$150 billion by 2030. GFI (2021) estimated that investments in 800 large-scale production plants would be needed to meet this target. Projections from other consultancies have estimated a market of around US$20–30 billion in the second half of the of the 2020s (Grichnik et al, 2021).[6] Despite the highly speculative and sometimes promotional nature of these projections, there is consensus that the most important markets will be in Asia and especially China. For the Good Food Institute (GFI APAC, 2022), this already became evident in 2022 with the large US$100 million financing to China's Starfield and Next Gen Foods of Singapore (Zhang, 2022). Calculations of the size of the Chinese market for alternative proteins in the early 2020s made by the global company ADM (2022) and EUROMONITOR (2021) are around US$12–15 billion, which appear to include traditional plant-based substitutes such as tofu.

Despite the confusion of these market projections, it is clear from an analysis of the investments that Asia is becoming a new hub for alternative proteins, with its primary hub in Singapore and secondary hubs in Hong Kong, Shanghai, and Beijing. Decisive in this has been the Singapore government's promotion of high-tech options in the pursuit of greater food self-sufficiency, both for climate-controlled agriculture and alternative proteins. The goal of reducing its dependence on food imports from over 90 per cent to 70 per cent by 2030 is driving the Singapore government to implement development, funding, and regulatory measures that are transforming Singapore into a global centre for research and development and also for the production and launching of food innovations (GFI APAC, 2021).

The Singapore-based state investment fund Temasek, which manages over US$280 billion in assets, has been one of the leading global financers of alternative proteins, participating in rounds of support for Impossible Foods, Perfect Day, and Upside Foods. Since 2013 Temasek has invested over US$8 billion in agfood start-ups, and funds a life sciences laboratory with 225 researchers, affiliated with the National University of Singapore. It has also created the Asia Sustainable Foods Platform that serves as an incubator and has entered a joint venture with ADM and the German alternative protein company Cremer. Next Gen Foods, a start-up from Singapore, is setting up an R&D centre on the Temasek platform made possible by the US$100 million it raised in its last funding round in 2022 (Poinski, 2022).

Other leading companies in this segment are investing in innovation centres in Singapore – ADM, Perfect Day, Avant Meats, and Liberty Produce in the climate-controlled agriculture sector. Eat Just, with regulatory approval, launched its cultured meat at Singapore's 1880 restaurant and has a production plant on the island. In 2022, it began construction of a new plant, the largest in Singapore, at an estimated cost of US$120 million to produce the two types of chicken already approved and its alternative eggs that it has been marketing in Singapore, Hong Kong, and China since 2018. Impossible Foods and Beyond Meat market their products in Singapore where they are also testing their new pork launches. With its large Chinese population, the Singapore market becomes an excellent platform for entering China (Tracxn, 2024).

If Singapore has Temasek, in Hong Kong Lever VC and Horizons Ventures are leading initiatives in venture capital. Lever VC, also based in New York, had raised a total of US$80 million by 2021 to back plant-based and cultured meats and had a portfolio of 19 alternative protein start-ups. Horizons Ventures has funded Impossible Foods, Eat Just, and Perfect Day and in 2021 provided funding for Nourish Ingredients, a start-up from Australia, which identifies crucial lipids to reproduce the flavours of meat. Lever VC has also invested in Avant Meats, the first cell culture meat start-up with a focus on seafood and whose motto is products 'without animal cruelty, heavy metals or micro plastics'. Avant Meats hopes to have a commercial product by 2023. Hong Kong's most important start-up is OmniFoods, from the company Green Monday,[7] which defines itself as 'a platform with a multi-dimensional social model of risk', combining venture capital activities, the production of alternative proteins, and a network of 'plant-based concept' retail/restaurants called Green Common (Ho, 2021b).

In China the leading venture capital firms are Dao Foods, which funds 30 alternative protein start-ups, including Starfield, and Shanghai-based Bits x Bites, which among other start-ups funds Next Gen Foods and InnovoPro alternative plant proteins, in addition to Future Meat which develops cellular meat (Vegconomist, 2021a). Beyond Meat and Oatly, in the case of milk alternatives, entered the Chinese market via the Starbucks chain in 2020. Since then, Beyond Meat's products have been available online, in restaurants and fast food chains, and in retail. In 2021 it opened its 'state of the art' factory in Jiaxing near Shanghai, its first outside the United States, to supply the full range of its products, which also includes an R&D facility for developing new products attuned to Chinese food tastes (Lucas, 2020).

While Impossible Foods is still awaiting permission to enter the Chinese market, Beyond Meat needs to face the new regional start-ups such as OmniFoods from Green Monday and Zhenmeat that have a wider variety of products in line with the region's culinary practices.[8] By 2020, new food start-ups in China received US$127 million in funding, the vast majority in small amounts (except for Green Monday, which received US$70 million), typical of a sector beginning the path from research to market. By 2021 the average amounts increased, showing the progress of firms such as Jones Food Company, which received more than US$10 million, and that together with CellX and Avant Meats develops cellular meat including seafood, much more important in Asian cuisines. In 2022, the rapid advance of this sector was evident with the funding of US$100 million to Starfield, a start-up that produces, among other products, a plant-based pastrami and is already present in more than 14,000 outlets based on partnerships with established brands. Starfield plans to build its own factory in Xiaogan, Hubei (Zhang, 2022).

Traditional vegan product companies such as Ningbo Sulian Food and Whole Perfect Food (Qishan), are already targeting this new market, partnering with the new start-ups and their raw material suppliers, with the advantage of having consolidated popular brands (GFI APAC, 2020).

Global food companies that had already entered these markets in the North are also present in the Chinese market. Nestlé promotes its product line Harvest Gourmet and in 2021 announced plans to build a plant-based food factory in Tianjin (Ellis, 2020a), and Unilever's The Vegetarian Butcher line is also present. More surprising perhaps is the presence of global traders: ADM (which as we saw in Chapter 4 already has a partnership with Brazil's Marfrig to produce plant-based burgers); and Cargill with its new PlantEver product line and its positioning as a supplier of 'private-label' products for local brands (Ellis, 2020b). DuPont also joins this group of global companies transitioning into ingredients and nutrition and entering the alternative protein market (Ferrer, 2020).

The speed with which this market has developed in China is reflected in the establishment of voluntary guidelines for plant-based meats that were announced in June 2021. Issued by a state-affiliated industry group, the Institute for Food Science and Technology, they allow the use of the word 'meat' along with 'plant-based' adjectives, ban the use of animal-derived ingredients, and limit the use of 'non-plant' ingredients to 10 per cent of the total product weight (Ho, 2021c).

The Chinese state's interest in meat alternatives was registered as early as 2017 when it closed a cooperation agreement with alternative protein companies in Israel worth US$300 million. The Five-Year Agriculture Plan launched in 2022 includes for the first time support for cellular meat as a measure to address food security in the country. And in a speech in 2022 Xi Jinping also advocated the development of alternative proteins:

> [...] it is necessary to expand from traditional crops and livestock and poultry resources to more abundant biological resources, develop biotechnology and bio-industry, and seek energy and protein from plants, animals, and micro-organisms. (Zhang, 2020)

Doubts regarding the continued dynamism of alternative protein markets began to emerge in the trade press in Northern countries in 2022. For some analysts, the post-COVID-19 upturn in activity could be the explanation with the return of the practice of eating out. Others assessed that consumers who tried these products enthusiastically in 2020 did not become regular consumers in 2021 either for taste or price reasons. The same discussions can be identified in relation to the Chinese alternative protein market. It is too early to draw conclusions yet, especially as companies are constantly reformulating and improving their products in the light of consumer feedback (Che, 2021).

With the new positions adopted by the Chinese state, central figures such as David Yeung, founder of OmniFoods, suggest the possibility of state support similar to that of alternative energy, in the form of subsidies and access to institutional markets to achieve the necessary scale and price competitivity. This would be coherent with the set of measures to curb meat consumption already adopted by the Chinese government (Vegconomist, 2020).

Besides directly aiming to contain consumption, the Chinese government is taking a series of measures to reduce its dependence on imports for the animal protein chain. Two measures are especially relevant in terms of their impacts on Brazil as a large exporter of animal feed. The first was a decision to lower the protein content of animal feed – by 1.5 per cent for pigs and 1 per cent for poultry – which would imply a reduction of no less than 11 million tonnes of soy meal, or 14 million tonnes of the grain (Wilkinson et al, 2022). The second, longer-term possibility, but not so long-term because the technology seems to have been proven, aims at a more radical substitution of feeds reminiscent of the efforts to develop single-cell protein in the 1970s. This involves the use of exhaust gas from petrochemical industries and sectors dependent on this input and its transformation into a *Clostridium autoethanogenum* cellular protein, which can be produced on an industrial scale directly as a substitute for soy. As it is produced from carbon capture, it would also be an important weapon for reducing greenhouse gas emissions (State Council, PRC, 2021). In Chapter 6, we analyse Brazil's position in the face of these global transformations in the animal protein sector.

6

Brazil on the Wrong Side of the Tracks? Maybe Not So Much

The explosion of Chinese demand for animal feed in the first decade of the 2000s launched Brazil onto the global stage as the granary of a world now of emerging countries in transition to a diet based on animal protein. At the same time, as a driver of renewable energy in the form of sugarcane-based ethanol, Brazil presented itself as a model of green development for African and Central American countries. It was argued that this huge expansion of its agricultural commodity exports would be achieved in a sustainable manner compatible with the preservation of the Amazon forest, based on the sugar industry's commitments not to enter the Amazon region, and the 'Soy Moratorium', signed by global trading companies and international NGOs, not to accept soybeans from deforested areas in the Amazon region, a commitment subsequently extended to cattle ranches with the signing of the Cattle Pact (Wilkinson and Herrera, 2010).

This image of Brazil as a global agribusiness powerhouse is in stark contrast with the vision of an urban-industrial Brazil under the hegemony of the São Paulo bourgeoisie that was consolidated throughout the 20th century (Mello, 1982; Castro and Souza, 1985; Tavares, 1998). It also contrasts with the view widely disseminated in literature and academia of a backward rural world dominated by large properties in the form of unproductive latifundia that also oppressed indigenous peoples and small producers (Guimarães, 1968) and that, in its most recent expression, would have been responsible for the progressive destruction of the forests and biodiversity of Brazil's biomes (Heredia et al, 2010).

There are two contrasting lines of analysis on the evolution of the dominant actors of the agri-food system in Brazil that help better to explain the economic and political centrality of Brazilian agribusinesses in the 21st century, even if, as we will see, both fail to integrate in their analyses a vision of urban-industrial Brazil. These two trends were born in the academic environment of São Paulo, the country's economic centre.

The first line of interpretation was elaborated at the Institute of Economics of the University of Campinas (Unicamp) with a fundamental focus on the transformations in agriculture resulting from the development of domestic input (chemical and genetic) and agricultural machinery industries. Two major structural changes are identified: the internalization of these upstream industries in Brazil that guarantees agricultural autonomy in relation to the availability of foreign exchange; and the feasibility of a technical modernization of agriculture without breaking the pattern of large properties consolidated since the colonial period. The notion of 'conservative modernization' was coined to capture this process, and the analytical framework favoured to understand the new interdependence between industry and agriculture was the 'agro-industrial complex', drawing on the French tradition of *filière*, or chain, that integrates industrial and agricultural activities in a single economic dynamic (Graziano da Silva, 1982; Kageyama et al, 1990).[1]

The notion of 'conservative modernization' serves to explain the continuity of the agrarian structure based on large properties, the inheritors of *sesmarias*, enormous donations of land that characterized the colonial occupation, while avoiding a transition to modernity via classic agrarian reform (Abramovay, 1992). This continuity is expressed in the maintenance of extremely negative indices of land concentration, measured by the 'Gini index', even in the context of modernization (Hoffman, 2015). Thus, the transition from slavery to the use of wage labour and then to mechanization took place without lasting changes in the agrarian order despite strong periodic contestations (Costa and Santos, 1998; Navarro, 2014).

This structural continuity was combined with a major geographical transformation in the migration of the main crops from the North and Northeast to the Southeast region. Rubber, which characterized the integration of the Amazon region into world markets by temporarily creating the sumptuous capital cities of Manaus and Belem for the rubber elite in the late 19th century, was reborn in the São Paulo plantations, now oriented to the emerging domestic market for the automobile and road transport industries (Martinez, 2006; Somain and Droulers, 2016). Coffee, which entered Brazil through the north of the country, became established during the colonial and slavery era around Rio de Janeiro and was later consolidated in São Paulo and further south in the state of Paraná based on wage labour (Silva, 1976). Cotton, for so long the mainstay of the economy of the semi-arid Northeast region, also migrated to the Southeast region, where it became part of the plantation economy, and then later returned to the Northeast in the form of large irrigated properties in the state of Bahia (Gonçalves and Ramos, 2008).

The most iconic product of the colonial period that defined Brazil as an exporter of agricultural commodities to world markets – sugarcane – suffers the same fate. Born in the Northeast and celebrated/demonized in literary classics (Rego, 1932) and social sciences (Freyre, 2002), sugarcane became the most important product of São Paulo state agriculture and the spearhead of Brazil's 'green development' diplomacy at the beginning of the 21st century (Paiva and Manduca, 2010). One should not forget either the orange plantations in São Paulo, originally consumed *in natura*, but now produced as a ubiquitous input for the global breakfast in the urban-industrial world of Northern countries (Mergulhão, 2018).

The second current of analysis was born in the University of São Paulo (USP), marked not by the technification of agriculture from the 1970s but by the 'liberal' reforms initiated by the Collor government in the 1990s (Delgado, 2012). Until the 1980s, agri-food activity was highly regulated. We can take the cases of wheat and milk, in which prices and quotas as well as quality standards were subject to public regulation covering farmers, importers of grain, flour, and milk powder, mills, and dairy cooperatives, and even the sale of 'French bread', and 'milk in a plastic bag' (Wilkinson, 1996; Café et al, 2003).

At the beginning of the 1990s, the agri-food markets in Brazil were abruptly deregulated following a parallel movement of deregulation in international agricultural commodity markets. Producers, cooperatives, and companies now had to negotiate directly among themselves on both the price and the quality of their products. Whereas before, all the stages of the chains were intermediated by the State, from the 1990s onwards the actors had to deal directly with their suppliers and clients and, at the same time, ensure stability among all actors in the chain. The issues of 'coordination' become the watchwords, and the postgraduate programme on agri-food systems (PENSA) at USP was created under the coordination of Décio Zylbersztajn and Elizabeth Farina precisely to train staff specialized in strategies for coordinating agribusiness players, already organized in a new Brazilian Association of Agribusiness (ABAG) (Zylbersztajn and Scare, 2003; Pompeia, 2021).

As we saw in Chapter 1, the 1990s were a period of stagnation in the commodity export markets of Northern countries, in which quality strategies were seen as a solution that would allow the renewal of markets through segmentation and product differentiation. A range of demographic and income factors favoured this shift – the ageing population, health issues, and new subjectivities around wellbeing (Wilkinson, 1999). In line with the advice of international organizations to segment commodity markets via quality strategies and to promote 'non-traditional' export products, the PENSA programme reflected this option in the promotion of quality strategies in traditional (milk, coffee, wines) and non-traditional chains (fruits and seafoods) (Nassar et al, 1999). The commercial integration of the Southern Cone countries within the Mercosur, starting in 1986 and formalized in 1991, accelerated the pressures for new standards and levels of quality, especially in dairy and beef cattle (Wilkinson, 2000). In a similar fashion to the Unicamp thinkers, PENSA adopted the approach of 'agro-industrial complexes' to capture the new relationship between agriculture and upstream and downstream industries but chose the more orthodox tradition of Davis and Goldberg (1957) and adopted the method of case studies of firms that these initiated at Harvard University.

If the 1980s in Brazil were seen economically as a lost decade of low growth and uncontrolled inflation, politically the country witnessed the peaceful but enthusiastic transition from the military dictatorship to a democratic regime anchored in a new constitution, in addition to the emergence of civil society and the explosion of social movements as from the last years of the dictatorship. Demands that had been repressed for decades, in particular agrarian reform, redirected the attention of agrarian studies to the victims of 'modernization' and 'agribusiness' and identified a new subject, family farming, as the bearer of an alternative project for the development of agriculture (Guanziroli et al, 2001).

Once again, São Paulo's academia provided the historical and theoretical basis by revisiting the processes of rural modernization in Northern countries and identifying the transformation of the peasantry into family farms able to incorporate 'technical progress' without promoting exclusionary land concentration and where gains of scale could be achieved through the association of producers in cooperatives (Veiga, 1991; Abramovay, 1992). Its viability in Brazil, however, was not expressed in the conservative modernization of the state of São Paulo but in the transplantation of the European model of family farming to the southern states of Brazil based on the massive immigration that began in the last quarter of the 19th century and continued throughout the first decades of the 20th century. There, in the hills of Rio Grande do Sul, Santa Catarina, and Paraná, a polyculture of family farmers, mostly German and Italian, was consolidated, organized in more or less egalitarian colonies, with strong associative practices (Schneider and Cassol, 2013). It was in this environment that the cooperatives were born, and later in the 1980s the associated social movements focused on demands for agrarian reform and policies to support family farming (de Medeiros, 2003).

We have already seen that the 1990s were marked by stagnation in the traditional commodity chains, which led to the collapse of the cotton/livestock economy in the Northeast and the decline of international markets for commodities such as traditional coffee. Thus, the explosion of movements around agrarian reform in the wake of democratization found a propitious environment for the negotiation of land for settlements (Sauer, 2010). During the governments of Fernando Henrique Cardoso (1995–2002), around 3,500 acts of expropriation were decreed, involving more than 20 million hectares (Cattelan et al, 2020). But if the land market in traditional regions favoured a policy of promoting settlements, the social and religious movements, the

Landless Workers' Movement (MST) and the Pastoral Land Commission (CPT), organized around the banner of agrarian reform and leading land occupations, emerged from a new reality – the increasing difficulties of farmers in the southern states to reproduce their way of life (Grisa and Schneider, 2015).

In parallel with the actions in favour of agrarian reform, the concept of 'family farming' was being refined in the academic world in centres such as the CPDA at UFRRJ, the graduate programme in rural development (PGDR) at Federal University of Rio Grande do Sul (UFRGS), and in the research network of the Social Research Exchange Project in Agriculture (PIPSA), and took political form in the National Programme for the Strengthening of Family Agriculture (PRONAF) launched during the Fernando Henrique Cardoso (FHC) government, formulated by the team around Carlos Guanziroli, professor at the Fluminense Federal University in Rio de Janeiro (Guanziroli et al, 2001).

In this way, the new face of agribusiness represented by ABAG and PENSA had as its counterpart the defence of modern agriculture based on family farming. Besides the proposal for agrarian reform, the defence of a development model based on family agriculture included the promotion of alternatives to the large poultry and pork agroindustries that were consolidating in the southern states (Wilkinson, 1996) and the promotion of the French model of geographical indications (GIs), in which the quality of products is closely associated with the artisanal production traditions of family farming (Wilkinson, Niederle and Mascarenhas, 2016). In contrast to agribusinesses and their agrichemicals, organic markets were promoted (Fonseca, 2005), and against the poverty associated with integration into traditional commodity chains, fair trade and versions of the solidarity economy were encouraged (Mascarenhas, 2007). Family farming with its traditional products was presented as the mainstay of domestic food supply, while agribusiness was attacked as sacrificing the domestic market for the benefit of exports, often for animal consumption, reinforcing unsustainable diets in Northern countries and threatening the environment in Brazil (França et al, 2009; Hoffman, 2015; Mitidiero Júnior et al, 2017).

However, as was to become clear when analysing the main beneficiaries of PRONAF, the strongest segments of family farming were already firmly integrated into agribusinesses, either as suppliers of poultry, pigs, and tobacco, based on integration contracts, or as producers of soybean and corn for feed (Delgado et al, 2010). However, for most family farmers it was becoming increasingly difficult to achieve the production scales required by agribusinesses. Many producers resorted to milk production as an alternative, but from the mid-1990s, this sector also advanced towards scales of operation that led to the expulsion of a third of producers between 1996 and 2006 in the southern states (Wilkinson, 1997).

The fragility of soybean farming in the Global South became evident from the clandestine entry of transgenic seeds from Argentina, which were legalized there as early as the 1990s. A strong movement 'for a Brazil free of transgenics' prevented their legalization in Brazil until the mid-2000s (Pessanha and Wilkinson, 2005). Even so, it was not possible to avoid their adoption, even in agrarian reform settlements, given the promise of saving costs on chemical inputs. This, however, was only one of the expressions of the continuous migration of the soybean/corn and meat complexes to the Centre-West of the country, with the consequent loss of competitiveness of the Southern region, which had been the cradle of the agroindustrial chains that made the Brazilian transition to an animal protein diet possible (Testa et al, 1996).

The 1990s and the first decade of the 2000s witnessed vibrant social movements articulated with international trends. They encompassed both distributive issues and the values associated with artisan agroindustry and pesticide-free agriculture and promoted new markets for organics, fair trade, and GIs (Wilkinson, 2011).

Brazil played a leading role in all these movements and became an international reference. Within the International Federation of Organic Agriculture Movements (IFOAM), Brazilian networks promoted an original system of participatory certification, based on peer-recognition protocols in organic production networks. The Ecovida Agroecology Network, with 340 farmer groups involving 4,500 families and the participation of 20 NGOs, gave rise to 120 organic fairs strengthening direct ties with consumers and achieved acceptance of its products in mainstream retail (Oliveira et al, 2020). In the case of fair trade, besides integrating into the international systems FLO (Fairtrade Labelling Organizations International) and IFAT (International Federation of Alternative Traders, now the World Fair Trade Organization, WFTO), Brazil followed Mexico's example and developed a national system for the Brazilian market. Under Lula's government, the fair trade movement was integrated into public policies for the promotion of the solidarity economy led by the academic/militant Paul Singer (Mascarenhas, 2007).

In cooperation with France, a strong national network was created to promote geographical indications, a form of collective intellectual property that is legitimized through the identification of a product – in our case, agricultural products – with the territory where they are produced. This network trained staff at various levels of the federal government (MAPA [Ministry of Agriculture], INPI [National Institute of Industrial Property]) and helped with GI recognition procedures, which reached 80 in 2020, with the first Brazilian GI being granted in 2002. The recognition and regulation by federal law of the artisan production of raw milk cheeses are also due to the network created around GIs (Wilkinson et al, 2017). Renowned chefs have been engaged in the promotion of GI products, and today Canastra cheese from the state of Minas Gerais and other artisan cheeses, which in the 1990s were still being sold clandestinely at degraded prices, can be found on the menus of restaurants and in delicatessens at exorbitant prices. In Brazil, the Slow Food movement, which was born in Italy in opposition to the spread of fast food in that country and quickly became internationalized, also emerged from the networks mobilized around geographical indications.

During the long period of the Lula and Rousseff governments (2003–2016) there was a growing convergence between social movements and public policies as NGO staff and associated academics took on government or advisory positions. In fact, this convergence dates to the end of the dictatorship with the institutionalization of policies for agrarian reform and other social policies. The year 1993 became an emblematic moment in this sense. On the one hand, the government of Itamar Franco (1993–1994) created the National Council for Food Security (CONSEA), a theme that would become a key axis of both policies and social mobilizations in the Lula governments. On the other hand, in the same year, a distinctly urban movement against hunger emerged, launched by Herbert 'Betinho' de Souza and IBASE (Brazilian Institute of Social and Economic Analysis) – Action of Citizenship Against Hunger and Misery and For Life – which became the most successful movement in terms of popular mobilization on food during the 1990s. From an urban perspective, this movement of 'Betinho' identified the solution in the 'democratization of the land', establishing ties with rural movements around the agrarian reform, especially the MST, as well as the promotion of family agriculture in the PRONAF policies promoted by the Cardoso government as from 1996 (Jardim Pinto, 2005; Ação de Cidadania, 2013).

In light of these initiatives, it is easier to understand why the first book published by ABAG, also in 1993, was entitled *Food Security: An Agribusiness Approach* (ABAG, 1993). The themes of social movements and associated policies were already setting the agenda of the dominant agri-food system.

The question of agrarian reform had polarized the Brazilian countryside since democratization between the MST's strategy of direct action and the intimidation, violence, and assassinations on the part of the large landowners organized in the Rural Democratic Union (UDR) created in 1985 to oppose agrarian reform (Bruno, 1997). At the same time, a vision of the complementarity between family farming and agribusiness began to emerge, with each side, however, having a different understanding of its content. For ABAG, family farming could be welcomed as a junior partner of agribusinesses, while the promoters of family farming saw this sector as the mainstay of domestic food supply against the export orientation of agribusiness. This complementarity initially took shape with the launch of PRONAF in 1996 and was institutionalized with the creation of the Ministry of Agrarian Development and Family Agriculture (MDA) in 2000, which integrated the set of actions around family farming until 2016 (Grisa, 2018; Mederios and Grisa, 2019).

The electoral campaign that brought Lula to government in 2003 included the commitment to eradicate hunger, and the issue of food security became one of the central axes of his government with the launch first of the Zero Hunger programme and then the Bolsa Família (family allowance). CONSEA closed during the second FHC government, was reinstated and densified with the promotion of councils at the municipal level, and became the focus of agglutination of NGOs and social movements mobilized on this theme. In contrast to the 'Betinho' movement of the 1990s, CONSEA focused on public policies and the legal recognition of rights around food security, enshrined in law in 2006. By repeating its action in the new social movements around food, Brazil became a reference for food security policies, especially with Graziano da Silva, one of the creators of these policies, first as director of the Food and Agriculture Organization of the United Nations (FAO) in Latin America, and later as Director-General of the FAO in Rome.

CONSEA innovated by including the nutritional issue in its definition of food security. Although this was initially in the context of traditional discussions on malnutrition and undernourishment, a broadening of the definition made it possible to establish connections with new and typically urban debates on food consumption (Maluf et al, 2021). The Consumer Protection Institute (IDEC) was created in 1987 and since its inception has given great attention to the issue of food consumption; in 1997, the federal government regulated the National System of Consumer Protection. In the academic world, the National Meeting of Consumer Studies (ENEC) was launched in 2004 and created a national network around its biannual meetings in which the theme of food became central (Portilho, 2005; Barbosa et al, 2021).

The 'Betinho' campaign had revealed the prevalence of hunger in large urban centres, but equally worrisome were the high rates of obesity, diabetes, and cardiovascular problems, especially among the urban poor, that were associated with the increased consumption of food industry products. In the Guide for a Healthy Diet, launched in 2006 by the federal government, Brazil, like many other countries, prioritized the consumption of fresh products as well as a reduction in the consumption of animal protein without specific references to the food industry. In 2010 Carlos Monteiro and his team at USP correlated these new diseases directly with the food industry, not focusing nutritional content but pointing as a criterion for classification the degree of processing of their products and identifying 'ultra-processed' foods as the villains to be avoided. In the second edition of the Guide in 2014, Brazil adopted this classification called Nova, and later in 2019 an

FAO publication backed this approach internationally. Several countries have adopted this classification, and the identification of ultra-processed foods as primarily responsible for the new non-communicable and typically urban diseases has been widely welcomed among opinion leaders and has been the focus of academic debates internationally (Bortoletto Martins et al, 2013; FAO, 2019).

Already in the 1970s, the opening of the agricultural and ranching frontier in the Centre-West of the country received a strong stimulus from the cooperation program between Brazil and a Japan eager to create a new source of grains supply (Wilkinson and Rama, 2012). Its actual occupation, however, was due more to the growth in domestic demand for meat and feed with the transition to an animal protein diet, resultant on the rapid pace of urbanization, which led to the displacement of the agricultural grain frontier towards the Centre and North of the country. Colonization projects and successive migration from the South region transformed family farmers into medium and large producers specializing in grains and livestock. In the process, the 'family farm' of the South was reborn in the Centre-West as an increasingly strong segment of agribusiness and became more autonomous in relation to the 'São Paulo' agribusiness model. The adaptation of soybean varieties to Midwest latitudes, a triumph of national research, and the legalization of transgenics in 2005 consolidated the no-till farming model, facilitating the management of increasingly larger properties (Wilkinson and Pereira, 2018).

In the first decade of the 2000s, there began a new boom cycle in agricultural commodities fuelled by Chinese demand on the one hand, and by the promotion of biofuels, whether from sugarcane in Brazil or from corn in the United States, on the other. Food security policies and the strengthening of family farming coexisted with the celebration of Brazilian agribusiness as the world's granary and promise of green energy development. In this context, sugarcane from São Paulo and soybean from the Midwest found a common voice in the person of Roberto Rodrigues, leader of ABAG and minister of agriculture in Lula's first government, and in their respective associations, Unica (Brazilian Sugarcane Industry Association) and ICONE (International Trade and Negotiations Institute) in São Paulo state, or Abiove (Brazilian Vegetable Oils Industry) and Aprosoja (Association of Soybean Producers) in the Midwest (Wilkinson, 1997).

Until the 2008 financial crisis, the sugarcane sector with its geopolitical promise of biofuels was the leading agribusiness sector, even advancing into cattle ranching and soybean areas in the Centre-West. However, with the financial crisis, sugarcane became one of the hardest hit sectors. New investments were frozen, which led to a high level of indebtedness, the precursor to a strong wave of acquisitions and concentration in the sector (Wilkinson and Herrera, 2010). With the support of the Brazilian

Development Bank, the leading white meat companies Perdigão and Sadia found a way out of the crisis, which had left Sadia heavily in debt, by their merger creating Brasil Foods (BRF). The soy sector, in stark contrast, expanded exuberantly under the impact of growing and seemingly inexhaustible demand from China, becoming the locomotive of Brazilian agribusiness.

Roberto Rodrigues remained at the Ministry of Agriculture almost until the end of the first Lula government when he was succeeded in 2006 by Reinhold Stephanes, from Paraná, also representing agribusiness in the Southeast. After him, however, agribusiness in the Centre-West took the reins with a succession of ministers all linked to the region: Blairo Maggi, Katia Abreu, and Teresa Cristina. In the 1980s, the new faces of agribusiness were the input/machinery industries and the traders/processors in which national companies and cooperatives stood out: Agroceres, in seeds; cooperatives, such as Cotrijuí (which pioneered the opening of the frontier in the Midwest); and Ceval, which was the largest grain processor not only in Brazil but in Latin America. Since the 1990s, for various reasons – indebtedness, the new genetic basis of research, the deregulation of markets – the leading companies in these sectors gave way to the transnationals and only maintained their leadership in the white meats segment, with a new generation of companies emerging in the beef sector (Wilkinson, 2000).

The combination of the Kandir Law in 1996 encouraging the export of soybeans and the new scales of agricultural production, which allowed large farmers to invest outside the farm in inputs, transport, and logistics, saw the strengthening of a new class of medium and large farmers able to accumulate capital and invest, if not as competitors, at least as junior partners to the large traders, both in upstream segments and also downstream of agricultural activity. The Maggi Group, whose founder was a classic emigrant from the South, now with 250,000 hectares and heavy involvement in the logistics of exports, became wholly integrated into the spirit of the ABAG association and into the initiatives of global traders such as the soy moratorium. Thousands of other medium-sized producers, on the other hand, became strong enough not to need the support of cooperatives and to have their own voice but felt cornered by the capacity of large groups to control the prices of both inputs and outputs.

Many of these farmers rebelled against the social and environmental restrictions on their expansion and became easy targets for a Bolsonaro government, which from 2018 onwards identified and stirred up these feelings, resurrecting the worst moments of the UDR's mobilizations. We are dealing here not only with a class movement that mobilizes soybean growers through its producer organization Aprosoja against ABAG and Abiove, but one which also takes on a regional and cultural dimension that deepens the potential for broader conflicts (Wilkinson et al, 2022).

As soybean/corn moves up into Brazil's Northeast and North, the financialization of this frontier land becomes more evident with a prominent role for companies specialized in the purchase and preparation of land for cultivation, and for agricultural companies listed on the stock exchange. China, in its strategy to establish greater control over these grain chains, tried to invest directly in Brazilian agricultural lands until it was barred by the decision in 2010 to reaffirm the impediments to the acquisition of land by foreigners contained in Law 5,709/1971. Since 2015 there have been efforts to make this access more flexible, and a project to this effect was approved in the Senate. In the face of this impediment, the main control strategies by Chinese actors have been the acquisition of companies in Brazil, the entry of large Chinese companies into the grain chains, together with associated investments in logistics and transportation. COFCO, with its investments in the Port of Santo, which are expected to begin operations in 2025, will be able to export up to 14 million tons of soybeans, or more than 15 per cent of Brazilian exports (Wilkinson, Wesz Júnior and Lopane, 2016).

The three approaches to the modernization of Brazilian agriculture that we have described all fail to situate their analyses within a vision of the great transition, in which Brazil was moving from a rural to an urban–industrial society in a period of only 50 years, half the time that this process took in the Northern countries. Thirty years later, from the 1980s, China underwent the same transition in half the time it took Brazil, with a population five times larger, a process which is changing the dynamics of the global agri-food system in unexpected and unprecedented ways (Wilkinson and Wesz Júnior, 2013).

The coffee economy in São Paulo, based on wage labour and mass immigration especially of Italians and Japanese, led to a rapid urbanization in the early 20th century and saw the emergence of basic industries linked to the coffee trade and also an industry of basic consumer goods, especially textiles and food, which during a large part of the 20th century accounted for around 20 per cent of Brazilian GDP (Rama and Wilkinson, 2019). The food industry has been studied by researchers such as Walter Belik (1998) from Unicamp and above all Elizabeth Farina (1988) and her students in the PENSA programme, but unfortunately it has never been integrated into the main agri-food system approaches discussed. On the contrary, it has been analysed from an industrial economy point of view, with emphasis on the dynamics of foreign direct investments (FDI), à la Dunning (Viegas, 2005).

We can identify four moments in the development of the Brazilian food industry. First, a surge of industrialization that accompanied the great European and Japanese immigration at the turn of the century. In a second moment, starting in the 1950s, there was the consolidation of the food industry in the context of the industrial policy of import substitution and the consequent acceleration of urbanization. Even with the presence of multinationals, national companies predominated during this period. The stabilization of inflation, the deregulation of domestic markets and the opening of international trade from the 1990s onwards led to a restructuring of the food industry now under the leadership of transnational companies but with strong national companies in key sectors, such as animal protein. From the second decade of the 2000s, we can identify the emergence of a new generation of Brazilian companies that value 'natural' and 'healthy' products, especially products of Brazilian origin (Wilkinson, 2022).

Throughout this trajectory, there has been little reflection on the food industry as an integral part of the agri-food system and a certain naturalization of its role as a simple adaptor of agricultural supplies to urban conditions, fundamentally through the scaling up of artisan activities. Thus, within an industrial economics perspective, the food industry has always been treated (with the notable exception of Ruth Rama (2008)) as a traditional branch, at most a receiver of innovations coming from other dynamic and innovative sectors. In Brazil, the food industry is organized separately in the Brazilian Food Industry Association (ABIA).

We showed in the first chapters that strategies of market segmentation and product differentiation from the 1980s onwards, even if initially dominated by the leading companies, opened space for a new generation of start-ups that bet on a clearer identification with values associated with health, well-being, and environmental preservation. An early example in this direction in Brazil was the creation of the Natura company at the end of the 1960s, which took up the banner of the environment and respect for traditional peoples in the creation of cosmetics lines from natural products.[2] The Rio 92 Earth Summit established the environment as a central concern in Brazil and saw the emergence of a variety of institutes, foundations, and NGOs as spin-offs of companies (Grupo Orsa) or oriented to promote sustainability and social responsibility in the business world (Ethos Institute, Friends of the Earth, Imaflora, Imazon). These organizations were fundamental in mobilizing meat packing plants and large supermarket chains in favour of the Cattle Pact with respect to the Amazon mentioned at the beginning of this chapter (Araújo et al, 2015). With the creation of the Akatu Institute, an offspring of the Ethos Institute, the focus becomes directed towards the notion of conscious consumption, and the institute receives support from leading food companies, such as Unilever and Nestlé.[3]

Later than in Northern countries, but not very much so, the second decade of the 2000s saw the emergence of a new generation of start-up food companies in Brazil. In 2019 Liga Insights already counts 322 new companies in the Brazilian food system, with 43 of these dedicated to new food products. The 2020–2021 report of Liga Ventures' start-up Scanner profiles 40 of these start-ups, all but one of which were created since 2015 and all of which are avowedly 'mission-oriented' around healthiness or the climate and environment. Of these firms, 25 per cent define themselves as plant-based, 20 per cent natural beverages, with cocoa products, ice cream, and snacks adding a further 20 per cent. Regarding technological content, two firms produce nutrient-rich beverages, one applying an advanced pressing system, the other artificial intelligence, and a third, Sustineri Piscis, grows fish meat from cells (Liga Insights, 2022).

In its report on food start-ups in Brazil, Forbes highlights six firms – again, all explicitly 'mission-oriented' – Liv Up, Raízs, Foodz, Pratí, Beleaf, and BeGreen. These are start-ups at various positions in the food chain – healthy food delivery, direct contracts with organic producers, a 'community assisted agriculture' model, convenience products with healthiness, health recipes and vertical farming (Del Carmen, 2021).

The mapping of start-ups in the Brazilian agribusiness sector for 2020–2021 carried out by Radar Agtech Brasil identified 275 start-ups in the category of 'innovative food and new food trends'. When identifying the start-ups that have benefited from investment rounds, however, only 13 start-ups are mentioned in the 'innovative foods' segment, suggesting that companies with higher technological density are still in a minority, which coincides with the data presented in other surveys (Radar Agtech, 2022).

Radar Agtech includes a profile of investors, incubators, and accelerators that reveals an innovation ecosystem already consolidated in Brazil, although strongly concentrated in the state of São Paulo. 337 investment rounds were identified, benefiting 223 agritechs, most of them oriented to agriculture, especially in the 'Agtech Valley' of Piracicaba, another reflection of the economic power of agribusiness in Brazil. On the other hand, the high number of new food companies is consistent with a Sebrae[4] survey that pointed to 'alternative food' as 'one of the most promising businesses in the country', with a 20 per cent yearly growth rate (Sebrae, 2015).

In Chapter 1, we addressed the emergence and explosive growth of microbreweries in Europe and the United States challenging the large global beer companies, notable for their rejection of the standardized products of the big brands and their focus on the pleasures of craft activity and the localism it promotes. Brazil is not so different and in 2010 already counted 266 microbreweries, a number that rose to 679 in 2017 according to the sector's association, Abracerva. The possibilities for articulation with the new Brazilian foodtechs are being explored by Gran Moar, created in 2017, which uses malt bagasse from a craft brewery to produce a high-protein flour (Lucas, 2020).

In the previous chapters, we have shown that the phenomenon of new food start-ups corresponds to the growing centrality of a series of consumer values that heritage firms were not able to or did not initially want to meet. Brazil is also experiencing a strong increase in vegetarianism/veganism as well as the search for healthy, natural, and environmentally friendly products. A survey by Euromonitor in 2018 estimated that 14 per cent of the population, something around 30 million people, declared themselves vegetarian or vegan (Kurzweil, 2019). In 2020, research by the QualiBest Institute and Galunion concluded that 75 per cent of consumers prioritized healthiness and that 68 per cent take into account concerns around the environment. Good intentions, of course, do not necessarily lead to new eating practices, but this survey shows that there is a favourable environment for the adoption of new products.[5]

Initially, the response of leading food companies in Brazil, as in Northern countries, was to acquire the successful start-ups. An emblematic case in Brazil was the purchase in 2016 of the natural juice company Do Bem by Ambev. Do Bem, created in 2007, had become consolidated in the markets of the Centre-South, but lacked the scale to expand, while Ambev felt the need to reinforce its presence in the fast-growing natural juice segment. In recognition of the differentiated profile of this market and in line with internationally consolidated practices noted in Chapter 1, Ambev maintained management of the brand under the control of the former owners (Caldas, 2017).

Although acquisitions may be one of the outcomes, the breadth of this new innovation ecosystem in food means that leading companies are becoming investors and promoters of start-ups. In the words of Daniela Pizzolatto from Danone in Brazil: 'start-ups are bringing in innovations with a speed that the sector would never have done without them'.[6] Eduardo Gil, from Mondelez, echoes this sentiment: 'corporations don't have the speed to pivot, which makes it essential to collaborate with start-ups' (Augusto and Coutinho, 2022).

In the ranking established by the 100 Open Start-ups website (TOP, 2022), leading food companies are among the one hundred corporations that most invest in this ecosystem in Brazil – Ambev, Nestlé, BRF, Unilever, Danone, Burger King, Cargill, and Magazine Luiza (which invests in supplements and food delivery and was responsible for three acquisitions in this sector in 2021).

Marketing surveys by ABIA and Euromonitor indicate that Brazil is the fourth or sixth largest market for 'healthy' products, and the conquest of the Brazilian market has become the goal even of foodtech start-ups from neighbouring countries. NotCo, the first Chilean unicorn that received US$30 million from Amazon's Bezos investment fund and benefits from a total funding of US$115 million, has launched its plant-based milk and meats in Brazil and is now striving to establish its presence in the North American market. NotCo uses its own artificial intelligence system to track plant properties (Exame Marketing, 2022). Tomorrow Foods from Argentina, which sees NotCo as its closest competitor, also plans to enter the Brazilian market with its products, which include plant alternatives to mayonnaise, eggs, milk, and burgers (Stucchi, 2023).

Despite its per capita meat consumption being among the highest in the world, Brazil has entered with force into the market for plant-based proteins whose beginning can be identified with the creation in 2019 in Rio de Janeiro of Future Farm (Fazenda Futuro), which launched its products (highlighting its Future Burger) with a view to the mainstream ('flexitarians') and not to niche vegetarians or vegans. In the words of its founder, Marcos Leta: '[w]e created the Future Farm to compete with meatpackers, not with companies that manufacture vegetarian or vegan products' (Fonseca, 2021).

In this case, it is clearly a matter of a product innovation strategy based on the consumption trends of an urban Brazil, which clashes with the vision of 'agribusiness' Brazil.

In the same year, the vegan Bruno Fonseca, who had already created the company Eat Clean to produce peanuts and almond paste, launched The New Butchers, which produces salmon and chicken from peas (100 per cent and without gluten) and does not use soy because it is identified with GMOs and the use of glyphosate. At first, it imported 80 per cent of its ingredients, but these were quickly reduced to 10 per cent. Peas are still imported, but the company plans to develop a Brazilian supply chain. It began with 1,200 points of sale in partnership with the supermarket chains Pão de Açúcar, Carrefour, Angeloni, and the horticultural chain Oba Oba, increasing to 8,000 points in 16 states of the Federation in 2021. Even though vegan, the market focus, as in the case of Future Farm, is to the mainstream with its competitors being the large meatpacking plants. In 2021, it received funding from Lever VC, a global investor in alternative proteins, and also from Paulo Veras, CEO of 99 Taxi, the only Brazilian unicorn, which allowed for the construction of a new factory increasing production to 80 tons per month (Fleischmann, 2020).

Fazenda Futuro has experienced explosive growth, combining proprietary know-how 'True Texture Technology' and extrusion machinery from Germany, and now operates in 24 countries through 10,000 outlets. As of 2019, it has raised US$89 million in funding (from the BTG Brazilian investment bank and from the Monashees Fund among other sources) and is valued at US$400 million. Following world trends, all the Brazilian global meat players are now investing heavily in this sector.

In 2019, Marfrig launched its Rebel Whopper burger in partnership with ADM to be sold in Burger King chains. In the same year, it also launched the Revolution burger in partnership with Outback Steakhouse. Together with ADM, Marfrig has already created the company Plant Plus Foods with a view to entering the North American market. BRF and JBS have launched an entire line of products: burgers (beef and chicken), nuggets, sausages, and kebabs. The São Paulo company Superbom, a traditional producer of vegan/vegetarian food, also launched its gourmet burger, which took a year to develop with investments of R$9 million in 2019. This burger does not use soy and its protein base is peas, which is becoming a favourite protein for plant-based options (Azevedo, 2021). The Incredible line by Seara (JBS) already dominates the Brazilian plant-based meat market with over 60 per cent, followed by Veg&tal from BRF, and is the only company to launch whole fillet-style products, both beef and chicken.

JBS, in turn, acquired Vivera for EUR341 million, the third largest producer of plant-based proteins in Europe, with three plants and an R&D centre. It also acquired Biotech Foods from Spain, specialized in cultivated meat. In the United States, the company created the company Planterra Foods to sell the products of the Incrível line (Beefpoint, 2021).[7] JBS's most notable investment, however, is the construction of a biotechnology research, development, and innovation centre for food and protein in Brazil (in Santa Catarina, where the Seara firm, now part of JBS, was born) at the cost of US$60 million, perhaps repaying the public support it has received in Brazil to become a world leader.

In addition to its participation in this plant-based protein segment with Veg&tal, including agreements with the food delivery start-ups Liv Up and Pratí, BRF has entered a partnership with Aleph Farms, an Israeli cultivated meat company, which indicates its openness to an even more radical break with the traditional meat chain (Best, 2021).

The global importance of the Brazilian market for plant-based meat became clear with the arrival of the North American company Beyond Meat, leader of the new generation of start-up companies, challenging the hegemony of the large Brazilian meatpackers. When it entered, however, it recognized that it was no longer breaking into a new market, but entering a segment already dominated by national and global players. Consequently, it adopted a niche strategy entering the premium segment in São Paulo in partnership with the St. Marche chain. Its 226-gram burger costs R$65.90 against R$19.99 for the Seara burger of 310 grams and R$17.99 for Fazenda Futura's 230-gram burger (Fitch Solutions, 2020). The market in Brazil already offers 93 brands of vegetable alternatives, and even though 'meat' predominates, there are also alternatives for fish, eggs, milk, and dairy products (GFI, 2023).

One uncertainty that hovers over the sector, especially in the case of moving forward with cellular meats, is the vagueness of the regulatory framework, which persists equally in the United States but which in Europe can be more easily negotiated in the 'novel foods' regulation which is already in operation.[8] In Brazil, the Ministry of Agriculture has begun discussions on the regulation of the plant-based alternatives market in 2021. Frightened by the advances of this market, several members of the 'rural caucus' have initiated bills, still being discussed in Congress, to prohibit the use of the terms, 'meat' and 'milk' in the case of plant-based products (Arioch, 2021), together with a more radical bill to outlaw research into the marketing of cell-based protein.[9]

Despite its image, dominated by the vastness of its countryside, its rivers and its forests, Brazil has one of the world's highest levels of urbanization, around 85 per cent, which prevails even in the regions of the agricultural frontier. The vigorous growth in Brazil of plant-based markets and the no less vigorous growth of consumption trends based on health and environmental concerns may become decisive factors as urban sensibilities reject the more predatory practices of the soybean and cattle-raising chains.

As we saw in Chapter 3, global agribusiness companies (Cargill, ADM, Tyson), which include Brazilian meat companies (Marfrig, Minerva, and JBS) as well as global food companies (Nestlé, Unilever) are not only adapting to, but actively promoting the alternative protein market with their own products, support for start-ups, and inhouse investment in research, development, and innovation.[10] More than meat companies, Tyson, Marfrig, Minerva, and JBS see themselves as protein companies, which loosens their identification with a specific sector of feed (soy, above all) and livestock. Tensions in Brazilian agribusiness between the agricultural link (soybean farmers and cattle ranchers) and the industrial components are currently fuelled by political polarizations but may assume a more economic focus as the various markets for alternative proteins reach maturity.

7

Countryside–City Revisited

In Chapter 6 we have shown how the ongoing transformations in the Brazilian agri-food system can only be properly understood once the urban dynamics are integrated into the analysis. Throughout the book, we also draw attention to the radical implications of the ongoing agri-food innovations for the redefinition of the place of the urban in the organization of the food system.

Independently of these considerations, the theme of urban agriculture had already been imposed by the emergence of urban groups from the 1970s onwards claiming the right to grow food for their subsistence. In the North, the combination of deindustrialization and the phenomenon of 'food deserts', neighbourhoods with only fast-food outlets, led community and religious groups to stimulate the production of food and small-scale livestock farming on vacant and abandoned land. This resulted in the emergence of the food justice movement, which has generated an important academic literature (Lyson, 2004; McClintock, 2010; Ladner, 2011; Cockrall-King, 2012) in addition to public policies for its promotion and regulation, as in the case of Paris where temporary contracts allow a short-term 'nomadic' agriculture (Demailly and Darly, 2017).

In developing countries and especially on the African continent, the acceleration of emigration from the countryside to the cities has been associated with only fragile integration into the urban labour market, placing pressure on populations newly arrived in the cities to develop forms of urban agriculture for their own survival. International organizations such as the FAO have highlighted this phenomenon, and calculations of the global number of farmers who generate an income from urban agriculture vary between 100 million and 200 million (UNDP, 1996; Orsini et al, 2013).

At the same time, local governments and urban planners are becoming more aware of environmental and food security issues. One example was the Resilient Cities Congress in Bonn in 2013, which called for 'the development and implementation of a holistic approach to the development of urban food systems to ensure food security and stimulate local biodiversity' (ICLEI, 2013). Another was the network created around the Milan Urban Food Policy Pact in 2015, with over 200 cities committed to re-examining their food supply and distribution systems.[1] A lively debate around the concept of smart cities, often seen as proposing only technological solutions without integrating the social actions associated with movements around urban agriculture, form part of the discussions of this network (Deakin et al, 2016; Maye, 2019).

A new generation of architects, for whom the city is not about 'bricks and concrete' but is seen as a biological organism, is responding to competitions and elaborating projects to visualize smart cities, where renewable energies, the environment, and food production are integrated into day-to-day urban life (Viljoen and Bohn, 2014). The Belgian architect Vincent Callebaut and his team are dedicated to smart city projects, including a vision of Paris in 2050 where all these elements are integrated through the principle of biomimicry, which can be appreciated on his website (Callebaut et al, 2015). Even if they are not realized, these projects create imaginaries and inspire countless other initiatives in the same spirit.

An iconic character in this sense is C.J. Lim, professor at the Bartlett School of Architecture in London and director of Studio 8 Architects, dedicated to rethinking architecture and urban planning from a vision of the integration between nature and the built spaces where food systems are central, as can be seen in the title of his book published in 2014, *Food City*. In another publication commissioned by the Chinese and South Korean governments, *Smart Cities, Resilient Landscapes and Eco-Warriors*, Lim and Liu (2019) coordinated a series of international studies in which the city is conceived from the needs of its citizens with a central focus on the reintegration of food production into the urban environment. In a playful satirical vision, Lim devised a Food Parliament hovering above London and more precisely its Houses of Parliament, where all governance activities as well as the social and spatial organization of the city are decided based on the priority given to food (Lim et al, 2015).[2]

The reassessment of the place of food in the contemporary urban context is being accompanied by a historical and prehistorical interrogation of city–countryside relations. On the one hand, the predominant narrative about cities is one that privileges a vision based on the Industrial Revolution that establishes a polarization between the rural and the urban, between agriculture and industry, production and consumption, resources and waste, a relationship that combines social and economic conflicts with ecological antagonisms. From this perspective, however, we lose sight of the enormous heterogeneity of urbanization processes and the degree to which cities have internalized an important part of their food needs, a theme that will be discussed later.

On the other hand, the classic works of Gordon Childe (1950) and Lewis Mumford (1961) consecrated an interpretation of the emergence of cities as being the result of an 'agricultural revolution', in which the domestication of plants and animals led to the generation of food surpluses, allowing for a division of labour and the emergence of groups dedicated to non-agricultural activities. Freed from the spatial constraints of the land, these activities became concentrated in urban centres and new social classes that subjected the countryside to their needs. Alternative interpretations question this view by highlighting cultural, religious, and trade motives rather than the existence of an agricultural surplus to explain the break from clan life in favour of a sociability that was both broader in scope and involved greater everyday proximity (Aslan, 2018).

The urbanist Jane Jacobs was perhaps the first to call into question the orthodoxy on the origin of agriculture by developing a bold hypothesis reversing the causality between countryside and city. Jacobs was inspired by excavations at the Çatalhöyük site in Turkey that testify to the emergence of cities 7,000 years before the common era, and 3,500 years before the great civilizations of the Fertile Crescent that began with the Sumerians (Mellaart, 1967; Collins, 2021). In Neolithic times, the most precious commodity was the volcanic stone obsidian, serving as weapon, ornament, mirror, and instrument for hunting, which stimulated trade, including long distance trade in that same era (Renfrew et al, 1968; Sherratt, 2005). The urban settlement of the city imagined by Jacobs would have arisen precisely to defend access to the deposits of obsidian. The peoples, who were drawn to the city to access the obsidian would normally bring hides, animals, and seeds as a basis of exchange. It would be in this urban environment with the arrival and coexistence of a multiplicity of varieties of seeds and animals that the process of selection and domestication would have taken place. Thus, agriculture and animal husbandry would be an urban by-product of long-distance trade and only at a subsequent stage would be 'outsourced' from the city, creating the speciality of agriculture (Jacobs, 1969).[3]

In 2021, Graeber and Wengrow published a book with the not at all modest title *The Dawn of Everything: A New History of Humanity*, in which they not only challenge head-on the classical notion of the 'agricultural revolution' but also confront its most negative interpretation in the works of Yuval Harari (2014) and Jared Diamond (1987). Like Jacobs, Graeber and Wengrow are inspired by the lessons to be drawn from the excavations of Çatalhöyük. For them too, urban settlements arise at a time when these peoples combined some agriculture with the continuation of hunting and foraging activities. Contrary to Harrari, who argues that it was wheat that domesticated humans by subjecting them to its demands, and Diamond, for whom agriculture was 'the worst mistake in the history of the human race', Graeber and Wengrow (2021) highlight the playfulness of the first forms of integrating agriculture into a still hunter and forager lifestyle. According to the authors, this agriculture was developed on the banks of lakes and rivers that were periodically flooded leaving fertile ground where all that was needed was to scatter the seeds.

Against the notion of an agricultural revolution, these authors draw attention to the fact that this modest, undemanding agriculture, which was combined with a continuation of hunting/fishing and gathering practices, lasted no less than 3,500 years and only then did it give way to large-scale agriculture. This type of agriculture required little in terms of management and was hardly compatible with the establishment of fixed farms and the private appropriation of surpluses given the seasonal and locational variability of floods. Just as or more important than the grain were the stalks used for various non-food purposes and mixed with clay to build their houses. More than agriculture, the authors argue, these were gardens that required a botanical rather than agricultural outlook and where, they add, the presence of women predominated. Thus, according to Graeber and Wengrow (2021, p 236), there was no agricultural revolution. For 3,500 years rudimentary agriculture coexisted with urban settlements whose *raison d'être* was not agriculture but 'hunting, gathering, fishing, trading and other things'.

It is estimated that the city of Çatalhöyük had between 5,000 and 7,000 inhabitants and persisted for 1,500 years with houses being periodically demolished and rebuilt. Some houses appear to have accumulated more artefacts, but there is no evidence of larger houses or separate neighbourhoods. Nor is there evidence of a central authority, which leads the authors to conclude that the city was organized in an egalitarian fashion around each household unit. The proliferation of statues of women in the houses suggests a special deference to older women. Analyses of food scraps and skeletons point to a parity among all in terms of diet and health. Although most of the diet came from agriculture, the house paintings celebrated the hunting of wild animals by men. In the higher lands not far from Çatalhöyük, the huge stone monuments of Göbekli Tepe with their carvings of ferocious male animals and human skulls suggest radically different worldviews and forms of organization. These two social groups that coexisted in nearby ecosystems and knew each other through trade seem to have opted for different models of collective life, and, in the authors' hypothesis, perhaps consciously chose opposite paths.

The contrast between Çatalhöyük and Göbekli Tepe is just one small example of a broader argument developed over more than 600 pages on urbanization dynamics and countryside–city relationships. Graeber and Wengrow (2021) present data from all continents to defend the thesis that urbanization processes throughout history have been of the most varied kinds. Depending on the seasons, the same groups could adopt different forms of sedentarism. For centuries, if not millennia, the same social groups, living in large concentrations, combined fishing, hunting, and gathering with agriculture and lived together without a central administration. In a similar position to Jane Jacobs, the authors speculate that extensive agriculture was adopted to supply already consolidated towns. And often, according to these authors, societies opted for forms of urban life that consciously differentiated themselves from their neighbours, in a process which they define as *schismogenesis*.

What is important for our analysis is the questioning of the classical interpretations of the agricultural revolution. The authors show with a wealth of empirical material that for thousands of years agriculture remained a minor and seasonal component side by side with hunting, gathering, fishing, and vegetable gardens. Urbanization was consolidated in this context and for millennia reproduced itself without evidence of the emergence of a state, in the form of a central administration.

The expansion and growing importance of agriculture in turn, can be interpreted as the result of the decisions of already urbanized societies. It is not only a matter of food supply but of the supply of inputs for urban activities – alcoholic beverages, textiles, and products of urban cooking and proto-industry: bread, cheese, and yoghurt – all Neolithic innovations.

For Graeber and Wengrow (2021, p 285), the second great phase of urbanization, around 5,000 BCE, is due to the increasing stabilization of river flows and sea levels that created large fertile areas, the deltas, integrating rivers and seas. Again, they identify important variations in urbanization processes and draw attention to the fact that the largest cities at this time were located not in Eurasia, but in Mesoamerica, a technologically much more backward region, with no wheeled transport, no draught animals, and a much less developed metallurgy.

We do not need to follow the authors' entire analysis, which continues for another 400 pages. What is important for us is their demonstration of the variability of the forms of urbanization, of the autonomy of this urbanization in relation to agriculture, and the possible inversion of causal relations, as well as the centrality of rivers and seas for the location of cities. They argue that this second wave of urbanization consisted mainly of networks of cities located along the rivers, specialized in different crafts, which stimulated trade and the development of counting and accounting systems. All this, they argue, preceded the emergence of the great urban civilizations with their centralized and hierarchical administrations.

The location of these cities on rivers and in coastal areas stems from the antiquity of navigation techniques, which in turn stimulated trade between networks of cities and explains the weight of fish protein in urban diets. With the improvement of navigation techniques, urban life could be viable based on long supply circuits. Subsequently, Greek cities developed colonization strategies, where selected groups of their citizens were sent to create settlements, especially in Sicily, to develop an agriculture directed specifically to the needs of the cities (Benjamin, 2006). The Roman Empire, where Rome at its height had over a million inhabitants, depended almost entirely on the agricultural regions of its provinces, mainly Egypt and Spain. Temin (2012), based on a meticulous analysis of the wheat trade in the Roman Empire, estimates that 4,000 vessels of wheat per year were needed to supply Rome's needs. During the medieval period, Braudel (1982) draws attention to the total dependence of the European 'city-states', such as Venice, on the food supply of distant regions. Thus, since antiquity large cities have depended on long supply routes.

The heterogeneity of forms of urbanization is not limited to geographical and technological considerations. Max Weber (1958) showed that the dynamics of the city could vary also depending on its politico-social structure, whether it was organized around the temple, a military garrison, political power, long-distance trade, or local markets. With the consolidation of the 'world economy' à la Braudel and Wallerstein, colonial relations created very specific characteristics for urbanization and the dynamics of food supply, as in the case of Brazil where urbanization was reduced to essential administrative functions and subordinated to the rhythm of the rural economy, which in turn arose to meet the urban demand of Europe (Freyre, 2002).

With the consolidation of colonial systems and even more so with the Industrial Revolution, states rather than cities assume responsibility for food supply in Europe. Industrialization brought with it an acceleration of urbanization on a new scale that became generalized with the industrial appropriation of activities previously carried out in the countryside and in villages, and the development of new industrial activities that urban life itself stimulated. Beginning in the second half of the 18th century, especially in England, the central question was the ability of agriculture to keep up with the new demand for food, considering the restrictions on productivity increases identified by Malthus and Ricardo. In England, the countryside and the city were seen as antagonistic realities, expressed politically in the demand for open ports to import grain. It was the renowned chemist Liebig (1840) who repositioned the debate by defining the productivity of the land as a function of its chemical components – nitrogen, phosphorus, and potassium. This opened the possibility of improving productivity with inputs from outside the property that would eventually be produced industrially.

Initially enthusiastic about this possibility of improving productivity, Liebig became increasingly critical of what he saw as the inevitable exhaustion of the soil. The antagonism between country and city came now to be seen in terms of a polarization between production in the countryside on the one hand and consumption in the city on the other, whereby the resources and nutrients generated in the countryside are transformed into waste in the city and discharged into rivers and seas far from the production areas. Thus, to the social antagonism of farmers versus industrialists, was added the notion of an environmental antagonism between countryside and city, which Marx theorized and Bellamy Foster (1999) christened 'a metabolic rupture', a line of analysis that is renewed today in the context of the crises surrounding the environment and climate.

The notion of metabolic rupture emphasizes the countryside–city polarization, but historical studies show an important presence of agricultural production and animal husbandry in the urban context. In a classic work, von Thünen (1826), established an ideal typology of relations between city and countryside in which he saw the production of the countryside organized in concentric circles around the city with the relative proximity of agricultural products being determined by criteria of perishability and transportability. Clearly, this is only valid for one of the various types of cities that we have identified and corresponds to what Raymond Williams (1973) called the market town in his classic study *The Country and the City*. Even though there are many critics of von Thünen's abstract model, the two variables of perishability and means of transportation offer important insights. On these criteria, von Thünen places dairy products and horticulture in the first circle, which corresponds to the peri-urban, what today we would call the green belt.

The coexistence of horticulture with urban life, even under constant pressure from the real estate sector, is evidenced throughout this period, beginning with the promotion of garden plots in Germany to reinforce the working-class diet, a policy that spread across Europe and assumed an important role during the two world wars. It is estimated that the 'victory gardens' in the United States accounted for 40 per cent of the national production of horticulture during the Second World War (McClintock, 2010). Even at the end of the 19th century, Paris maintained a strong commercial horticulture sector in the Marais district, including the export of its products to the London market. What enabled this production in the heart of the French capital was the presence (according to the 1890 census) of no less than 90,000 horses, whose manure was collected and used for vegetable production. In fact, since time immemorial and also throughout the 19th century, highly perishable products, such as milk and meat, were produced in urban environments (Atkins, 2012).

Transformations in the two variables identified by von Thünen – perishability and transport – definitively changed both his scheme and the relationship between food production and the city. In first place came the radical innovation of the railway system, quickly adopted worldwide, which allowed for the arrival of perishable goods from ever greater distances. Later, new refrigeration techniques combined with the steamship made it possible to import fresh meat into Europe even from Argentina. The fatal blow, however, was the disappearance of the horse from the cities with the invention of the car and the electric tramway, which eliminated a precious source of fertilizer, and radicalized the metabolic break between city and countryside.

Just as important as the innovations in transportation and refrigeration were the public health measures adopted since the early 19th century (Daviron et al, 2017). The transmission of diseases that ravaged the inhabitants of cities in that century was identified with the nauseating smells of the animals raised and slaughtered in them. Regulations were introduced that led to the closure of dairies and slaughterhouses and the prohibition of the raising of small animals in homes and backyards. It was, therefore, only from the 20th century that animals, the source of meat and dairy products, were finally driven out of cities in European countries and in the United States.[4] The only urban animals allowed from then on would be pets, which, throughout that century, acquired more and more citizenship rights and were even nourished by the food industry and no longer by table scraps.

In the book organized by Daviron et al (2017) we see how, in the European case throughout the medieval period, cities had a protagonist role in the organization of their food systems. With the consolidation of the nation states and even more so from the colonial expansion and the industrial revolution, food became a national issue subject to food supply policies, which lasted for much of the 20th century.

From the 1980s on, cities have assumed a more interventionist role in food issues. A series of factors can be identified that converge in this direction. Deindustrialization and the consequent unemployment in many Northern cities, which led to the emergence of the food justice movement, has already been mentioned. The promotion of agriculture on urban wasteland challenges urban land use patterns just as these cities are confronted with the need to rethink their urban models. Deindustrialization was only one component of a more general shift towards the deregulation of economic activities and less national state intervention, which placed more responsibility on local governments. It is from this period that criticism of the dominant food system becomes more acute, in relation both to its production patterns and its implications for consumption. Thus, notions of short circuits and farmers markets, the criticism of ultra-processed products and soft drinks, especially for children, the pressure for local governments to value fair trade products, all these issues have pushed for responses at the local level. A central focus has been on institutional markets that articulate with social movements and promote new values around food and its identification with health and the environment. Hundreds of towns in England have embraced fair trade products in their public events, and movements around food in schools have been described as the 'school food revolution' by Morgan and Sonnino (2010).

In the case of Brazil and China, the two countries identified throughout this book as constituting the new axis of the global agri-food system, a similar protagonism of cities can be identified. In an earlier publication (Wilkinson, 2021), I highlighted the role of municipal governments in Brazil, stimulated even more by the social renewal that followed the end of the military dictatorship and the approval of a new constitution. The food policies of the local government of Belo Horizonte became a world reference in the academic and policy literature (Sonnino, 2009). Notable in its policies was a systemic focus on the food system from the perspective of consumption, in terms both of access and quality, targeting the poorest urban populations. Thus, canteens with low prices and universal access were created in central areas of the city to cater for the thousands of people who previously went to work without breakfast. A complementary programme for families registered as low-income subsidized access to a basic basket of non-perishable food goods. The children were attended not only by a school lunch programme that in 2007 served 40 million meals to 155,000 students in 218 public schools, but also through a specific programme to combat malnutrition among children under five years old. A 'food bank' which distributed 600 tons of treated fresh food leftovers through 108 charities completed these access policies (Rocha and Lessa, 2009).

The programme also intervened in market mechanisms to ensure the delivery of fresh food to underserved neighbourhoods (the food deserts) by the private sector. Traders were licensed to sell their products in more affluent neighbourhoods on the condition that they also serve poor neighbourhoods from a list of products with prices agreed with the municipality. Direct sales from peri-urban family farmers were made possible through open air markets organized by the municipality with monitored prices (Rocha and Lessa, 2009). This systemic policy based on urban food needs has made the example of Belo Horizonte an international reference disseminated both by organizations such as FAO and by notable figures such as the previously mentioned C.J. Lim.

The Grand Canal, which links Beijing to Hangzhou (1,776 kilometres) and integrates the southern farmlands with the political centre in the north, bears witness to the centrality of food security for the Chinese state. Its construction was begun in the 5th century BCE, but the interconnection of its various parts had to wait until the Sui dynasty a thousand years later. However, the administrative responsibilities of municipal cities in China traditionally encompassed the surrounding agricultural areas, and historically local and regional authorities were responsible for the food security of their localities. A survey of Shanghai in the 1990s, as we noted in Chapter 5 on China, estimated that 41 per cent of the workforce was engaged in agriculture, 80 per cent of which was part-time. One hundred per cent of poultry, eggs, and milk and 80 per cent of vegetables and freshwater fisheries were produced within 10 kilometres of the city centre (Cai and Zhang, 2000). Thus, even though essential grains had been organized at the national level since ancient times, the bulk of perishable products in China were still produced on the outskirts of cities.

Shanghai, like the rest of China, is seeing its area for agriculture shrink dramatically with urban growth. To respond to this, Sasaki, an American architectural firm, was commissioned to develop an agri-urban project in an area of more than 100 hectares in the city, the so-called Sunqiao district, between the airport and the central region of the city, aiming at the development of vertical farms integrated with residential, leisure, cultural, and educational areas. Sunqiao was a traditional agricultural area in Shanghai. Thus, the project aims to maintain the agricultural vocation of the area in a manner compatible with the evolution of the city, where aquaponics, seaweed farms, floating greenhouses, green walls, seed banks, and vertical farming will coexist with residential, commercial, and leisure areas (Adjie et al, 2021).

Local governments in Northern countries were forced to rethink the vocation of their cities as a result of the varied impacts of deindustrialization. Quickly, however, the new issues of energy, the environment, climate, and quality of life became incorporated, requiring more holistic visions that were becoming feasible with the wave of innovations that hit the transport, construction, and energy sectors. Urban design has been revolutionized by digitalization, converging around the notion of smart cities, progressing to the goal of green cities, and now extending to that of food cities, as we have seen in the examples of Vincent Callebout and J.C. Lim.

Considering these trends, the author and a colleague elaborated an initial typology of the different social forces and technological resources, driving the integration of food production and distribution within the urban space (Wilkinson and Lopane, 2018):[5]

1. peri-urban agriculture or the green belt;
2. self-provisioning responses to marginalization by transformations in urban life – food justice movement;
3. individual or collective initiatives, the fruit of new subjectivities around individual and planetary health and wellbeing;
4. public policies and planning, Belo Horizonte, and Shanghai style;
5. the emergence of 'agritecture' and the integration of food in the projects and imaginaries of cities;
6. initiatives from the new food technological frontier.

Peri-urban agriculture was discussed using the von Thünen model. It is a traditional component of urban life that is constantly threatened by real estate expansion despite ongoing efforts to regulate these spaces in the form of 'green belts', as in the 'city gardens' promoted by Ebenezer Howard (1902) in the United Kingdom. Pluriactivity characterizes this sector, as a result both of urban employment opportunities and the need to generate incomes compatible with urban life. Today, this traditional urban segment has become a privileged locus for the promotion of short agri-food circuits and community-supported agriculture. It is also becoming an important source of supply for institutional markets, as well as contracts between producers and restaurants, with a growing role for ecological chefs (Curtis and Cowee, 2009).

The emergence of urban agriculture movements promoted by marginalized groups in the deindustrialization processes in Northern countries and by the livelihood needs of newly arrived migrants in the cities of the Global South has already been discussed. These initiatives can be incorporated into public policies (as in the case of the vegetable gardens in Rio de Janeiro) and endorsed by the recognition of temporary contracts (as in the case of Paris already mentioned) or maintained with the support of community groups. Besides their economic importance, the evaluations of these initiatives highlight their social value to communities and vulnerable individuals (Lagneau et al, 2015; Reece, 2018; Lohrberg et al, 2020).

Throughout these pages, the importance of new patterns of food consumption that are being adopted in the interests of establishing greater control over food has been a constant theme. Urban allotments promoted for the working class in earlier times are now being reclaimed by the middle classes for their own fruit and vegetable production. In Chapter 3, we emphasized the modular character of climate-controlled agriculture equipment, which allows for its insertion into many different contexts of everyday urban life – in apartments, on balconies, in flats, in collective facilities (canteens, condominiums) – and in containers for commercial or retail purposes. The inputs and information for these activities, as well as the equipment, are available online.

The example of Belo Horizonte demonstrated how local public policies focused on access to food to transform cities into powerful environments for the promotion of short production and consumption circuits. These institutional markets – school, hospital, and prison meals – present, at the same time, great challenges of both scale and quality, which can open up opportunities for modern climate-controlled agriculture systems.

The fifth category identified is constituted by the generation of architects and urban designers mentioned at the beginning of this chapter, who elaborate new visions of sustainable urban living based on the possibilities opened up by scientific and technological frontiers. In this sense, they become a valuable input for public policies that are often stuck in sectoral choices within the confines of existing urban structures. At the same time, they present a fresh perspective on ways to integrate climate-controlled agriculture and alternative proteins into everyday urban life.

The last category deals primarily with new enterprises in alternative proteins and climate-controlled agriculture. In the two chapters devoted to these developments (3 and 4), the focus was mainly on the compatibility of these enterprises with the economic reality of urban life. In this sense, vertical production is shown to be compatible with urban rents and can be complemented by the strategy of using buildings abandoned by deindustrialization or similarly abandoned port areas to compensate for costs that have not yet been addressed, especially energy costs. Alternative proteins production is like that of any fermentation company, such as a brewery. Upside Foods' new plant for cultured meat, discussed in Chapter 4, emphasizes its compatibility with the urban environment and has purposely opted for a transparent architecture that allows visitors to follow the production process. In addition, the raw material for the fermentation plants can come from urban food waste, constituting a circular economy, as in the example of the insect plant in China mentioned in Chapter 4 and the microbrewery discussed in Chapter 6.

These ventures also adopt the traditional pattern of dedicated plants aiming to maximize the scale of operations. Architects and designers become crucial in this context since they broaden the vision for policy making, imagining ways to integrate the new possibilities of producing food into everyday urban life. These innovations can then be appropriated by individual and collective initiatives to reintegrate food production and consumption in a decentralized way into the various facilities of the urban space.

The typology presented previously highlights the diversity of actors and interests at stake in promoting urban food systems that will certainly reproduce all the conflicts already evident in the agribusiness world – use or not of chemical inputs, GMOs, concentration of production, economic power, social and environmental impacts, as well as the regulation of these activities – and most likely new ones, some of which are already evident: can agriculture without the use of soil be accepted as organic? Can alternative proteins be called meat and fish?

Beyond the ethical and health issues, the beneficial impact for the environment has led many people to support radical solutions for animal protein production. It is estimated that almost 80 per cent of the world's agricultural land is used for livestock production and that 40 per cent of the world's grain goes into feed. Agriculture and cattle-raising already occupy almost 40 per cent of the world's land. The cultivation of only a limited number of plants and animals by agriculture with production methods that are harmful to other species is leading to an extinction rate a thousand times higher than in untouched environments (Monbiot, 2022). The same agricultural methods are responsible for the deforestation of tropical forests, as well as land and water pollution. Equal damage is also evident in large-scale fishing in the rivers and the seas.

With the switch to alternative proteins, one can expect a drastically reduced pressure on vulnerable ecosystems. Declining feed markets and increasing direct consumption of grains and oilseed crops will accelerate demand for organic and non-GMO protein products and for other protein sources, accelerating the end of the soy monopoly. A ProVeg survey of 20 associations representing over 300,000 farmers in Europe indicates a willingness to support a transition to alternative proteins if it were to be financially viable (ProVeg, 2022).

In addition to these transformations in agriculture, the decline in the consumption of animal protein opens up the prospect for policies to restore threatened ecosystems. Some protagonists of climate-controlled agriculture, such as Despommier and the CEO of Nordic Harvest, see this as the possibility for a rewilding process in which ecosystems rebuild themselves autonomously. Others advocate a model in which agriculture coexists with untouched areas. In Europe, the United States, and other countries there are public policies to promote areas dedicated to rewilding, and the topic already occupies the mainstream of academic debates (Kremen, 2015; Prior and Ward, 2016; Vogt, 2021; Corson et al, 2022). Rewilding policies are also being adopted in the urban context (Coughlan, 2021). The various crises that are affecting the global organization of food supply and are reaching a breaking point in a world dominated by COVID-19, geopolitical tensions, Russia's invasion of Ukraine, and threats to the Suez Canal trade route may also slow the pace of rewilding as all countries seek greater levels of food self-sufficiency.

Many factors converge to stimulate new thinking on the relations between countryside and city. Archaeological discoveries and technological advances have brought the Sumerians out of the shadows and identified waves of urbanization before the great civilizations of Mesopotamia – in Latin America in the Caral-Supe civilization in Peru (Solis, 2006), in Mesopotamia itself, in the 4,000-year-old BCE mega-sites of Trypillia in Ukraine, and in other regions of central Europe (Müller et al, 2016) – together with the indications of urbanization coinciding with the adoption of agriculture, as in the example of Çatalhöyük. Urban settlements in what are still hunter–gatherer societies, less centralized forms of urban organization, and even evidence of counting and accounting underpinning trade in networks of smaller towns point to a variability in rural–city relations overshadowed by the model of the great Mesopotamian civilizations.

Unemployment brought on by deindustrialization in Northern cities, combined with the lack of jobs for new waves of urban migration in Southern countries, has reintroduced food production into the urban context, an everyday practice in cities until the end of the 19th century. This subsistence, small-scale, local agriculture has been stimulated by community organizations and then supported by public policies and international organizations as an essential component of food security for millions of urban citizens. For many analysts, urban agriculture is as important for health and wellbeing in urban life as it is for its direct contribution to food security and as a source of income.

Globalization has loosened the standards of 'post-two-world-wars' national regulation, giving more importance to cities as a policy focus precisely when new issues, such as the climate, stimulate radically new visions of urbanization made possible by the digital revolution and captured in the notion of smart cities and green cities. The questioning of dependence on long food supply chains in Northern cities, as well as the rapid urbanization in regions with little endowment of land and water, is placing food at the centre of urban concerns. The notion of 'food cities' today is becoming more integrated into visions of green cities and smart cities, eminently compatible with climate-controlled agriculture innovations and alternative protein sources.

Conclusion

The 2019–2020 biennium saw accelerated growth in the ecosystems of innovation of both climate-controlled agriculture and alternative proteins. The number of new start-ups, the volume of investments, and the growth in markets created an atmosphere of euphoria regarding their disruptive possibilities. The high point was the public launching on the New York Stock Exchange in May 2019 of the leading company in alternative proteins, Beyond Meat. The initial offering of US$25 per share was quickly oversubscribed, and by closing time the stock had risen to US$65. A year later, with ups and downs, the stock was valued at US$91.53. Beyond Meat, worth an estimated US$14 billion, had become mainstream, present in 50 countries, and distributed by major brands – McDonald's, Starbucks, KFC – in both the North and in Asia.

Contrary to expectations, 2021 did not repeat the performance of previous years and sales of plant-based meats in the United States that had increased 46 per cent in 2020 over the previous year stagnated in 2021, up just 0.5 per cent. An influential *Financial Times* article in January 2022 sounded the alarm by suggesting that alternative protein markets might have already peaked. One explanation advanced by the authors Terazono and Evans draws on the Gartner hype cycle of new technologies developed by the consultancy firm of the same name.[1] This cycle identifies five phases, all bearing fanciful names: 'innovation trigger'; 'peak of inflated expectations' 'valley of disillusionment'; 'slope of enlightenment'; 'plateau of productivity'. According to this interpretation, the beginning of 2022 corresponded to the 'valley of disillusionment'. In an optimistic view, this would pave the way for a period of consolidation and subsequent increase in efficiency leading to a resumption of growth but at a more moderate rate. At the start of 2022, Beyond Meat was worth less than US$4 billion and in 2023 its shares dropped to below US$10 and its valuation to under US$1.5 billion. On the other hand, investments in the sector in 2021 increased, reaching US$4.8 billion according to the AgFunder 2022 report, with a significant increase in public funding by various countries of over US$600 million based on GFI's calculations. The fate of individual leader firms, therefore, should not be confused with the performance of the sector as a whole, characterized by the continued proliferation of start-ups involved in an ever larger range of activities and in increasingly varied geographical, institutional, and political contexts.[2]

A month before the *Financial Times* article, Henry Gordon-Smith of consultancy Agritecture had developed a similar analysis of the climate-controlled agriculture sector, also using the Gartner cycle. In this case too there were disappointments around public launches in 2021 (AeroFarms and AppHarvest), but the central problem identified was the difficulty of achieving operational profitability given the high costs of upfront investments, especially energy costs. In a similar vein to alternative proteins, Gordon-Smith concluded that although we are now in the 'valley of disillusionment', we can expect a pick-up after a period of restructuring (Gordon-Smith, 2021).

Both assessments emphasize the persistence of 'fundamentals' in demand (demography, urbanization) and supply (negative climate impacts and scarcity of natural resources in key growth regions) to justify optimism about the advance of these sectors in a post-hype phase. On the other hand, the conjuncture has changed dramatically. The combination of COVID-19, Russia's invasion of Ukraine, and more recently the Israeli response to the Hamas massacre is increasing the danger of a global recession and calls into question a model of innovation that depends on the ready availability of venture capital.[3] The same factors, however, increase the risks of a structural dependency on long supply chains, which may accelerate investments in the alternative food supply systems analysed here by these capital-rich and resource-poor states, notably China and the Middle East.[4]

Economic and geopolitical factors will not be the only determinants of the scope and speed of diffusion of the innovations examined in this book. Chapter 1 showed how the incorporation of the 'new biotechnologies' in the 1980s was rejected when it implied their presence in final foods, and they were finally restricted to their agricultural applications in the form of transgenic varieties for animal feed and non-food crops. This rejection already pointed to the growing hegemony of the combined interests of final food companies, large retail chains, public health policies, the scientific world, and to changes in consumers' own values expressed in the demand for organic markets, fair trade, 'origin', and 'natural' products.

First indications in the case of alternative proteins suggest more varied responses than in the case of transgenics. In the so-called grey press, which comprises publications of committed organizations, even though they are increasingly produced by academics with considerable analytical rigour, the new innovations are criticized for various reasons: for increasing economic concentration and power, for representing the continuation of junk food production, for leading to the co-option of start-ups by incumbent leaders (ETC Group, 2019; IPES, 2022). On the other hand, the PETA movement against animal cruelty actively promotes the development of cellular animal protein. Perhaps the most eloquent advocacy for the adoption of technologies to produce alternative proteins comes from the columnist of the *Guardian* in the UK, George Monbiot (2022), whose book *Regenesis* sees the adoption of protein precision fermentation as the only possibility for diminishing the dominance of the feed and animal protein sectors, paving the way for a policy of rewilding – the handing back of agricultural land so that nature can recompose itself at its leisure, leading to a regeneration of biodiversity and a mitigation of the effects of greenhouse gases.

Our analysis has identified an increasing tension between the global meat firms, which are repositioning themselves as protein producers and investing heavily in the range of alternative proteins, and the animal feed and cattle-rearing farming sectors. In country after country the latter's associations have called for legislation restricting the use of labelling that situates these alternative products within traditional protein categories. In Italy, a mass mobilization of rural organizations has led to the banning and criminalization of cellular protein products. Similar legislation has been proposed in Uruguay and Brazil, although in Brazil, JBS, the world's leading animal protein company, is investing heavily in cellular meat both in Europe and in Brazil. Cellular meat is in danger of becoming an issue in the agendas of broader political polarizations.

At different moments in this text, I have indicated issues that have become central in a wide-ranging academic literature focused primarily on alternative proteins. These were commented and referenced only in notes, since my central concern was to situate the innovations in alternative proteins and climate-controlled agriculture within a general interpretation of the transformations in the global agri-food system. In this conclusion, I will briefly reflect on the way my interpretation converges or contrasts with key contributions in this literature.

While neither underestimating the degree of oligopolization in the agri-food system nor the risks of its increase as the convergence of digital and genetic technologies advances, several qualifying conclusions emerge from my analysis.[5] Economic concentration in agri-food is to be expected to the extent that nature cedes control to technology, although, as we also suggest, periods of transition and the nature of the innovations under consideration create opportunities for radical decentralization. In the case of agri-food, we have argued that shifts in economic power from supply to demand within the agri-food system, combined with the influence of civil society in its various expressions, on markets and public policy, has limited – while in no way eliminating – the transformation of economic concentration into political power.[6] In practice, the leading players have been induced to adopt societal agendas and targets on food quality and climate issues.

Nor is it clear that this wave of innovation will be readily domesticated by the incumbent actors. Food industry acquisitions of start-ups are a reality, but we have shown that the innovation ecosystem is a much broader phenomenon and fuelled by an investment model that ensures considerable autonomy for innovators and has seen start-ups transformed into global players in only half a decade. Food industry leaders explicitly recognize this and are increasingly adopting the new investment model (incubators, accelerators) to keep abreast of the innovation frontier. In addition, while Northern actors still predominate, food innovation hubs have become consolidated in the Middle East and Asia and are increasingly driven by public policy priorities and investment funds.[7]

Important research has been carried out on alternative proteins with a focus on the Silicon Valley innovation model.[8] These investigations have variously made use of discourse analysis and the formation of agendas, notions of performativity where the discourse creates its own reality, and associated approaches whereby the construction of imaginaries moulds the investment climate. The specifics of the Silicon Valley finance-driven innovation model are vividly captured in detailed ethnographic studies – the promise of technological solutions to global problems as being also the promise of 'unicorn'-style financial returns. The importance of 'hype'-driven investment is clearly attested in the fortunes of Beyond Meat, and other examples could de adduced. On the other hand, there is little analysis of the reality checks provided by the organization of successive rounds of funding which are premised on the achievement of clearly defined targets.

In these analyses, advanced technology innovation is reduced to the notion of 'tech fixes' which do not confront the huge inequalities built into the organization of the agri-food system. While this is true, the implications of a widespread adoption of alternative proteins for reducing carbon emissions and industrial animal slaughter, and for the liberation of land and water from cattle-raising, sheep-grazing, and largescale animal-feed monoculture, and the consequent recuperation of biodiversity are downplayed or ignored.

The objective of these innovations, as we have argued throughout the analysis conducted here, is not to reinforce an existing niche market for vegans and vegetarians but to impact the mainstream markets of animal protein consumption. Current technological possibilities and dominant patterns of meat consumption converge on fast and convenience foods – burgers, chicken nuggets, kibbehs, meatballs, and minced meat. The aim is not to change food habits but to change the content of the food while preserving the pleasures associated with these forms of meat consumption. The disruptive character of these innovations relates to the upstream consequences of the widespread adoption of alternative proteins for the climate, biodiversity, and the preservation of natural resources.

Occupying the mainstream is central to the product innovation strategy and therefore agreements with the dominant players in the food, retail, and fast food sectors for mass production and distribution are imperative. The interpretation of such agreements as co-option on the part of the incumbent players misses the intent of these product innovations. That the incumbent players themselves are moving to occupy these markets only reinforces the importance of these product innovations. Mainstream outlets, however, may be content with the introduction of these products only as niche market sectors. A study in Brazil, for example, has shown that retail simultaneously stocks alternative 'meat' protein while organizing the promotion of traditional meat products (Reis et al, 2023).[9]

Alternative protein products have been criticized for reproducing the health problems associated with fast, convenience, and ultra-processed foods. The notion of alternative proteins as 'software' is relevant here, and continuous improvement in the nutritional content is possible given the greater flexibility when using plants, microorganisms, or animal cells as opposed to whole animals. It is to be supposed that innovating firms, although primarily motivated by environmental and animal welfare concerns, will be sensitive to critiques of their products on health grounds. Nevertheless, we have already seen that consumer and public policy pressure on health is leading to a reformulation of these popular products. The negative categorization of certain foods as ultra-processed has gained strong currency in recent years. How the new technologies for producing alternative proteins will fare in this light is still uncertain, since, as in additive manufacturing, in a number of their routes foods are built up from the molecular and cellular levels.

In Chapter 1, note 7 we referred to a range of publications in the societal transitions literature which focuses on novel foods and particularly alternative (meat and milk) proteins. Drawing on earlier evolutionary economics, this current analyses transitions through a multilevel schema which consists of emerging niches, established regimes, and the broader institutional context, the landscape. Of particular concern is the interaction between emerging niches and established regimes, and a problematizing of the transition from niche to mainstream. Detailed case studies map the varied interactions between niche and mainstream players and also capture the complexities of the agri-food value chains, identifying the diverse interests of retail and food industry actors and especially the relative autonomy of these actors in relation to the affected farming interests. In all these aspects, these contributions converge with the analysis developed here. The niche mainstream focus, however, does not capture the originality and the magnitude of the agri-food innovation ecosystem driven by finance capital, largely independent even of the incumbent actors. Nor does it capture the way in which this ecosystem is being reproduced in contexts very different from that of the Silicon Valley model where capital-rich countries are confronted by questions of food security demanding radically new solutions.

In the case of climate-controlled agriculture and vertical farming, the academic literature focuses mainly on questions of technical and economic feasibility within a perspective of their sustainability (Jürkenbeck et al, 2019). There are also several studies on the perceptions of consumers, but the limited diffusion as yet of vertical farming make them rather speculative (Specht et al, 2016). The RUAF Global Partnership on Sustainable Urban Agriculture and Food Systems, which groups together a large part of the movements around urban agriculture, issued a policy brief in 2021 calling for investment and innovation in climate-controlled agriculture, which is posited as a complement rather than a substitute to traditional agriculture, 'capable of providing fresh produce and niche commodities for both high- and low-income consumers' (Halliday, 2022, p 55). The topic, however, occupies little space in their journal and, when mentioned, emphasizes the possibilities of low-technology-intensive options and modular systems (the minimally structured and modular vertical farm [MSM-VF]) (Cuello and Liu, 2014), mainly targeting communities in low-income urban neighbourhoods in Asia and Africa.

We have drawn attention on several occasions to the concept of 'agritecture', associated with Henry Gordon-Smith, which deals with the integration of food production into everyday urban life, in the home, at school, at work, and in retail outlets. In Chapter 3 on vertical farming, mention was made of the efforts of urban designers to rethink cities based on decentralized energy and food production systems. In an opposite dynamic, the large investments in vertical agriculture production at scales such that only a few factories and companies could supply a whole country's demand for the range of fresh produce that makes up our salads, links these initiatives directly to the organizational logic of the large supermarkets. In this context, as the obstacles of 'nature' (land, space, sun) are progressively overcome, economic concentration extends to agri-food production so that it resembles other dominant economic activities.

We have pointed to many indications that the innovations analysed here might lead to far greater levels of economic concentration. Even in this case, a shift to a food system which radically reduces its dependence on land and water with all their accompanying negative externalities and equally radically reduces carbon emissions would be a decisive contribution to the maintenance of a liveable planet. At the same time, in our analysis of both climate-controlled agriculture and alternative proteins we have shown the potential for modular systems. On the model of microbreweries, fermentation systems, and cellular bioreactors using decentralized energy supply and information systems could be integrated into the various patterns of communal and domestic life. Similar developments have been registered in the case of climate-controlled agriculture which we discussed in Chapter 3.

The future of cellular meat may be key in this sense since scalability is proving a greater challenge than originally anticipated. A recent report by Reynolds and Fassler (2023) suggests that Upside, a leading firm in this sector discussed in Chapter 4 whose cellular chicken has been approved for marketing in the United States, is still unable to use the large-scale bioreactors of its showpiece factory in San Francisco. Fassler (2024) extends this critique to other leading cellular protein firms and presents us with what he considers an obituary of cell cultured proteins. These setbacks for production at scale, which may or may not be temporary however (the Israeli firms were not analysed in the article), create opportunities for more decentralized strategies. Meatable, a Dutch cellular meat start-up that claims to have the most advanced technology to date, is currently working with a 50-litre bioreactor with plans to increase this in the short term to 500 litres (Watson, 2023). It is with this scale in mind that the RESPECTfarms project has also been initiated in the Netherlands, Germany, Belgium, and Switzerland, with funding from the European Union. The idea here is to promote a new model of cellular meat farming where bioreactor production is combined with the rearing of small donor herds and the farming of culture media for cellular meat cultivation (Green Queen Team, 2023).[10] The same idea was already promoted by van der Weele and Tramper in their 2014 article titled 'Cultured meat: Every village its own factory?'

On concluding this book, the perspectives both in relation to the evolution of the respective markets for alternative proteins and climate-controlled agriculture and the positioning of the various social movements and their organizations are still unclear. In the interpretation of the evolution of the agri-food system from the 1970s presented in Chapter 1, the centrality of the movements contesting the dominant model was highlighted. The first indications in the grey press and in academic production suggest more nuanced responses to alternative proteins and climate-controlled agriculture than in the case of transgenics. Today, the dynamics of innovation go beyond the control of the traditional leading firms and even beyond the markets of the North. This is expressed above all in the shift in the axis of the agri-food system globally towards the South and Asia, with the complementary roles of Brazil and China constituting the key poles. The wave of innovation initiated primarily in the North and by private actors is being rapidly complemented by innovation hubs in regions of the world where higher population density faces greater scarcity of natural resources. In this context, states and public policies combine with private innovation ecosystems to scale up, accelerate, and adapt innovations to the conditions of their markets. This diffusion of sources of innovation, combined with the exacerbation of geopolitical relations threatening supply chains, in addition to the acceleration and amplification of climate change effects, creates favourable conditions for their continued advance.

Notes

Introduction

[1] Two other experimental routes can be mentioned: i) the production of proteins from the air where CO_2 is captured and transformed into protein via fermentation; ii) the insertion of genes for animal proteins into plants.

[2] The Nordic countries, which confront similarly severe resource restrictions, are also important sources of innovation in both vertical farming and alternative proteins.

Chapter 1

[1] My analysis has been influenced by many years of immersion in economic sociology approaches, particularly those associated with Mark Granovetter (1985), where markets and economic activity are alternately embedded in social practices, and especially social networks, or are socially constructed by interested actors. In either case, from this perspective, markets are forms of social action and not adequately analysed as arenas in which a special type of 'economic' behaviour, or special laws 'of accumulation', for example, apply. In a complementary fashion, the work of Viviana Zelizer (1994), in a series of tightly argued case studies, demonstrates how economic life, including money, can become domesticated by social and cultural values. This is particularly the case of food practices, which condense social and cultural relations in a particularly intense manner. In agri-food studies these issues have been played out in recurrent debates on the interrelation between production and consumption (Goodman, 2002; Lockie, 2002) and the contestability of markets (Marsden et al, 2000). The notion of new economic social movements that have as their objective the construction of alternative economic networks and are not reducible to demands directed at the state was developed during my studies of fair trade and organics and was initially stimulated by the work of Gendron (2004).

[2] *quilombolas*: Communities created by fugitives from slavery.

[3] https://www.fao.org/nutrition/education/food-based-dietary-guidelines

[4] https://www.fao.org/nutrition/education/food-based-dietary-guidelines

[5] https://www.carrefour.com/en/group/food-transition

[6] Harriet Friedmann (2005) posited the emergence of a green capitalism able to absorb some of the demands of the social movements, particularly those focused on the environment. For many, however, greening is reduced to 'greenwashing', an approach which draws on discourse analysis. Other authors have focused on the key role of agenda setting in the mobilization of economic interests. Much of the literature on alternative proteins focuses on this theme, and quite rightly so since its model of innovation based on a financialized ecosystem explicitly promotes 'hype' as a mechanism for attracting investment and is intrinsic to the 'fail quick' logic of such investment (Stephens and Ruivenkamp, 2016; Sexton, 2020; Guthman and Biltekoff, 2021; Sippel and Dolinga, 2023). An important

strand of economic sociology focuses on the 'performative' nature of discourse (Callon, 2017), arguing that discourse provides both the stimulus and the legitimation for economic action. At a more theoretical level, the work of Jens Beckert (2017) emphasizes the centrality of discourse in creating expectations which reduce uncertainty and mould the future in ways favourable to investment. While firms continuously resort to greenwashing, which needs to be permanently monitored and exposed, the analysis developed here points to the ways in which sustainability goals are becoming embodied in the daily practices of firms.

[7] If Granovetter (1985) and Zelizer (1994) analyse the way economic activity is immersed in social and cultural networks, Fligstein (2001) and Callon (2017) in different ways show how informal and formal understandings based on asymmetric interests and power negotiate specific social spaces within which economic practices can proceed. Fligstein focuses on the conditions which allow 'new entrants' to challenge the 'incumbent' actors dominating the social space in question. Callon, for his part, shows how social spaces can be constructed that even approximate to the rare conditions of the 'perfect market' of neoclassical theory. At the same time, he insists that the demarcation of any space or arena is an exclusionary process, creating the basis for future contestation around the interests and values excluded. On my understanding, the new economic social movements which I analyse are fuelled by these excluded interests and values. Fligstein's 'new entrants' can be analysed within this framework and the 'mission-oriented' entrepreneurs, discussed in this and the following chapter, assume, initially at least, some of the trappings of social movements. Inspired by Geels' work on innovation and transitions (2004), there is now an extensive literature exploring the shifts from niche to mainstream markets in the context of food and alternative proteins (Wild et al, 2014; Bui et al, 2016; El Bilali, 2019; Mylan et al, 2019; Boukid, 2020; Chiles et al, 2021; Lonkila and Kaljonen, 2021; Bulah et al, 2023; Dueñas-Ocampo et al, 2023; Reis et al, 2023). While sympathetic to these approaches, our analysis suggests that the current innovation wave was born on a scale which cannot be convincingly confined to the niche–regime categories.

[8] What Sexton defines as 'non-stuff' (2016).

[9] https://exame.com/tecnologia/cientistas-comecam-corrida-para-melhorar-refrigerantes-diet/

[10] The information in this section was derived from a search of various internet sources including company homepages and Wikipedia entries. The interpretation of their significance is that of the author.

[11] https://en.wikipedia.org/wiki/H%C3%A4agen-Dazs

[12] https://en.wikipedia.org/wiki/Ben_%26_Jerry%27s

[13] https://en.wikipedia.org/wiki/Chobani

[14] https://www.chobani.com/impact/our-causes

[15] https://www.chobani.com/impact/incubator

[16] An ironic response given Unilever's origin in the radical product innovation of margarine replacing butter.

[17] https://en.wikipedia.org/wiki/Eat_Just

[18] https://en.wikipedia.org/wiki/Hain_Celestial_Group

Chapter 2

[1] https://www.dw.com/en/golden-rice-a-shining-solution-or-an-impending-danger/a-18670353

[2] These authors, to whom we should add the works of Guthman and Biltekoff (2021), Fairbairn, Kish and Guthman (2022), and Sippel and Dolinga (2023), are right to stress the central role of 'financialized imaginaries', as these latter describe them, in the attraction

of investment, but they limit themselves to a description of the way these narratives are constructed and promoted and do not focus on the mechanisms put in place by venture capital firms to ensure close monitoring and a step-by-step investment process that depends on satisfying specified targets. Beyond the hype and the techno-optimism which is explicitly embraced is the guiding principle that viability must be quickly established, expressed in the catch phrase 'fail quick'.

3   The breakdown by categories becomes somewhat confusing as the report oscillates between the initial choice of 15 categories and then presents tables with only 6 and others with 11. Even more confusing is the division of the 15 categories into two broad categories of upstream and downstream, where innovative foods are situated upstream, contrary to much of the academic literature that situates them as downstream based on the distinction between before and after farming activities.

4   https://en.wikipedia.org/wiki/Rich_Products

5   Research carried out on the companies' own websites.

6   https://thriveagrifood.com/thrive-top-50-report/

7   https://www.linkedin.com/company/chobani-incubator/

8   https://www.theunileverfoundry.com/home.html

9   https://astanor.com/team/eric-archambeau/

10   https://astanor.com/entrepreneurs

11   https://www.agriinvestor.com/ospraie-weighs-public-and-private-options-for-agtech-venture-strategy/; http://solarimpulse.com/companies/agroecology-capital; http://start-life.nl/new-partnership-with-shift-invest/

12   www.nestle.com/sustainability/nutrition-health/tasty-healthy-food

13   As we will see in Chapter 6, similar reactions, triggered by the Bolsonaro government, came from the soybean sector in Brazil in reaction to parallel 'zero deforestation' movements in the Cerrados and the Amazon rainforest.

14   https://newclimate.org/resources/publications/corporate-climate-responsibility-monitor-2022

15   On the other hand, Unilever has already made three bids in 2022, all rejected, to acquire the health business of GlaxoSmithKline and it seems that the company, today with most of its sales outside the Europe/United States axis, is prioritizing its non-food health and wellness division (Silva, 2022).

Chapter 3

1   It should not be forgotten, however, that almost all the technologies of what was to become vertical farming were developed under NASA space programs and remained in the public domain, which explains the explosion of private sector initiatives since the second decade of the new millennium.

2   Or perhaps more accurately, Despommier reinvented the notion. In his fascinating dissertation, Ng Wil Szen reproduces a drawing of vertical farming published in *Life* magazine in 1909 and attributes the authorship of the definition to Gilbert Ellis Bailey in 1915, even though he preferred underground farming, another option that became relevant in the new millennium in the production of fungi and mushrooms, popular in promoting alternatives to animal protein (Ng, 2017). For another version of the 'prehistory' of vertical farming, see also Van Gerreway, Boon and Geelen (2022).

3   https://www.aerofarms.com/about-us/

4   https://www.verticalfield.com/vertically-grown-rice-comes-to-vietnam-with-vertical-field/

5   Here, the concern with vertical farming in the urban context is creating a new speciality called 'agritecture', which integrates agriculture into the architectural design of cities and

converges with broader proposals for green cities, a theme discussed in the last chapter of this book.

[6] https://fischerfarms.co.uk/fischer-farms-breaks-ground-on-worlds-largest-vertical-farm/
[7] http://www.fastcompany.com/90713239/
[8] https://www.statista.com/outlook/cmo/food/vegetables/united-states
[9] https://en.wikipedia.org/wiki/Haitz%27s_law
[10] Information gleaned from multiple websites.
[11] https://www.facebook.com/urbancropsolutions
[12] https://www.aerofarms.com/our-intellectual-property/
[13] Surveyed on these companies' websites.
[14] These firms in Europe (Infarm and others) have been especially hard hit by the hikes in energy prices and the economic problems resulting from Russia's invasion of Ukraine, leading to some closures, as in the case of Agricool, the French container farming company.
[15] Agrilution was acquired in 2019 by Miele, a leading German company specializing in high-quality household products. It ceased trading in 2023.
[16] https://www.ourfoodfuture.gov.sg
[17] https://www.gartner.co.uk/en/methodologies/gartner-hype-cycle

Chapter 4

[1] The first radical product innovation in this chain was the substitution of margarine for butter by Unilever based first on animal fat and later on vegetable oils (Goodman et al, 1987).
[2] For comprehensive analyses of the history of vegetarianism, see *The Bloodless Revolution* (Stuart, 2008) and *Vegetarianism: A History* (Spencer, 2016).
[3] https://foodandwine.com/search?q=History+vegetarianism
[4] The ethics of meat-eating has taken a new turn with the possibility of producing meat through the multiplication of cells acquired from a simple biopsy of a living animal, a point forcibly made by Dutkiewicz and Rosenberg in the title of their article on the subject: 'The sadism of eating real meat over lab meat' (2021). See also Heidemann et al (2020).
[5] The flexitarian strategy is based on the feasibility of direct product substitution, which is highly debated in a range of social science literature. For the 'systems of provision' approach espoused Bayliss and Fine (2020), the organization of the supply side heavily influences the possibilities and limits of product substitution. Social practice theory (Shove et al, 2021), as its title suggests, emphasizes the social nature of consumption and the importance of considering values and skills. The sustainable transition literature for its part (Geels et al, 2015), argues that microlevel behavioural changes must be accompanied by a restructuring of the sociotechnical systems within which they are situated. Income and educational factors would also influence the rhythm and extensions of product substitution. Alternative proteins and the notion of flexitarianism provide an excellent testing ground for these different approaches.
[6] Resort to the patenting of these innovative processes has been seen critically as a new closing of the 'commons' of microorganisms (Dutkiewicz, 2019). Sexton (2020) also sees the recourse to patents rather than open-sourcing as an effect of the subjection of food start-ups to the Silicon Valley model of financialized innovation. It should be recognized, however, that while the food industry as a whole is seen as traditional, leading food firms have long sported large portfolios of patents (Nestlé: 48,621; Unilever: 43,123).
[7] New Wave Foods ceased trading in February 2024.
[8] Almond production concentrated in the Central Valley of the state of California is also criticized for being a monoculture that requires large amounts of water, in a state with

great water scarcity, and pesticides, which in turn cause a high percentage of commercial bee deaths (McGivney, 2020).

[9] Büchs et al (2023) analyse the adoption of alternative fluid milks in the UK and show how these alternatives may complement and not substitute for cow's milk. They also show the relevance of skill acquirements, and institutional and business forms of provision, together with the influence of gender, income, and education.

[10] Impossible Foods, as of 2024 still awaited regulatory approval for marketing of its heme burger in Europe and China.

[11] https://golden.com/query/plant-based-meat-companies-RE9

[12] In instigating articles Sexton (2020) and Fairbairn et al (2022) provide critical presentations of the notion of food as software understood as an adaptation to the pressures of the Silicon Valley-style financialization of the innovation process. While this is undoubtedly true, it is the convergence of big data digitalization and advances in synthetic biology which brings food innovation closer to the model of software innovation.

[13] http://www.grandviewresearch.com

[14] Some companies, such as Moolec Science, are betting on the introduction of animal molecules into plants such as soy and argue that this route is more effective than precision fermentation because it can harness the entire infrastructure of a chain such as soy to achieve production at scale (Watson, 2022). These companies are still in the testing phase, a much slower process than for microorganisms. Other firms are researching tobacco with the same objectives.

[15] The new generation of insecticides (neonicotinoids) introduced in the 1990s to substitute the banned DDT has had devastating impacts on all types of insects, including pollinizers, especially bees. It is not simply a case of what some authors have called 'insectinction' but of the fate of a decisive link in the larger food chain which also threatens the predators of these insects and so on successively (Gordon, 2022).

Chapter 5

[1] https://www.asiapacificex.com/products/crude-palm-oil-futures

[2] World Integrated Trade Solution, World Bank (https://wits.worldbank.org)

[3] http://dg.cnsoc.org/article/2016b.html

[4] This paragraph is based on Natrajan's article cited here.

[5] https://www.caas.cn/en/ResearchInnovation/ASTIP/index.htm

[6] Also see: https://www.grandviewresearch.com/industry-analysis/alternative-protein-market-report

[7] Also a social movement, present in 100 countries, that promotes Mondays without animal protein.

[8] https://zhenmeat.com

Chapter 6

[1] Bernardo Sorj, then at the Federal University of Minas Gerais, also developed a research programme with the 'agroindustrial chains' approach, a concept that informed two ambitious Latin American research programmes initiated in 1978 by Raul Vigorito (1983) and Gonzalo Arroyo et al (1985) respectively, which were important influences on this research that focused on the contractual integration of family farming in the agribusinesses in the states of Minas Gerais, Santa Catarina, and Rio Grande do Sul (Sorj, 1980).

[2] http://www.natura.com.br

[3] https://akatu.org.br

[4] Sebrae was originally a public federal institution for the support of small and medium firms. In the 1990s its statute was changed, becoming a private organization financed by industry but maintaining the same mission.

[5] An article by Teixeira et al (2024) presenting the results of research into 'flexitarians' in Brazil concludes that 'flexitarianism can serve as a pivotal catalyst in the transition towards a more sustainable food system' and identifies a strong connection between environmental concerns and the adoption of flexitarianism. At the same time, they caution that the main demographic of self-identified flexitarians are women, with a prevalence of white women, and further that, given the extremely regressive income distribution in the country, a reduction in meat consumption should not be interpreted as a sign of flexitarianism. Legumes are identified as the main alternative to meats.

[6] https://blog.openstartups.net/2022/05/06/cultura-e-inovacao-na-danone/

[7] JBS closed this line of products in 2022 due to falling sales in the United States.

[8] In 2023 the United States authorised the marketing of two cultivated meat products, and Brazil regulated the registration of novel foods and ingredients including those from cell cultivation and fermentation.

[9] Alternative proteins are promoting a new area of debate on the 'ontology' of these new foods. Different marketing strategies, legislations, and regulations are producing a multiplicity of meats, milks, and fish (Jönsson, 2016; Jönsson et al, 2019).

[10] Morais-da-Silva et al (2022), in a study identifying the social impacts of alternative meats adoption in Brazil, based on in depth interviews with experts in the meats and alternative meats sectors, highlighted a wide range of opportunities (transition to a higher value protein economy, diversification of agricultural production, less use of pesticides, qualified jobs) while recognizing the importance of associated challenges (especially unemployment in the low-qualified jobs of the existing workforce), both of which would require positive policy interventions.

Chapter 7

[1] https://www.milanurbanfoodpolicypact.org

[2] One of the examples most highlighted by Lim are the popular restaurants created by municipal governments in Brazil and, above all, the experience of public food policies in the city of Belo Horizonte, which has become an international reference and will be discussed later.

[3] Neil Brenner (2014) developed the concept of 'planetary urbanization' to capture the way in which the 'rural' has been remade by urban dynamics.

[4] Steele (2013, p 23) quotes the following account of an 'extraordinary piggery at Kensington', London by George Dodd from 1856: 'inhabited by a population of 1000 or 1200 persons, all engaged in the rearing of pigs; the pigs usually outnumbered the people three to one, and had their sties mixed up with the dwelling-houses; some of the pigs lived in the houses and even under the beds'.

[5] In the original formulation, points 4 and 5 were conflated, but the new imagery being created around the notion of smart cities becomes an increasingly important influence.

Conclusion

[1] https://www.gartner.co.uk/en/methodologies/gartner-hype-cycle

[2] A good example is the 'beef rice' announced by South Korean researchers in 2024: a hybrid rice containing meat muscle and fat cells, which they claim could provide a complete meal especially for situations of extreme food insecurity (Sample, 2024).

[3] We could also add the intrinsic volatility of venture capital's interest, which in 2023 had artificial intelligence in its sights.

[4] Russia's blocking of Ukraine's grain exports has dramatized the vulnerability of many countries dependent on long trade circuits.

[5] A powerful contribution by my friend and colleague David Goodman (2023) published in this series, provides a detailed and forceful argument which concludes that 'the current

wave of innovation driven by the convergence of digital and molecular technologies has been contained within the hegemonic model of agriculture and food' (p 94). While we share an understanding of the way the convergence of digital and molecular technologies has accelerated the processes of 'appropriationism' and 'substitutionism' identified in our earlier book *From Farming to Biotechnology* (1987), my analysis suggests that the future is less foreclosed, and that the diffusion of these innovations in themselves would bring enormous benefits for the climate, biodiversity, the restoration of natural resources, new urban–rural relations, and most importantly for food security.

[6] Systems theory provides a different and equally important critique of economic concentration to the extent that the latter is generally accompanied by the elimination of a plurality (redundancy) of actors and markets in the name of efficiency. COVID-19 and the consequent breakdown in agri-food supply systems revealed this vulnerability.

[7] The view that incumbent leading players not only subsequently co-opt innovative food start-ups but mould the ecosystem as a whole is the conclusion of an in-depth study of the Silicon Valley case (Fairbairn and Reisman, 2024). The authors correctly show that alliances with the incumbent global players are a necessary step in the start-up strategy to occupy mainstream global markets, with all the risks that such alliances involve. These start-ups, however, do not propose to change the nature of the markets but focus on changing the content of existing products and their life- and planet-threatening externalities.

[8] For the references see Chapter 2 and especially note 2.

[9] In Chapter 1 I show how the success of new entrants, such as Ben & Jerry's and Chobani depended on independent marketing and distribution strategies.

[10] The Dutch cell culture firm Mosa Meat is also a partner.

References

ABAG. (1993) *Segurança alimentar: Uma abordagem de agribusiness*, São Paulo: Abag.

Abramovay, R. (1992) *Paradigmas do capitalismo agrário em questão*, São Paulo: Unicamp.

Ação de Cidadania. (2013) 'Nossa história', Ação de Cidadania, [online] 1 October, Available from: https://www.acaodacidadania.org.br

ADM. (2022) 'Emerging trends that will shape the protein alternatives market in the year ahead', ADM, [online] January, Available from: https://www.adm.com/globalassets/news/adm-stories/final-adm-story-alternative-protein-outlook-020122.pdf

Adjie, K.R.P., Srinaga, F. and Mensana, A. (2021) 'Building-integrated agriculture's role in supporting urban food cycle', *IOP conference series: Earth Environment Science*, 881, 012037. doi.org/10.1088/1755-1315/881/1/012037

AgFunder. (2022) 'AgFunder AgriFoodTech Investment Report', AgFunder, [online] 24 March, Available from: https://agfunder.com/research/2022-agfunder-agrifoodtech-investment-report/

Aglietta, M. and Bai, G. (2013) *China's Development: Capitalism and Empire*, Abingdon: Routledge.

Aguilar, J.C. (ed) (2022) 'Sovereign wealth funds 2021: Changes and challenges accelerated by the Covid-19 pandemic', Madrid: IE University.

Albrecht, C. (2019) 'Miele Acquires Consumer Indoor Vertical Farm Company Agrilution', The Spoon, [online] 9 December, Available from: https://thespoon.tech/miele-acquires-consumer-indoor-vertical-farm-company-agrilution/

Alfranca, O., Rama, R. and von Tunzelmann, N. (2005) 'Innovation in food and beverage multinationals', in R. Rama (ed) *Multinational Agribusinesses*, New York: Haworth Press, pp 115–48.

Alkon, A.H. and Agyeman, J. (eds) (2011) *Cultivating Food Justice: Race, Class, and Sustainability*, Cambridge, MA: MIT Press.

Allaire, G. and Boyer, R. (1995) *La grande transformation de l'agriculture*, Paris: INRA.

Allied Market Research. (2023) 'Vertical farming market size, forecast analysis 2032', Allied Market Research, [online] Last modified 19 November, Available from: https://www.alliedmarketresearch.com/vertical-farming-market) Accessed: 20 September 2022.

Alonso, I.O. (2021) 'The environmental impacts of greenhouse agriculture in Almería, Spain', FoodUnfolded, [online] 23 September (last modifed 26 February 2024), Available from: https://www.foodunfolded.com/article/the-environmental-impacts-of-greenhouse-agriculture-in-almeria-spain

Antos, M. (2021) 'Kalera acquires Vindara to unlock the "power of the seed" and drive explosive growth in the vertical farming industry', GlobeNewsWire, [online] 24 February, Available from: https://www.globenewswire.com/news-release/2021/02/24/2181084/0/en/Kalera-Acquires-Vindara-to-Unlock-the-Power-of-the-Seed-and-Drive-Explosive-Growth-in-the-Vertical-Farming-Industry.html

Araújo, G.C. de, Souza, M.T.S. and Pimenta, A.S. (2015) 'Cadeia de suprimentos verde e as ações do pacto da pecuária do programa "Conexões sustentáveis" São Paulo – Amazônia', *Revista em Agronegócios e Meio-Ambiente*, 8: 137–57. https://doi.org/10.17765/2176-9168.2015v8nEd.esp.p137-157

Arioch, D. (2021) 'Para deputado, PL que proíbe termo "carne vegetal" já deveria ter sido aprovado', Vegazeta, [online] 19 April, Available from: https://vegazeta.com.br/para-deputado-pl-que-proibe-termo-carne-vegetal-ja-deveria-ter-sido-aprovado/

Arroyo, G., Rama, R., Rello, F. and Aceituno, G. (1985) *Agricultura y alimentos en América Latina: El poder de las transnacionales*, Mexico City: Universidad Nacional Autónoma de México.

Aslan, R. (2018) *Deus: Uma história humana*, Rio de Janeiro: Zahar.

Atkins, P. (2012) 'Animal waste and nuisance in nineteenth century London', in P. Atkins (ed) *Animal Cities: Beastly Urban Histories*, Farnham: Ashgate.

Augusto, R. and Coutinho, C. (2022) 'A evolução das startups no setor de Food Techs', PricewaterhouseCoopers Brasil, [online], Available from: https://www.pwc.com.br/pt/estudos/setores-atividades/produtos-consumo-varejo/2022/a-evolucao-das-startups-no-setor-de-food-2021-22.pdf

Axworthy, N. (2022) 'This startup is disrupting the $89 billion cheese industry with the same technology as Perfect Day', VegNews, [online] 12 May, Available from: https://vegnews.com/2022/5/change-foods-cheese-industry-casein-technology

Azevedo, D. (2021) 'Brazilian giants invest in alternative proteins', Poultry World, [online] 3 May, Available from: https://www.poultryworld.net/poultry/brazilian-giants-invest-in-alternative-proteins/

Barbosa, L., Portilho, F., Galindo, F. and Borges, S. (eds) (2021) *Encontros e caminhos dos estudos do consumo no Brasil*, Rio de Janeiro: ESPM/E-Papers.

Barrientos, S., Gereffi, G. and Rossi, A. (2010) *Economic and Social Upgrading in Global Production Networks: Developing a Framework for Analysis*, Capturing the Gains, University of Manchester, working paper 2010/03.

Bayer. (2023) 'Unfold joins De Ruiter', Bayer, [online] 7 September, Available from: https://www.vegetables.bayer.com/us/en-us/resources/news/unfold-joins-de-ruiter.html

Bayliss, K. and Fine, B. (2020) *A Guide to the Systems of Provision Approach: Who Gets What, How and Why*, London: Palgrave Macmillan.

BBC News. (2020) 'China launches "clean plate" campaign against food waste', BBC News, [online] 13 August, Available from: https://www.bbc.com/news/world-asia-china-53761295

Beckert, J. (2017) *Imagined Futures: Fictional Expectations and Capitalist Dynamics*, Cambridge, MA: Harvard.

Beefpoint. (2021) 'Seara eleva aposta no crescente mercado de proteínas plant based', Beefpoint, [online] 15 October, Available from: https://www.beefpoint.com.br/seara-eleva-aposta-no-crescente-mercado-de-protei nas-plant-based/

Belik, W. (1998) 'O novo panorama competitivo da indústria de alimentos no Brasil', in C.H.P. Mello (ed) *Reestruturação industrial*, Caderno PUC: Economia, São Paulo: Educ.

Bellamy Foster, J. (1999) 'Marx's theory of metabolic rift. Classical foundations of environmental sociology', *American Journal of Sociology*, 105(2): 366–405. https://doi.org/10.1086/210315

Benjamin, S. (2006) *Sicily: Three Thousand Years of Human History*, Hanover, NH: Steerforth Press.

Berman, A. (2018) 'Major agriculture companies partner to use blockchain in grain trading', Cointelegraph, [online] 25 October, Available from: https://cointelegraph.com/news/major-agriculture-companies-partner-to-use-blo ckchain-in-grain-trading

Best, D. (2021) 'Meat giant BRF inks tie-up with cell-cultured firm Aleph Farms', Just Food Magazine, [online] 4 March, Available from: https://www.just-food.com/news/meat-giant-brf-inks-tie-up-with-cell-cultu red-firm-aleph-farms/

BEUC. (2016) 'Annual report 2015', BEUC, [online] 17 May, Available from: https://www.beuc.eu/sites/default/files/publications/beuc-x-2016-046_beuc_annual_report_2015_en.pdf

Bijman, W.J.J. (2001) 'How biotechnology is changing the structure of the seed industry', *International Journal of Biotechnology*, 3(1/2): 82–94. doi.org/10.1504/IJBT.2001.000153

Boekhout, R. (2021) 'When will vertical farming become profitable?' Vertical Farm Daily, [online] 14 May, Available from: https://www.verticalfarmda ily.com/article/9321424/when-will-vertical-farming-become-profitable/

Boltanski, L. and Chiapello, È. (1999) *Le nouvel esprit du capitalisme*, Paris: Gallimard.

Bonani, B. (2019) 'Beyond Meat (BYND): O Melhor IPO De 2019 e Você Ficou De Fora?', Investing.com, [online] 7 December, Available from: https://br.investing.com/analysis/beyond-meat-bynd-o-melhor-ipo-de-2019-e-voce-ficou-de-fora-200432695

Bond, C. (2021) 'Upside Foods develops animal-free cell growth medium', The Spoon [online] 15 December, Available from: https://thespoon.tech/upside-foods-develops-animal-free-cell-growth-medium/

Borak, M. (2018) 'Why are Chinese tech companies so much into raising pigs?' *South China Morning Post*, 22 November.

Bortoletto Martins, A.P., Levy, R.B., Claro, R.M., Moubarac, J.C. and Monteiro, C.A. (2013) 'Participação crescente de produtos ultraprocessados na dieta brasileira (1987–2009)', *Revista de Saúde Pública*, 47(4): 656–65. https://doi.org/10.1590/S0034-8910.2013047004968

Boukid, F. (2020) 'Plant-based meat analogues: From niche to mainstream', *European Food Research and Technology*, 247: 297–308.

Braudel, F. (1982) *Civilization and Capitalism 15th–18 Century, Volume 2: The Wheels of Commerce*, translated by S. Reynolds, New York: Harper & Row.

Brenner, N. (ed) *Implosions/Explosions: Towards a Study of Planetary Urbanization*, Berlin: Jovis Verlag.

Briney, A. (2020) 'History and overview of the Green Revolution: How agricultural practices changed in the 20th century,' ThoughtCo., [online] 22 January, Available from: https://www.thoughtco.com/green-revolution-overview-1434948

Brown, L.R. (1970) *Seeds of Change: The Green Revolution and development in the 1970s*. New York: Praeger.

Bruno, R. (1997) *Senhores da terra, senhores da guerra: A nova face política das elites agroindustriais no Brasil*, Rio de Janeiro: Forense Universitária.

Büchs, M., Middlemiss, L., Mylan, J. and Stevens, L. (2023) 'Sustainable consumption by product substitution? An exploration of the appropriation of plant-based "mylk" in everyday life', *Consumption and Society*, 2(1): 78–101. https://doi.org/10.1332/PREN9891

Bui, S., Cardona, A., Lamine, C. and Cerf, M. (2016) 'Sustainability transition: Insights on processes of niche-regime interaction and regime reconfiguration in agri-food systems', *Journal of Rural Studies*, 48: 92–103. https://doi.org/10.1016/j.jrurstud.2016.10.003

Bulah, B.M., Tziva, M., Bidmon, C. and Hekkert, M.P. (2023) 'Incumbent entry modes and entry timing in sustainable niches: The plant-based protein transition in the United States, Netherlands, and United Kingdom', *Environmental Innovation and Societal Transitions*, 48: 100735. https://doi.org/10.1016/j.eist.2023.100735

Café, S.L., Fonseca, P.S.M. da, Amaral, G.F., Motta, M.F. dos S.R., Roque, C.A.L. and Ormond, J.G.P. (2003) 'Cadeia produtiva do trigo', BNDES Setorial, Rio de Janeiro, 18, pp 193–220.

Cai, Y.-Z. and Zhang, Z. (2000) 'Shanghai: Trends towards specialized and capital-intensive urban agriculture', in N. Bakker, M. Dubbeling, S. Gündel, U. Sabel-Koschella and H. de Zeeuw (eds) *Growing Cities, Growing Food: Urban Agriculture on the Policy Agenda*, Feldafing: DSE pp 467–75.

Caldas, E. (2017) 'Do Bem depois da Ambev', Época Negócios, [online] 19 June, Available from: https://epocanegocios.globo.com/Empresa/noti cia/2017/06/do-bem-depois-da-ambev.html

Callebaut, V., Martin, A., Zaini, F. and Delrieu, M. (2015) 'Paris smart city 2050', Vincent Callebaut Architectures, [online] 1 January, Available from: https://vincent.callebaut.org/object/150105_parissmartcity2050/ parissmartcity2050/projects

Callon, M. (ed) (1998) *The Laws of the Markets*, Oxford: Blackwell

Callon, M. (2017) *L'Emprise des marchés: Comprendre leur fonctionnement pour pouvoir les changer*, Paris: La Découverte.

Castro, A.B. de and Souza, F.E.P. de. (1985) *A economia brasileira em marcha forçada*, Rio de Janeiro: Paz e Terra.

Cattelan, R., Moraes, M.L. and Rossoni, R.A. (2020) 'A reforma agrária nos ciclos políticos do Brasil, 1995–2019', *Revista NERA*, 23(55): 138–64. https://doi.org/10.47946/rnera.v0i55.6907

CCICED. (2016) 'China's role in greening global value chains', Beijing: China Council for International Cooperation on Environment and Development. https://cciced.eco/research/special-policy-study/chinas-role-in-green ing-global-value-chains/

Charlton, E. (2019) 'This is why Denmark, Sweden and Germany are considering a meat tax', World Economic Forum, [online] 28 August, Available from: https://www.weforum.org/agenda/2019/08/meat-tax-denmark-sweden-and-germany/

Charnley, B. and Radick, G. (2013) 'Intellectual property, plant breeding and the marketing of Mendelian genetics', Studies in History and Philosophy of Science Part A, 44(2): 222–33.

Charvatova, V. (2018) 'A brief history of plant milks', Vegan Food and Living, [online] 23 April, Available from: https://www.veganfoodandliv ing.com/features/a-brief-history-of-plant-milks/

Che, C. (2021) 'Does plant-based meat have a future in China?', The China Project, [online] 25 June, Available from: https://thechinaproject.com/ 2021/06/25/does-plant-based-meat-have-a-future-in-china/

Childe, V.G. (1950) 'The urban revolution', *The Town Planning Review*, 21(1): 3–17. https://www.jstor.org/stable/40102108

Chiles, R.M., Broad, G., Gagnon, M., Negowetti, N., Glenna, L., Griffin, M.A.M., Tami-Barrera, L., Baker, S. and Beck, K. (2021) 'Democratizing ownership and participation in the 4th Industrial Revolution: Challenges and opportunities in cellular agriculture', *Agriculture and Human Values*, 38(4): 943–61. https://doi.org/10.1007/s10460-021-10237-7

Cockrall-King, J. (2012) *Food and the City: Urban Agriculture and the New Food Revolution*, New York: Prometheus Books.

Collins, P. (2021) *The Sumerians*, London: Reaktion Books.

Conexão Planeta. (2016) 'China lança campanha para reduzir em 50% o consumo de carne vermelha', Conexão Planeta [online] 27 June, Available from: https://conexaoplaneta.com.br/blog/china-lanca-campanha-para-reduzir-em-50-o-consumo-de-carne-vermelha/

Conrad, D. (2012) 'China in Copenhagen: Reconciling the "Beijing climate revolution" and the "Copenhagen climate obstinacy"', *The China Quarterly*, 210: 435–55. https://doi.org/10.1017/S0305741012000458

Corporate European Observatory. (2016) 'A spoonful of sugar: How the food lobby fights sugar regulation in the EU', [online] July, Available from: https://corporateeurope.org/sites/default/files/a_spoonful_of_sugar_final.pdf

Corson, M.S., Mondière, A., Morel, L. and van der Werf, H. (2022) 'Beyond agroecology: Agricultural rewilding, a prospect for livestock systems', *Agricultural Systems*, 199, 103410. https://doi.org/10.1016/j.agsy.2022.103410

Costa, L.F.C. and Santos, R. (eds) (1998) *Política e Reforma Agrária*, Rio de Janeiro: Mauad.

Costa, M. (2022) 'The State of food manufacturing in 2022', Food Engineering, [online] 6 July, Available from: https://www.foodengineeringmag.com/articles/100394-the-state-of-food-manufacturing-in-2022

Coughlan, A. (2021) 'Urban rewilding: A solution to the world's ecological and mental health crises?', Earth.org, [online] 8 February, Available from: http://www.earth.org/urban-rewilding

Coyne, A. (2024a) 'Hatching new ideas – Big Food's incubator and accelerator programmes', Just Food Magazine, [online] 20 March, Available from: https://www.just-food.com/newsletters/hatching-new-ideas-big-food-incubator-and-accelerator-programmes/

Coyne, A. (2024b) 'Big Food's stake in the future – in-house-venture-capital funds' investments', Just Food Magazine, [online] 20 March, Available from: https://www.just-food.com/features/big-foods-stake-in-the-future-in-house-venture-capital-funds/

Crumpacker, M. (2019) 'A look back at the amazing history of greenhouses', Medium, [online] 27 June, Available from: https://medium.com/@MarkCrumpacker/a-look-back-at-the-amazing-history-of-greenhouses-adf301162a7b

Cuello, J.L. and Liu, X. (2014) 'Re-imagineering the vertical farm: A novel strategy in the design and development of vertical farms', *Urban Agriculture*, 28: 61, Available from: https://ruaf.org/assets/2019/11/Urban-Agriculture-Magazine-no.-28-GROW-the-City.-Innovations-in-Urban-Agriculture.pdf

Curtis, K.R. and Cowee, M.W. (2009) 'Direct marketing local food to chefs: Chef preferences and perceived obstacles', *Journal of Distribution Research*, 40(2): 26–36. http://dx.doi.org/10.22004/ag.econ.99784

Dabhade, A. (2021) 'What is making flexitarians in the US and UK shift towards a meatless diet?', YouGov, [online] 31 May, Available from: https://yougov.co.uk/consumer/articles/36188-what-making-flexitarians-us-and-uk-shift-towards-m

Dagevos, H. (2021) 'Finding flexitarians: Current studies on meat eaters and meat reducers', *Trends in Food Science and Technology*, 114: 530–39. https://doi.org/10.1016/j.tifs.2021.06.021

Danstrup, L. (2021) 'Novozymes is combining cutting-edge science and business expertise to help feed the world sustainably', Novozymes, [online] 21 September, Available from: https://www.novozymes.com/en/news/novozymes-combining-cutting-edge-science-and-business-expertise-help-feed-world-sustainably

Daviron, B., Perrin, C. and Soulard, C.-T. (2017) 'History of urban food policy in Europe, from the ancient city to the industrial city', in C. Brand, et al (eds) *Designing Urban Food Policies: Concepts and Approaches*, Cham: Springer. https://doi.org/10.1007/978-3-030-13958-2_2

Davis, J.H. and Goldberg, R.A. (1957) *A Concept of Agribusiness*, Boston: Harvard University Press.

Deakin, M., Borrelli, N. and Diamantini, D. (eds) (2016) *The Governance of City Food Systems: Case Studies from Around the World*, Milan: Fondazione Giangiacomo Feltrinelli.

De Bernardi, P. and Azucar, D. (2020) *Innovation in Food Ecosystems: Entrepreneurship for a Sustainable Future*, Cham: Springer. https://doi.org/10.1007/978-3-030-33502-1

Deininger, K., Nizalov, D. and Singh, S.K. (2013) 'Are mega farms the future of global agriculture? Exploring the farm size–productivity relationship for large commercial farms in Ukraine', Washington D.C.: World Bank Group. https://doi.org/10.1596/1813-9450-6544

Del Carmen, G. (2021) '6 foodtechs brasileiras que estão revolucionando o mercado de refeições saudáveis', Forbes, [online] 12 August, Available from: https://forbes.com.br/forbes-tech/2021/08/6-foodtechs-brasileiras-que-estao-revolucionando-o-mercado-de-refeicoes-saudaveis/

Delgado, G.C. (2012) *Do 'capital financeiro na agricultura' à economia do agronegócio: mudanças cíclicas em meio século (1965–2012)*, Porto Alegre: UFRGS.

Delgado, N.G., Leite, S.P. and Wesz Júnior, V.J. (2010) 'Nota técnica: Produção agrícola', Rio de Janeiro: CPDA/UFRRJ.

Demailly, K.-E. and Darly, S. (2017) 'Urban agriculture on the move in Paris: The routes of temporary gardening in the neoliberal city', *ACME: An International Journal for Critical Geographies*, 16(2): 332–61. https://acme-journal.org/index.php/acme/article/view/1384

De Maria, M., Robinson, E.J.Z., Kangile, J.R., Kadigi, R.M.J., Dreoni, I., Couto, M., Howai, N., Peci, J. and Fiennes, S. (2020) 'Global Soybean Trade: the Geopolitics of a Bean', UK Research and Innovation Global Challenges Research Fund (UKRI GCRF) Trade, Development and the Environment Hub. Available from: https://trade-hub.new-production. wordpress-linode.linode.unep-wcmc.org/content/uploads/2024/01/Glo bal-Soybean-Trade-The-Geopolitcs-of-a-Bean-1.pdf

De Medeiros, L.S. (2003) 'Reforma agrária de mercado e movimentos sociais: aspectos da experiência brasileira', *ComCiência*, 44.

De Medeiros, L.S. (2015) 'Rural social movements, struggles for rights, and land reform in contemporary Brazilian history', in M. Carter (ed) *Challenging Social Inequality: The Landless Rural Workers Movement and Agrarian Reform in Brazil*, Durham, NC: Duke University Press, pp 68–89.

Despommier, D. (2010) *The Vertical Farm: Feeding the World in the 21st Century*, New York: St Martin's Press.

Diamond, J. (1987) 'The worst mistake in the history of the human race', *Discover Magazine*, May: 95–8.

Diamond, J. (2005) *Collapse: How Societies Choose to Fail or Succeed*, New York: Penguin.

DigitalFoodLab. (2021) *FoodTech Trends in 2021*. Available from: https:// www.digitalfoodlab.com/foodtech-trends-in-2021/

Domingues, M.S., Bermann, C. and Manfredini, S. (2014) 'A produção da soja no Brasil e sua relação com o desmatamento na Amazônia', *Presença Geográfica*, 1(1): 32–47. doi.org/10.36026/rpgeo.v1i1.2308

Donley, A. (2020) 'China proposes "soybean alliance" with Russia', World-grain.com, [online] 27 August, Available from: https://www.world-grain. com/articles/14152-china-proposes-soybean-alliance-with-russia

Dossey, A.T., Morales-Ramos, J.A. and Guadalupe Rojas, M. (eds) (2016) *Insects as Sustainable Food Ingredients: Production, Processing and Food Applications*, Amsterdam: Elsevier. https://doi.org/10.1016/ C2014-0-03534-4

Drinks Insight Network. (2021) 'PepsiCo to reduce sugar content in beverages across the EU', Drinks Insight Network, [online] 2 July, Available from: https:// www.drinks-insight-network.com/news/pepsico-beverages-eu/

Driver, E. (2021) 'East Africa wants to be the continent's maggot protein hub', Quartz, [online] 16 April, Available from: https://qz.com.africa/ 1996243/east-africa-wants-to-be-the-worlds-insect-protein-hub

Dueñas-Ocampo, S., Eichhorst, W. and Newton, P. (2023) 'Plant-based and cultivated meat in the United States: A review and research agenda through the lens of socio-technical transitions', *Journal of Cleaner Production*, 405: 136999. https://doi.org/10.1016/j.jclepro.2023.136999

Dunn, K. (2021) 'Impossible Foods wants to be "everywhere." First it has to get into China', Fortune, [online] 11 November, Available from: https://fortune.com/2021/11/11/impossible-foods-pork-china-hong-kong/

Dutkiewicz, J. (2019) 'Socialize lab meat', Jacobin, [online] 11 August, Available from: https://jacobin.com/2019/08/lab-meat-socialism-green-new-deal

Dutkiewicz, J. and Rosenberg, G.N. (2021) 'The sadism of eating real meat over lab meat', The New Republic, [online] 23 February, Available from: https://newrepublic.com/article/161452/sadism-eating-real-meat-lab-meat

EFSA. (2022) 'Added and free sugars should be as low as possible', European Food Safety Authority, [online] 28 February, Available from: https://www.efsa.europa.eu/en/news/added-and-free-sugars-should-be-low-possible

El Bilali, H. (2019) 'Research on agro-food sustainability transitions: A systematic review of research themes and an analysis of research gaps', *Journal of Cleaner Production*, 221: 353–64. https://doi.org/10.1016/j.jclepro.2019.02.232

Ellis, J. (2020a) 'Cargill unveils PlantEver plant-based brand for Chinese consumers, expands B2B offering', AgFunder News, [online] 4 May, Available from: https://agfundernews.com/cargill-unveils-plantever-plant-based-protein-brand-for-chinese-consumers-expands-b2b-offering

Ellis, J. (2020b) 'Nestlé enters Asian plant-based protein market with $103 m China investment', AgFunder News, 27 May, Available from: https://agfundernews.com/nestle-enters-asian-plant-based-protein-market-with-103m-china-investment

Engström, A. (2023) 'The Eating insects startups: Here is the list of Entopreneurs around the world!', Bugburger, [online] Last modified 18 March, Available from: https://www.bugburger.se/foretag/the-eating-insects-startups-here-is-the-list-of-entopreneurs-around-the-world/

ERS/USDA. (1999) 'US-Mexico sweetener trade mired in dispute', *Agricultural Outlook*, [online] September, Available from: https://www.ers.usda.gov/media/trslu0ge/us-mexico-sweetener-trade-mired-in-dispute.pdf

Escher, F. (2020) *Agricultura, alimentação e desenvolvimento rural na China e no Brasil: Uma análise institucional comparativa*, Curitiba: Appris.

Essick, K. (2021) 'Shiru closes $17m series A to develop novel plant-based food ingredients', PR Newswire, [online] 27 October, Available from: https://www.prnewswire.com/news-releases/shiru-closes-17m-series-a-to-develop-novel-plant-based-food-ingredients-301409247.html

ETC Group. (2005) 'Oligopoly, Inc. 2005'. ETC Group [online], Communiqué 91. Available from: www.etcgroup.org/sites/www.etcgroup. org/files/publication/44/01/oligopoly2005_16dec.05.pdf

ETC Group. (2019) 'Lab-grown meat and other petri-protein industries', ETC Group, [online] 1 April, Available from: https://www.etcgroup.org/ content/lab-grown-meat-and-other-petri-protein-industries

Euromonitor. (2021) 'Plant-based eating and alternative proteins', Euromonitor International, [online] July, Available from: https://www. euromonitor.com/plant-based-eating-and-alternative-proteins/report

Exame Agro. (2021) 'Bayer lança programa para captura de carbono na agricultura brasileira', Exame, [online] 27 May, Available from: https:// exame.com/agro/bayer-lanca-programa-para-captura-de-carbono-na-agri cultura-brasileira/

Exame Marketing. (2022) 'NotCo, de alimentos à base de plantas, amplia linha de não-leite no Brasil', Exame Marketing, [online] 7 April, Available from: https://exame.com/marketing/notco-de-alimentos-a-base-de-pla nta-amplia-linha-de-nao-leite-no-brasil/

Fairbairn, M. and Reisman, E. (2024) 'The incumbent advantage: Corporate power in agri-food tech', *The Journal of Peasant Studies*, 1–24. https://doi. org/10.1080/03066150.2024.2310146

Fairbairn, M., Kish, Z. and Guthman, J. (2022) 'Pitching agri-food tech: Performativity and non-disruptive disruption in Silicon Valley', *Journal of Cultural Economy*, 15(5), 652–70. https://doi.org/10.1080/17530 350.2022.2085142

FAIRR. (2022) 'Alternative proteins framework', FAIRR, [online] 7 September, Available from: https://www.fairr.org/tools/alternative-prote ins-framework

FAO (Food and Agriculture Organization). (2013) *Edible Insects: Future prospects for food and feed security*, Rome: FAO.

FAO. (2019) *Ultra-processed foods, diet quality, and health using the NOVA classification system*, Rome: FAO.

Farina, E.M.M.Q. (1988) 'O Sistema Agroindustrial de Alimentos', in *XVI Encontro Nacional de Economia 1988*, 3: 292–315.

Fassler, J. (2024) 'The revolution that died on its way to dinner', New York Times, [online] 9 February, Available from: https://www.nytimes.com/ 2024/02/09/opinion/eat-just-upside-foods-cultivated-meat.html

Feedstuffs. (2021) 'Memphis Meats now Upside Foods', [online] 17 May, Available from: https://www.feedstuffs.com/agribusiness-news/memp his-meats-now-upside-foods

Feingold, S. (2017) 'Field of machines: Researchers grow crop using only automation', CNN, [online] 7 October, Available from: https://edit ion.cnn.com/2017/10/07/world/automated-farm-harvest-england/ index.html

Ferrer, B. (2020) 'Davos 2020: DuPont discusses "seismic shifts" in the protein revolution', Food Ingredients 1st, [online] 23 January, Available from: https://www.foodingredientsfirst.com/news/davos-2020-dupont-discusses-seismic-shifts-in-the-protein-revolution.html

Fi Global Insights. (2019) 'Veganism 2.0: Animal-free food goes mainstream', Fi Global Insights, [online] 4 September, Available from: https://insights.figlobal.com/trends/veganism-20-animal-free-food-goes-mainstream

Finnerty, K. (2020) 'Could veganism be the solution to the climate crisis?', Ipsos, [online] 15 January, Available from: https://www.ipsos.com/en-uk/could-veganism-be-solution-climate-crisis

Fitch Solutions. (2020) 'Alternative protein: Beyond Meat playing catch-up as it enters Brazilian market', Fitch Solutions, [online] 31 July, Available from: https://www.fitchsolutions.com/bmi/consumer-retail/alternative-protein-beyond-meat-playing-catch-it-enters-brazilian-market-31-07-2020

Fleischhacker, S. (2007) 'Food Fight: The battle over redefining competitive foods', Journal of School Health, 77(3): 147–52. https://doi.org/10.1111/j.1746-1561.2007.00184.x

Fleischmann, I. (2020) 'A plant-based que "chegou de fininho" e quer construir a categoria no Brasil: The New Butchers', LABS News, [online] 16 December, Archived at: https://web.archive.org/web/20231209030305/https://labsnews.com/pt-br/artigos/negocios/a-plant-based-que-chegou-de-fininho-e-quer-construir-a-categoria-no-brasil-the-new-butchers/

Fligstein, N. (2001) The Architecture of Markets: An Economic Sociology of Twenty-First-Century Capitalist Societies, Princeton: Princeton University Press.

Fonseca, F. (2005) 'A institucionalização do mercado de orgânicos no mundo e no Brasil: uma interpretação', PhD thesis, CPDA/UFRRJ.

Fonseca, M. (2021) 'Fazenda futuro: Como a startup que aposta em carne de planta para superar frigoríficos já vale R$715 milhões', InfoMoney, [online] 21 July, Available from: https://www.infomoney.com.br/Do-Zero-Ao-Topo/Fazenda-Futuro-ComoA-Startup-Que-Aposta-Em-Carne-De-Planta-Para-Superar-Frigorificos-JaVale-R-715-Milhoes/

Food Manufacturing. (2018) 'Making sense of the clean label concept', Food Manufacturing, [online] 19 June, Available from: https://www.foodmanufacturing.com/labeling/blog/13166825/making-sense-of-the-clean-label-concept

Forward Fooding. (2021) 'The Fortune 500 of AgriFoodTech', Forward Fooding, [online], Available from: https://forwardfooding.com/foodtech500/

Foster, J.B. (1999) 'Marx's theory of metabolic rift: Classical foundations for environmental sociology', American Journal of Sociology, 105(2): 366–405.

França, C.G., Del Grossi, M.D. and Marques, V.P.M. (2009) O censo agropecuário de 2006 e a agricultura familiar no Brasil, Brasília: MDA.

Freyre, G. (2002) *Casa-Grande e Senzala*, Madrid: ALLCA XX. First published 1933.

Friedmann, H. (2005) 'From colonialism to green capitalism: Social movements and the emergence of food regimes', in F.H. Buttel and P. McMichael (eds) *New Directions in the Sociology of Global Development*, Leeds: Emerald, pp 227–64.

Fukuda-Parr, S. (ed) (2007) *The Gene Revolution: GM Crops and Unequal Development*, Abingdon: Routledge.

Garavaglia, C. and Swinnen, J. (2017) 'The craft beer revolution: An international perspective', *Choices*, 32(3): 1–8.

Geels, F.W. (2004) 'Understanding systems innovations: A critical literature review and a conceptual synthesis', in F.W. Geels, B. Elzen and K. Green (eds) *System Innovation and the Transition to Sustainability: Theory, Evidence and Policy*, Cheltenham: Edward Elgar Publishing, pp 19–47.

Geels, F.W., McMeekin, A., Mylan, J. and Southerton, D. (2015) 'A critical appraisal of sustainable consumption and production research: The reformist, revolutionary and reconfiguration positions', *Global Environmental Change*, 34: 1–12. https://doi.org/10.1016/j.gloenvcha.2015.04.013

Geller, M. (2017) '"Food revolution": Megabrands turn to small start-ups for big ideas', Reuters, [online] 24 May, Available from: http://www.reuters.com/article/idUSKBN18K19Q

Gendron, C. (2004) 'Le commerce équitable: Un nouveau mouvement social économique au cœur d'une autre mondialisation', *Les cahiers de la chaire économie et humanisme*, 2-2004, Montreal: Université du Québec à Montréal.

GFI (Good Food Institute). (2021) '2020 State of the industry report: Plant-based meat, eggs, and dairy', GFI, [online] May, Available from: https://gfi.org/wp-content/uploads/2021/05/COR-SOTIR-Plant-based-meat-eggs-and-dairy-2021-0504.pdf

GFI. (2023) '2022 State of the industry report: Cultivated meat and seafood', GFI [online] January, Available from: https://gfi.org/wp-content/uploads/2023/01/2022-Cultivated-Meat-State-of-the-Industry-Report-2-1.pdf

GFI APAC. (2020) 'Traditional Chinese plant-based companies leap into 2.0 protein era', GFI Asia Pacific, [online] 19 November, Available from: https://gfi-apac.org/traditional-chinese-plant-based-companies-leap-into-2-0-protein-era/

GFI APAC. (2021) 'Mapped: Singapore's plant-based meat B2B ecosystem', GFI Asia Pacific, [online] 14 December, Available from: https://gfi-apac.org/mapped-singapores-plant-based-meat-b2b-ecosystem/

Gilchrist, K. (2021) 'This multibillion-dollar company is selling lab-grown chicken in a world-first', CNBC Make It, [online] 1 March, Available from: https://www.cnbc.com/2021/03/01/eat-just-good-meat-sells-lab-grown-cultured-chicken-in-world-first.html

Glaeser, B. (ed) (1987) *The Green Revolution Revisited: Critique and Alternatives*, London: Routledge.

Glenn, E. and Yao, K. (2016) 'China loosens land transfer rules to spur larger, more efficient farms', Reuters, [online] 3 November, Available from: https://www.reuters.com/article/idUSKBN12Y09E/

Gonçalves, J.S. and Ramos, S.F.A. (2008) 'Algodão Brasileiro 1985–2005: surto de importação desencadeia mudanças estruturais na produção', *Informes Econômicos*, 38(1): 54–64.

Goodman, D. (2002) 'Rethinking food production-consumption: Integrative perspectives', *Sociologia Ruralis*. 42(4): 271–7. https://doi.org/10.1111/1467-9523.00216

Goodman, D. (2023) *Transforming Agriculture and Foodways: The Digital-Molecular Convergence*, Bristol: Bristol University Press.

Goodman, D., DuPuis, E.M. and Goodman, M.K. (2014) *Alternative Food Networks: Knowledge, Practice, and Politics*, Abingdon: Routledge.

Goodman, D., Sorj, B. and Wilkinson, J. (1987) *From Farming to Biotechnology: A Theory of Agro-Industrial Development*, London & New York: Blackwell.

Goodman, D., Sorj, B. and Wilkinson, J. (1990) *Da lavoura às biotecnologias: agricultura e indústria no sistema internacional*. Translated by C.E. Baesse de Souza and C. Schlottfeldt, Rio de Janeiro: Campus.

Gordon, E. (2022) 'Bye-bye firefly', *London Review of Books*, 44(9), [online] 12 May, Available from: https://www.lrb.co.uk/the-paper/v44/n09/edmund-gordon/bye-bye-firefly

Gordon-Smith, H. (2021) 'Vertical farming is headed for the "trough of disillusionment." Here's why that's a good thing', AgFunderNews, [online] 14 December, Available from: https://agfundernews.com/vertical-farming-is-headed-for-the-trough-of-disillusionment-heres-why-thats-a-good-thing

Gottlieb, R. and Joshi, A. (2010) *Food Justice*, Cambridge, MA: MIT Press.

Graeber, D. and Wengrow, D. (2021) *The Dawn of Everything: A New History of Humanity*, New York: Farrar, Straus and Giroux.

Granovetter, M. (1985) 'Economic action and social structure: The problem of embeddedness', *American Journal of Sociology*, 91(3): 481–510. https://www.jstor.org/stable/2780199

Grant, T. (2021) 'Explorando a produção de café na China', Perfect Daily Grind, [online] 3 May, Available from: https://www.perfectdailygrind.com/pt/2021/05/03/explorando-a-producao-de-cafe-na-china/

Gras, C. and Hernández, V. (eds) (2013) *El agro como negocio: Producción, sociedad y territorios en la globalización*, Buenos Aires: Editorial Biblos.

Graziano da Silva, J. (1982) *A modernização dolorosa: Estrutura agrária, fronteira agrícola e trabalhadores rurais no Brasil*, Rio de Janeiro: Zahar.

Greenpeace. (2007) 'How the palm oil industry is cooking the climate', Greenpeace, [online] November, Available from: https://www.greenpe ace.org/usa/wp-content/uploads/legacy/Global/usa/report/2010/2/ how-the-palm-oil-industry-is-c.pdf

Greenpeace. (2017) 'How the palm oil industry is still cooking the climate', Greenpeace, [online] November, Available from: https://www.greenpe ace.org/static/planet4-southeastasia-stateless/2019/04/0a48e8fb-0a48e 8fb-still-cooking-the-climate.pdf

Greenpeace European Unit. (2019) 'Feeding the problem: The dangerous intensification of animal farming in Europe', Greenpeace, [online] 12 February, Available from: https://www.greenpeace.org/static/planet4-eu-unit-stateless/2019/02/83254ee1-190212-feeding-the-problem-danger ous-intensification-of-animal-farming-in-europe.pdf

Green Queen Team. (2021) 'Q&A w/ Eugene Wang of Sophie's Bionutrients: Why we moved our production from Singapore to the Netherlands', Green Queen, [online] 12 November, Available from: https:// www.greenqueen.com.hk/sophies-bionutrients-eugene-wang/

Green Queen Team. (2023) 'RESPECTfarms: New project explores decentralizing cultivated meat by supporting farmers', Green Queen, [online] 15 January, Available from: https://www.greenqueen.com.hk/ decentralizing-cultivated-meat-respect-farmers/

Grichnik, D., Müller, E. and Schreiber, R. (2021) 'Alternative proteins: (Can) alternative proteins take over—one way out of the grand food challenges?' HSG FoodTech Lab, University St Gallen, Available from: https://cache. pressmailing.net/content/1df0576a-1eb4-475c-9009-f7029ab552a2/ White-Paper-Alternative-proteins.pdf

Grisa, C. (2018) 'Mudança nas políticas públicas para a agricultura familiar no Brasil', *Raízes*, 38(1): 36–50. https://doi.org/10.37370/raizes.2018.v38.37

Grisa, C. and Schneider, S. (2015) 'Três gerações de políticas públicas para a agricultura familiar e formas de interação entre sociedade e Estado no Brasil', in C. Grisa and S. Schneider (eds) *Políticas públicas de desenvolvimento rural no Brasil*, Porto Alegre: Editora da UFRGS, pp 19–50.

Grove, M. (2016) 'Sunqiao Urban Agricultural District', Sasaki, [online] 15 August, Available from: https://www.sasaki.com/projects/sunqiao-urban-agricultural-district/

Guanziroli, C., Romeiro, A., Buainain, A.M., di Sabbato, A. and Bittencourt, G. (2001) *Agricultura familiar e reforma agrária no século XXI*, Rio de Janeiro: Garamond.

Guimarães, A.P. (1968) *Quatro séculos de latifúndio*, Rio de Janeiro: Paz e Terra.

Gursel, I.V., Sturme, M., Hugenholtz, J., Bruins, M. (2022) 'Review and analysis of studies on sustainability of cultured meat', Wageningen: Wageningen Food & Biobased Research. https://doi.org/10.18174/563404

Guthman, J. and Biltekoff, C. (2021) 'Magical disruption? Alternative protein and the promise of dematerialization', *Environment and Planning E: Nature and Space*, 4(4): 1583–600. https://doi.org/10.1177/2514848620963125

Hall, C. (2020) 'Bayer, Temasek-based company Unfold enters vertical farming with $30m investment', Crunchbase News, [online] 12 August, Available from: https://news.crunchbase.com/startups/bayer-temasek-based-company-unfold-enters-vertical-farming-with-30m-investment/

Halliday, J. (2022) 'Controlled Environment Agriculture for sustainable development: a call for investment and innovation', *Urban Agriculture Magazine*, 38: 55–6, Available from: https://ruaf.org/2022/08/11/urban-agriculture-magazine-38-20-years-of-ruaf/

Harari, Y.N. (2014) *Sapiens: A Brief History of Humankind*, London: Harvill Secker.

Harding, R. (2020) 'Vertical farming finally grows up in Japan', Financial Times, [online] 23 January, Available from: https://www.ft.com/content/f80ea9d0-21a8-11ea-b8a1-584213ee7b2b

Heidemann, M.S., Molento, C.F.M., Reis, G.G. and Phillips, C.J.C. (2020) 'Uncoupling meat from animal slaughter and its impacts on human–animal relationships', *Frontiers in Psychology*, 11, article 1824. https://doi.org/10.3389/fpsyg.2020.01824

Henchion, M., Hayes, M., Mullen, A.M., Fenelon, M. and Tiwari, B. (2017) 'Future Protein Supply and Demand: Strategies and Factors Influencing a Sustainable Equilibrium', *Foods*, 6(7), 53. https://doi.org/10.3390/foods6070053

Henderson, R. (2020) *Reimagining Capitalism in a World on Fire*, New York: PublicAffairs.

Henderson, R.M. (2021) 'Changing the purpose of the corporation to rebalance capitalism', *Oxford Review of Economic Policy*, 37(4): 838–50. https://doi.org/10.1093/oxrep/grab034

Henesy, D. (2021) 'Almond milk: A medieval obsession', Seconds Food History, [online] 27 January, Available from: https://www.secondshistory.com/home/almond-milk-medieval-obsession

Henze, V. and Boyd, S. (2021) 'Plant-based Foods Market to Hit $162 Billion in Next Decade, Projects Bloomberg Intelligence', Bloomberg, [online] 11 August, Available from: https://www.bloomberg.com/company/press/plant-based-foods-market-to-hit-162-billion-in-next-decade-projects-bloomberg-intelligence/

Heredia, B., Palmeira, M., Leite., S.P. (2010) 'Sociedade e economia do "agronegócio" no Brasil', *Revista Brasileira de Ciências Sociais*, 25(74): 159–96.

Heynen, N., Kurtz, H.E. and Trauger, A. 'Food justice, hunger and the city', *Geography Compass*, 6:304–11. https://doi.org/10.1111/j.1749-8198.2012.00486.x

Hickman, G.W. (2019) 'International greenhouse vegetable production – statistics (2018 and 2019)', Cuesta Roble (Oak Hill) Consulting, [online] Available from: https://www.cuestaroble.com/statistics.html

Hindy, S. (2014) *The Craft Beer Revolution*. New York: Palgrave Macmillan.

HLPE. (2013) 'Biofuels and food security', Rome: FAO. https://openkn owledge.fao.org/server/api/core/bitstreams/3ae13a1c-0fae-4c33-b3c7-df5600b957ce/content

Ho, S. (2021a) 'U.S. animal agriculture subsidies soared in 2020 despite climate & health damage', Green Queen, [online] 16 April, Available from: https://www.greenqueen.com.hk/us-animal-agriculture-subsid ies-soared-in-2020-despite-climate-health-damage

Ho, S. (2021b) 'China establishes its first voluntary standard for plant-based meat products', Green Queen, [online] 21 April, Available from: https://greenqueen.com.hk/china-establishes-its-first-voluntary-standard-for-pla ntbased-meat-products/

Ho, S. (2021c) 'OmniPork slashes retail prices by double-digits & announces parity with pork', Green Queen, [online] 18 May, Available from: https://greenqueen.com.hk/omnipork-slashes-retail-prices-by-double-digits-announces-parity-with-pork/

Hoffman, R. (2015) 'A agricultura familiar produz 70% dos alimentos consumidos no Brasil?', *Segurança Alimentar e Nutricional*, 21(1): 417–21. https://doi.org/10.20396/san.v21i1.1386

Holm, L. and Møhl, M. (2000) 'The role of meat in everyday food culture: An analysis of an interview study in Copenhagen', *Appetite*, 34(3): 277–83. https://doi.org/10.1006/appe.2000.0324

Howard, E. (1902) *Garden Cities of To-Morrow*, London: Swan Sonnenschein & Co.

Howard, P.H. and Hendrickson, M.K. (2020) 'The state of concentration in global food and agriculture industries', in H. Herren and B. Haerlin (eds) *Transformation of Our Food Systems: The Making of a Paradigm Shift*, Washington, D.C.: IAASTD, pp 88–91.

Huang, Y. (2008) *Capitalism with Chinese Characteristics: Entrepreneurship and the State*, New York: Cambridge University Press.

ICLEI. (2013) 'Declaração de Solidariedade a Bogotá', ICLEI, [online] 20 December, Available from: https://americadosul.iclei.org/declaracao-de-solidariedade-a-bogota/

iJinshan. (2021) 'An orchard in Shanghai successfully grows bananas on water', WeChat, [online] 31 October, Available from: https://mp.weixin. qq.com/s/oUf-JztJUOD1koSn7vX1FA

IPES (International Panel of Experts on Sustainable Food Systems). (2017) 'Too Big to Feed'. Available from https://ipes-food.org/wp-content/uplo ads/2024/03/Concentration_FullReport.pdf

IPES. (2022) 'The Politics of Protein'. Available from: https://ipes-food. org/wp-content/uploads/2024/03/PoliticsOfProtein.pdf

Isaacson, W. (2022) *The Code Breaker: Jennifer Doudna, Gene Editing, and the Future of the Human Race*, New York: Simon & Schuster.

IstoÉ Dinheiro. (2016) 'Danone compra a WhiteWave Foods com o objetivo de liderar setor de alimentação orgânica', IstoÉ Dinheiro, [online] 7 July, Available from: https://istoedinheiro.com.br/danone-compra-a-whitew ave-foods-com-o-objetivo-de-liderar-setor-de-alimentacao-organica/

Jackson, L. (2021) 'France has become innovation nation for insect production', Global Seafood Alliance, [online] 26 July, Available from: https://www. globalseafood.org/advocate/france-has-become-innovation-nation-for-insect-production/

Jacobs, J. (1969) *The Economy of Cities*. New York: Knopf Doubleday.

Jank, M.S., Guo, P. and Miranda, S.H.G. (eds) (2020) *China-Brasil: Partnership on Agriculture and Food Security*, Piracicaba: ESALQ/USP.

Jardim Pinto, C.R. (2005) 'A sociedade civil e a luta contra a fome no Brasil (1993–2003)', *Sociedade e Estado*, 20(1): 195–228. https://doi.org/10.1590/S0102-69922005000100009

Jenkins, A. (2022) 'Resource sharing between vertical farms and the built environment', TU Delft, [online] 10 February, Available from: https:// www.tudelft.nl/en/stories/articles/resource-sharing-between-vertical-farms-and-the-built-environment

Jensen, M. (2001) 'History of hydroponics', University of Arizona Controlled Environment Agriculture Center, [online] 31 January, Available from: https://cales.arizona.edu/hydroponictomatoes/history.htm

Joly, P.-B. and Ducos, C. (1993) *Les artifices du vivant: Stratégies d'innovation dans l'industrie des semences*, Paris: Inra.

Jönsson, E. (2016) 'Benevolent technotopias and hitherto unimaginable meats: Tracing the promises of in vitro meat', *Social Studies of Science*, 46(5): 725–48. https://doi.org/10.1177/0306312716658561

Jönsson, E., Linné, T. and McCrow-Young, A. (2019) 'Many meats and many milks? The ontological politics of a proposed post-animal revolution', *Science as Culture*, 28(1): 70–97. https://doi.org/10.1080/09505431.2018.1544232.

Juma, C. (1989) *The Gene Hunters: Biotechnology and the Scramble for Seeds*, Princeton: Princeton University Press.

Jürkenbeck, K., Heumann, A. and Spiller, A. (2019) 'Sustainability matters: Consumer acceptance of different vertical farming systems', *Sustainability*, 11(15), 4502. https://doi.org/10.3390/su11154052

Kageyama, A. (1990) 'O novo padrão agrícola brasileiro: Do complexo rural aos complexos agroindustriais', in G.C. Delgado and W. Belik (eds) *Agricultura e políticas públicas*, Brasília: IPEA, pp 113–223.

Kaplinski, R., Terheggen, A. and Tijaja, J. (2010) 'What happens when the market shifts to China? The Gabon timber and the Thai cassava value chains', Policy Research working paper WPS5206, Washington, DC: World Bank.

Kateman, B. (2017) *The Reducetarian Solution*. Los Angeles: Tarcherperigee.

Kenney, M. (1988) *Biotechnology: The University-Industrial Complex*, New Haven, CT: Yale University Press.

Klapholz, S. (2019) 'Our commitment to nutrition and health: Sodium and the Impossible Burger', Impossible Foods, [online] 20 December, Available from: https://impossiblefoods.com/blog/sodium-and-the-impossible-burger

Klein, J. (2021) 'AeroFarms is trying to cultivate the future of vertical farming', GreenBiz, [online] 10 August, Available from: https://www.greenbiz.com/article/aerofarms-trying-cultivate-future-vertical-farming

Kloppenburg, J.R. (1988) *First the Seed: The political economy of plant biotechnology, 1492–2000*, Cambridge: Cambridge University Press.

Knell, M. (2021) 'The digital revolution and digitalized network society', *Review of Evolutionary Political Economy*, 2(1): 9–25. https://doi.org/10.1007/s43253-021-00037-4

Kremen, C. (2015) 'Reframing the landsparing/land-sharing debate for biodiversity conservation, *Annals of the New York Academy of Sciences*, 1355(1): 52–76. https://doi.org/10.1111/nyas.12845

Kurzweil, C. (2019) 'Consumidores Conscientes impulsionem vendas de produtos veganos', Euromonitor International, [online] 15 February, Available from: https://www.euromonitor.com/article/consumidores-conscientes-impulsionam-vendas-de-produtos-veganos

Ladner, P. (2011) *The Urban Food Revolution: Changing the Way We Feed Cities*, Gabriola Island, BC: New Society Publishers.

Lagneau, A., Barra, M. and Lecuir, G. (2015) *Agriculture urbaine: Vers une réconciliation ville-nature*, Lorient: Le passager clandestin.

Laing, R. (2021) 'Betting billions on the wrong farms', LinkedIn, [online] 12 August, Available from: https://www.linkedin.com/pulse/betting-billions-wrong-farms-rob-laing/

Lappé, F.M. (1971) *Diet for a Small Planet*, New York: Ballantine Books.

Lawrence, G. and Dixon, J. (2015) 'The political economy of agri-food: Supermarkets', in A. Bonanno and L. Busch (eds) *Handbook of the International Political Economy of Agriculture and Food*, Cheltenham: Edward Elgar Publishing, pp 213–31.

Lee, S. and Ham, S. (2021) 'Food service industry in the era of COVID-19: Trends and research implications', *Nutrition Research and Practice*, 15(Suppl 1): S22–S31. https://doi.org/10.4162/nrp.2021.15.S1.S22

Lerner, J. and Nanda, R. (2020) 'Venture capital's role in financing innovation: What we know and how much we still have to learn', *Journal of Economic Perspectives*, 34(3): 237–61. http://doi.org/10.1257/jep.34.3.237

Letterman, J. and White, T. (2020) 'U.S. Horticulture Operations Report $13.8 Billion in Sales', USDA/NASS, [online] 8 December, Available from: https://www.nass.usda.gov/newsroom/archive/2020/12-08-2020.php

Levkoe, C.Z. (2006) 'Learning democracy through food justice movements', *Agriculture and Human Values*, 23(1): 89–98. https://doi.org/10.1007/s10460-005-5871-5

Liebig, J. (1840) *Organic Chemistry in Its Applications to Agriculture and Physiology*, London: Taylor and Walton.

Liga Insights. (2022) 'Food Techs: As startups que atuam na alimentação' Liga Ventures, [online], 12 September, Available from: https://liga.ventures/insights/startups/food-techs-as-startups-que-atuam-na-alimentacao/

Lim, C.J. (2014) *Food City*, Abingdon: Routledge.

Lim, C.J. and Liu, E. (2019) *Smartcities, Resilient Landscapes and Eco-Warriors* (2nd edn), Abingdon: Routledge.

Lim, C.J., Tang, M., Bronner, P., Wang, J., Ng, G. and Cho, B. (2015) 'Food City: The Food Parliament', Bartlett School of Architecture, UCL, [online], Available from: https://www.ucl.ac.uk/bartlett/architecture/research/sustainable-urbanism-and-landscape/food-city-food-parliament

Liu, S., Zhang, M., Feng, F. and Tian, Z. (2020) 'Towards a "Green Revolution" for soybean', *Molecular Plant*, 13(5): 688–97. https://doi.org/10.1016/j.molp.2020.03.002

Lockie, S. (2002) '"The invisible mouth": Mobilizing "the consumer" in food production–consumption networks', *Sociologia Ruralis*, 42(4): 278–94. https://doi.org/10.1111/1467-9523.00217

Lohrberg, F., Licka, L., Scazzosi, L. and Tempe, A. (eds) (2020) *Urban Agriculture Europe*, Berlin: Jovis.

Lonkila, A. and Kaljonen, M. (2021) 'Promises of meat and milk alternatives: An integrative literature review on emergent research themes', *Agriculture and Human Values*, 38(3): 625–39. https://doi.org/10.1007/s10460-020-10184-9

Loria, K. (2017) 'Report: Smaller food brands outshine legacy competitors in innovation', Food Dive, [online] 22 May, Available from: https://www.fooddive.com/news/report-smaller-food-brands-outshine-legacy-competitors-in-innovation/443192/

Lu, M. (2021) 'The China multinational behind Oatly, the hottest oat milk brand in the U.S.', Nspirement, [online] 8 June, Available from: https://nspirement.com/2021/06/08/china-multinational-behind-oatly.html

Lucas, A. (2020) 'Beyond Meat enters grocery stores in mainland China through Alibaba partnership', CNBC, [online] 30 June, Available from: https://www.cnbc.com/2020/07/01/beyond-meat-enters-grocery-stores-in-mainland-china-through-alibaba-partnership.html

Lyson, T.A. (2004) Civic Agriculture: Reconnecting Farm, Food, and Community, Medford, MA: Tufts University Press.

Lyu, J. (2020) 'Agriculture 5.0 in China: New technology frontiers and the challenges to increase productivity', in M. Jank, P. Gui and S.H.G. de Miranda (eds) China-Brazil: Partnership on Agriculture and Food Security, Piracicaba: ESALQ/USP, pp 186–215.

Magnin, C. (2016) 'How big data will revolutionize the global food chain', McKinsey Digital, [online] 19 August, Available from: https://www.mckinsey.com/business-functions/mckinsey-digital/our-insights/how-big-data-will-revolutionize-the-global-food-chain

Magrini, M.-B., Anton, M., Chardigny, J.-M., Duc, G., Duru, M., Jeuffroy, M.-H., Meynard, J.-M., Micard, V. and Walrand, S. (2018) 'Pulses for sustainability: Breaking agriculture and food sectors out of lock-in', Frontiers in Sustainable Food Systems, 2, 64. https://doi.org/10.3389/fsufs.2018.00064

Malkan, S. (2020) 'Research from Tufts GDAE finds billion-dollar Alliance for a Green Revolution in Africa is not living up to its promises', U.S. Right to Know, [online] 20 July, Available from: https://usrtk.org/pesticides/gates-foundations-failing-green-revolution-in-africa-new-report/

Maluf, R.S., Zimmerman, S.A. and Jomalins, E. (2021) 'Emergência e evolução da política nacional de segurança alimentar e nutricional no Brasil (2003–2015)', Estudos Sociedade e Agricultura, 29(3): 517–44. https://doi.org/10.36920/esa-v29n3-2

Marsden, T., Flynn, A. and Harrison, M. (2000) Consuming Interests: The Social Provision of Food, London: UCL Press.

Marston, J. (2023) 'Brief: Container farming startup Freight Farms to go public for $147m via SPAC', AgFunder News, [online] 8 September, Available from: https://agfundernews.com/container-farming-tech-startup-freight-farms-to-go-public-via-spac

Martinez, A.A. (2006) 'Borracha: São Paulo é o maior produtor nacional', InfoBibos, [online] 20 March, Available from: http://www.infobibos.com.br/artigos/borracha/index.htm

Mascarenhas, G. (2007) 'O movimento do comércio justo e solidário no Brasil: Entre a solidariedade e o mercado', PhD thesis, CPDA/UFRRJ.

Mattinson, A. and Nott, G. (2020) 'Ocado boosts stake in vertical farming specialist Jones Food Co', The Grocer, [online] 28 August, Available from: https://www.thegrocer.co.uk/mergers-and-acquisitions/ocado-boosts-stake-in-vertical-farming-specialist-jones-food-co/647817.article

May, P., Boyd, E., Chang, M. and Veiga, F.C. (2005) 'Incorporando o desenvolvimento sustentável aos projetos de carbono florestal no Brasil e na Bolívia', *Estudos Sociedade e Agricultura*, 13(1): 5–50.

Maye, D. (2019) '"Smart food city": Conceptual relations between smart city planning, urban food systems and innovation theory', *City, Culture and Society*, 16: 18–24. https://doi.org/10.1016/j.ccs.2017.12.001

McBride, J., Berman, N. and Chatzky, A. (2020) 'China's massive Belt and Road Initiative', Council on Foreign Relations, [online] Last modified 2 February 2023, Available from: https://www.cfr.org/backgrounder/chinas-massive-belt-and-road-initiative

McClintock, N. (2010) 'Why farm the city? Theorizing urban agriculture through a lens of metabolic rift', *Cambridge Journal of Regions, Economy and Society*, 3(2): 191–207. https://doi.org/10.1093/cjres/rsq005

McGivney, A. (2020) '"Like sending bees to war": The deadly truth behind your almond milk obsession', The Guardian, [online] 8 January, Available from: https://www.theguardian.com/environment/2020/jan/07/honeybees-deaths-almonds-hives-aoe

McKay, B.M., Hall, R. and Liu, J. (eds) (2018) *Rural Transformations and Agro-Food Systems: The BRICS and Agrarian Change in the Global South*, Abingdon: Routledge.

McMichael, P. (2005) 'Global development and the corporate food regime', in F.H. Buttel and P. McMichael (eds) *New Directions in the Sociology of Global Development*, Leeds: Emerald, pp 265–99.

Medeiros, J.C. and Grisa, C. (2019) 'O Ministério do Desenvolvimento Agrário (MDA) e suas capacidades estatais na promoção do desenvolvimento rural', *Revista Campo-Território*, 14(34): 6–35.

Meinhold, B. (2013) 'Aeroponic vertical farm: High-Yield Terraced Rice Paddies For The Philippines', InHabitat, [online] 18 March, Available from: https://inhabitat.com/aeroponic-vertical-farm-high-yield-terraced-rice-paddies-for-the-philipines/

Mellaart, J. (1967) *Çatal Hüyük: A Neolithic Town in Anatolia*, New York: McGraw-Hill.

Mello, J.M.C. de. (1982) *O capitalismo tardio*, São Paulo: Brasiliense.

Mergulhão, A.D. (2018) 'Circuitos de produção da laranja no Brasil: Do cultivo aos produtos industriais destinados principalmente ao mercado internacional', *Estudos Geográficos*, 16(2): 141–55. https://doi.org/10.5016/estgeo.v16i2.13263

Meticulous Research. (2024) 'Edible insects market size, share, forecast, and trends analysis by product, insect type, application, and geography', Meticulous Research, [online] Last modified April 2024, Available from: https://meticulousresearch.com/product/edible-insects-market/-5156

Meyers, J. (2016) 'China's lucrative caffeine craze', BBC Worklife, [online] 29 June, Available from: https://www.bbc.com/worklife/article/20160 628-yuan-more-coffee-chinas-lucrative-caffeine-craze

Milman, O. and Leavenworth, S. 'China's plan to cut meat consumption by 50% cheered by climate campaigners', The Guardian, [online] 20 June, Available from: https://www.theguardian.com/world/2016/jun/20/chi nas-meat-consumption-climate-change

Mitidiero Junior, M.A., Barbosa, H.J.N. and de Sá, T.H. (2018) 'Quem produz comida para os brasileiros? 10 anos do censo agropecuário 2006', *Pegada: A Revista da Geografia do Trabalho*, 18(3): 7–77. https://doi.org/ 10.33026/peg.v18i3.5540

Mol, A.P.J. and Carter, N.T. (2006) 'China's environmental governance in transition', *Environmental Politics*, 15(2): 149–70. https://doi.org/10.1080/ 09644010600562765

Monbiot, G. (2022) *Regenesis*, London: Penguin.

Monteiro, A., Santos, S. and Gonçalves, P. (2021) 'Precision agriculture for crop and livestock farming—Brief review', *Animals*, 11(8): 2345. https:// doi.org/10.3390/ani11082345

Monteiro, C.A. and Cannon, G. (2012) 'The impact of transnational "big food" companies on the South: A view from Brazil', *PLoS Med*, 9(7): e1001252. https://doi.org/10.1371/journal.pmed.1001252

Morais-da-Silva, R.L., Reis, G.G., Sanctorum, H. and Molento, C.F.M. (2022) 'The social impacts of a transition from conventional to cultivated and plant-based meats: Evidence from Brazil', *Food Policy*, 111, 102337. https://doi.org/10.1016/j.foodpol.2022.102337

Morgan, K. and Sonnino, R. (2010) *The School Food Revolution: Public Food and the Challenge of Sustainable Development*, Abingdon: Routledge.

Mozaffarian, D., Angell, S.Y., Lang, T. and Rivera, J.A. (2018) 'Role of government policy nutrition – Barriers to and opportunities for heathier eating', *BMJ* 2018;361;k2426. https://doi.org/10.1136/bmj.k2426

Müller, J., Rassman, K. and Videiko, M. (eds) *Trypillia Mega-Sites and European Prehistory 4100–3400 BCE*, Abingdon: Routledge.

Mumford, L. (1961) *The City in History: Its Origins, Its Transformations, and Its Prospects*, San Diego: Harcourt, Brace and World.

Mylan, J., Morris, C., Beech, E. and Geels, F.W. (2019) 'Rage against the regime: Niche-regime interactions in the societal embedding of plant-based milk', *Environmental Innovation and Societal Transitions*, 31: 233–47. https:// doi.org/10.1016/j.eist.2018.11.001

Nassar, A.M., Zylbersztajn, D., Spers, E., Farina, E.M.M.Q. and Jank, M.S. *Cinco ensaios sobre a gestão de qualidade no agribusiness*, São Paulo: USP.

Natrajan, S. (2021) 'Urban agriculture, food security and sustainable urban food systems in China', Occasional paper 71, New Delhi: Institute of Chinese Studies. https://www.icsin.org/publications/urban-agriculture-food-security-and-sustainable-urban-food-systems-in-china

Naughton, B. (2006) *The Chinese Economy: Transitions and Growth*, Cambridge, MA: MIT.

Navarro, Z. (2014) 'Por que não houve (e nunca haverá) reforma agrária no Brasil?', in A.M. Buainain, E. Alves, J.M. da Silveira and Z. Navarro (eds) *O mundo rural no Brasil do século 21: A formação de um novo padrão agrário e agrícola*, Brasília: Unicamp/Embrapa, pp 695–724.

Nelson, K. (2019) 'Top consumer companies' palm oil sustainability claims go up in flames', Greenpeace, [online] 4 November, Available from: https://www.greenpeace.org/usa/news/top-consumer-companies-palm-oil-sustainability-claims-go-up-in-flames/

Neo, P. (2019) 'Healthier Milo: Nestlé Thailand invests US$6.6m in world-first "no added sugar" beverage version', FoodNavigator Asia, [online] 26 March, Available from: https://www.foodnavigator-asia.com/Article/2019/03/26/Healthier-Milo-Nestle-Thailand-invests-US-6.6m-in-world-first-no-added-sugar-beverage-version

Neslen, A. (2021) 'Vertical farming's sky-high ambitions cut short by EU organic rules', Politico, [online] 12 January, Available from: https://www.politico.eu/article/vertical-farming-eu-organic-rules-startups/

Nestlé. (2022) 'Our road to net zero', Nestlé, [online] 2 December, Available from: https://www.nestle.com/sustainability/climate-change/zero-environmental-impact

Nestlé CWA. (2018) 'Reducing sugar, sodium and fats', Nestlé CWA, [online] 22 March, Available from: http://www.nestle-cwa.com/en/cvs/impact/tastier-healthier/sugar-salt-fat

Newell, R. (2021) 'Grow your patent portfolio with vertical farming', Whitmer IP Group, [online] 9 August, Available from: https://www.whipgroup.com/blog/grow-your-patent-portfolio-with-vertical-farming/

Nex, S. (2018) 'The 10 biggest and best vertical farms', Maximum Yield, [online] 30 October, Archived at: https://web.archive.org/web/20221205084947/https://www.maximumyield.com/future-farming-the-biggest-and-best-vertical-farms/2/17389

Ng, W.S. (2017) 'Re-imagining future of vertical farming: Using modular design as the sustainable solution', Bachelors dissertation, University Sains Malaysia, Available from: https://issuu.com/ngwilszen/docs/re-imaging_future_of_vertical_farming-using_modula/34

O'Doherty Jensen, K. and Holm, L. (1999) 'Preferences, quantities and concerns: Socio-cultural perspectives on the gendered consumption of food', *European Journal of Clinical Nutrition*, 53(5): 351–9. https://doi.org/10.1038/sj.ejcn.1600767

OECD. (2016) 'Is precision agriculture the start of a new revolution?' in OECD (ed) 'Farm management practices to foster green growth', Paris: OECD Publishing, pp 137–59. https://doi.org/10.1787/978926 4238657-8-en

Olho No Araguaia. (2021) 'Maior fazenda vertical do mundo para suínos esta sendo concluída na China', Olho No Araguaia, [online] 11 July, Available from: https://olhonoaraguaia.com.br/negocios/maior-fazenda-vertical-do-mundo-para-suinos-esta-sendo-concluida-na-china/

Oliveira, D., Grisa, C. and Niederle, P. (2020) 'Inovações e novidades na construção de mercados para a agricultura familiar: Os casos da Rede Ecovida da Agroecologia e da RedeCoop', Redes, 25(1): 135–63. https://doi.org/10.17058/redes.v25i1.14248

Oliveira, G. de L.T. (2015) 'Chinese and other foreign investments in the Brazilian soybean complex', Brics Initiative for Critical Agrarian Studies (BICAS) working paper 9, Available from: https://www.tni.org/files/download/bicas_working_paper_9_oliveira.pdf

Orsini, F., Kahane, R., Nono-Womdim, R. and Gianquinto, G. (2013) 'Urban agriculture in the developing world: A review', Agronomy for Sustainable Development, 33: 695–720. https://doi.org/10.1007/s13 593-013-0143-z

Orzolek, M.D. (ed) (2017) A Guide to the Manufacture, Performance, and Potential of Plastics in Agriculture, Amsterdam: Elsevier.

Otero, G., Pechlaner, G. and Gürcan, E.C. (2015) 'The neoliberal diet: Fattening profits and people', in S.N. Haymes, M.V. de Haymes and R.J. Miller (eds) The Routledge Handbook of Poverty in the United States, New York: Routledge, pp 472–9.

Paiva, I. and Manduca, P.C. (2010) 'Análise da Diplomacia do Etanol no governo Lula a partir de diferentes perspectivas institucionalistas', João Pessoa: UFPB.

Panasonic Group. (2021) 'Growing vegetables in extreme conditions: Panasonic technology underpins a new model for plant factory systems', Panasonic Group, [online] 27 May, Available from: https://news.panasonic.com/glo bal/stories/969

Paris, H.S. and Janick, J. (2008) 'What the Roman emperor Tiberius grew in his greenhouses', in M. Pitrat (ed) Cucurbitaceae, Proceedings of the IXth EUCARPIA meeting on genetics and breeding of Cucurbitaceae, 21–24 May 2008, Avignon: INRA, pp 33–42.

Patel, R. (2012) 'The long Green Revolution', The Journal of Peasant Studies, 40(1): 1–63. https://doi.org/10.1080/03066150.2012.719224

Patton, D. (2020) 'Flush with cash, Chinese hog producer builds world's largest pig farm', Reuters, [online] 8 December, Available from: https://www.reuters.com/article/idUSKBN28H0C7/

Pearse, A. (1980) *Seeds of Plenty, Seeds of Want: Social and Economic Implications of the Green Revolution*, Oxford: Clarendon Press.

Perez-Aleman, P. and Sandilands, M. (2008) 'Building value at the top and the bottom of the global supply chain: MNC-NGO partnerships', *California Management Review*, 51(1): 24–49. https://doi.org/10.2307/41166467

Persson, J. 'Nordic harvest: Danish-Taiwanese indoor farming collaboration', ScandAsia, [online] 1 August, Available from: https://scandasia.com/nordic-harvest-danish-taiwanese-indoor-farming-collaboration/

Pessanha, L. and Wilkinson, J. (2005) *Transgênicos, recursos genéticos e segurança alimentar: O que está em jogo nos debates?*, Campinas: Armazém do Ipê.

Peters, A. (2019) 'If it looks like a steak and tastes like a steak, in this case, it's a mushroom', Fast Company, [online] 29 October, Available from: https://www.fastcompany.com/90421889/if-it-looks-like-a-steak-and-tastes-like-a-steak-in-this-case-its-a-mushroom

Pippinato, L., Gasco, L., Di Vita, G. and Mancuso, T. (2020) 'Current scenario in the European edible-insect industry: A preliminary study', *Journal of Insects as Food and Feed*, 6(4): 371–81. https://doi.org/10.3920/JIFF2020.0008

Plant Based Foods Association. (2022) '2022 U.S. Retail sales data for the plant-based foods industry', [online], Available from: https://plantbasedfoods.org/2022-retail-sales-data-plant-based-food

Poinski, M. (2022) 'Bel Brands gets into animal-free cheese with Perfect Day partnership', Food Dive, [online] 8 December, Available from: https://www.fooddive.com/news/bel-brands-animal-free-cheese-perfect-day/638258/

Pompeia, C. (2021) *Formação política do agronegócio*, São Paulo: Elefante.

Ponte, S. (2019) *Business, Power, and Sustainability in a World of Global Value Chains*, London: Zed Books.

Portilho, F. (2005) *Sustentabilidade ambiental, consumo e cidadania*, São Paulo: Cortez.

Poynton, S. (2016) 'Failure of Indonesia's palm oil commitment "not bad news" [commentary]', Mongabay. [online] 27 July, Available from: https://news.mongabay.com/2016/07/failure-of-indonesias-ipop-not-bad-news-commentary/

Prause, L., Hackfort, S. and Lindgren, M. (2021) 'Digitalization and the third food regime', *Agriculture and Human Values*, 38(3): 641–55. https://doi.org/10.1007/s10460-020-10161-2

Price, C. (2021) 'SEO cost calculator: How much should you budget for SEO services?', Search Engine Journal, [online] 7 May, Available from: https://www.searchenginejournal.com/seo-cost-calculator/264305/

Prior J. and Ward, K.J. (2016) 'Rethinking rewilding: A response to Jørgensen', *Geoforum*, 69: 132–5. https://doi.org/10.1016/j.geoforum.2015.12.003

ProVeg. (2022) 'New report: Farmers speak out about transition to alternative protein production', ProVeg International, [online] 22 June, Available from: https://proveg.org/press-release/new-report-farmers-speak-out-about-transition-to-alternative-protein-production/

Purdy, C. (2020) 'A startup says it's building a US pilot plant for cell-based meat', Quartz, [online] 22 January, Available from: https://qz.com/1788 892/memphis-meats-plans-to-build-the-first-us-cell-based-meat-plant

Quorn. (2019) 'A Revolutionary story', Quorn, [online] 4 May, Available from: https://www.quorn.co.uk/company

Radar Agtech. (2022) 'AgTech Brasil 2020/2021', RadarAgTech, [online], Available from: https://radaragtech.com.br/dados-2020-2021/

Ralph, E. (2021) 'The state of sugar and health taxes in 2021', Kerry, [online] 8 February, Available from: https://www.kerry.com/insights/kerrydigest/ 2018/the-state-of-sugar-and-health-taxes-around-the-world.html

Rama, R. (ed) (2008) *Handbook of Innovation in the Food and Drinks Industry*, New York: Haworth Press.

Rama, R. and Wilkinson, J. (2019) 'Innovation and disruptive technologies in the Brazilian agrofood sector,' *Systèmes alimentaires/Food Systems*, 4: 51–70. https://dx.doi.org/10.15122/isbn.978-2-406-09829-4.p.0051

Raphaely, T. and Marinova, D. (2014) 'Flexitarianism: A more moral dietary option', *International Journal of Sustainable Society*, 6(1/2): 189–211. http:// doi.org/10.1504/IJSSOC.2014.057846

Rastoin, J.-L., Ghersi, G., Perez, R. and Tozanli, S. (1998) *Structures, performances et stratégie des groupes agroalimentaires multinationaux*, Agrodata CD-ROM, Montpellier: CIHEAM-IAMM.

Raynolds, L.T., Murray, D. and Wilkinson, J. (eds) (2007) *Fair Trade: The Challenges of Transforming Globalization*, Abingdon: Routledge.

Reardon, T., Swinner, S., Vos, R. and Zilberman, D. (2021) 'Digital innovations accelerated by COVID-19 are revolutionizing food systems', International Food Policy Research Institute, [online] 8 June, Available from: https://www.ifpri.org/blog/digital-innovations-accelerated-covid-19-are-revolutionizing-food-systems-implications-un-food

Reece, J. (2018) 'Seeking food justice and a just city through local action in food systems: Opportunities, challenges, and transformation', *Journal of Agriculture, Food Systems and Community Development*, 8(B): 211–15. https:// doi.org/10.5304/jafscd.2018.08B.012

Reese, J. (2018) *The End of Animal Farming: How Scientists, Entrepreneurs, and Activists Are Building an Animal-Free Food System*, Boston, MA: Beacon Press.

Regalado, A. (2021) 'Is Ginkgo's synthetic-biology story worth $15 billion?' MIT Technology Review, [online] 24 August, Available from: https:// www.technologyreview.com/2021/08/24/1032308/is-ginkgos-synthe tic-biology-story-worth-15-billion/

Rego, J.L. (1932) *Menino de engenho*, reissued 2020, Lisbon: Global Editora.

Reis, G.G., Villar, E.G., Ryynänen, T. and Rodrigues, V.P. (2023) 'David vs Goliath: The challenges for plant-based meat companies competing with animal-based meat producers', *Journal of Cleaner Production*, 423: 138705. https://doi.org/10.1016/j.jclepro.2023.138705

Renfrew, C., Dixon, J.E. and Cann, J.R. (1968) 'Obsidian and the origins of trade', *Scientific American*, 218(3): 38–55. https://doi.org/10.1038/scientificamerican0368-38

Repko, M. (2022) 'Walmart makes an investment in vertical farming start-up Plenty', CNBC, [online] 25 January, Available from: https://www.cnbc.com/2022/01/25/walmart-makes-an-investment-in-vertical-farming-start-up-plenty.html

Reynolds, M. and Fassler, J. (2023) 'Insiders reveal major problems at lab-grown meat start-up Upside Foods', Wired, [online] 15 September, Available from: https://www.wired.com/story/upside-foods-lab-grown-chicken

Ridler, G. (2022) 'Vertical farming venture secures £21m investment', Food Manufacture, [online] 18 January, Available from: https://www.foodmanufacture.co.uk/Article/2022/01/18/Vertical-farming-venture-secures-21m-investment

Ritchie, H. and Roser, M. (2024) 'Half of the world's habitable land is used for agriculture', Our World in Data, [online] 16 February, Available from: https://ourworldindata.org/global-land-for-agriculture

Rocha, C. and Lessa, I. (2009) 'Urban governance for food security: The alternative food system in Belo Horizonte, Brazil', *International Planning Studies*, 14(4): 389–400. https://doi.org/10.1080/13563471003642787

Rosenfield, K. (2015) '75 projetos avançam no concurso "Reinventer Paris"', ArchDaily, [online] 21 September, Available from: https://www.archdaily.com.br/br/773837/75-projetos-avancam-no-concurso-reinventer-paris

Salviano, P. (2021) 'Evidências de práticas sustentáveis na produção da soja: Ações coletivas de atores locais no Município de Rio Verde-GO', PhD thesis, Rio de Janeiro: CPDA/UFRRJ.

Sample, I. (2024) 'Lab-grown "beef rice" could offer more sustainable protein source, say creators', Guardian, [online] 14 February, Available from: https://www.theguardian.com/environment/2024/feb/14/lab-grown-beef-rice-could-offer-more-sustainable-protein-source-say-creators

Sananbio. (2020) 'SANANBIO announces the availability of its unmanned vertical farming system UPLIFT to global growers', Cision NewsWire, [online] 16 July, Available from: https://www.newswire.ca/news-releases/sananbio-announces-the-availability-of-its-unmanned-vertical-farming-system-uplift-to-global-growers-832185351.html

Sauer, S. (2010) '"Reforma agrária de mercado" no Brasil: um sonho que se tornou dívida', *Estudos Sociedade e Agricultura*, 18(1): 98–126.

Schlosser, E. (2001) *Fast Food Nation: The Dark Side of the All-American Meal*, Boston: Houghton Mifflin.

Schneider, M. (2011) 'Feeding China's pigs: implications for the environment, China's small holder farmers and food security', Institute for Agriculture and Trade Policy [online] 17 May, Available from: www.iatp.org/sites/defa ult/files/2011_04_25_FeedingChinasPigs_0.pdf

Schneider, M. (2017) 'Dragon Head Enterprises and the state of agribusiness in China', *Journal of Agrarian Change*, 17(1): 3–21. doi.org/10.1111/joac.12151

Schneider, S. and Cassol, A. (2013) 'A agricultura familiar no Brasil', Serie Documentos de Trabalho 145, Grupo de Trabajo: Desarrollo con Cohesión Territorial, Programa Cohesión Territorial para el Desarrollo, Santiago: Rimisp.

Schurman, R.A. and Kelso, D.D.T. (eds) (2003) *Engineering Trouble: Biotechnology and Its Discontents*, Berkeley: University of California Press.

SCMP Style. (2018) 'How to show China's wine lovers a good time', South China Morning Post, [online] 22 September, Available from: https://www. scmp.com/magazines/style/travel-food/article/2164659/how-show-chi nas-wine-lovers-good-time

Sebrae. (2015) 'Alimentação saudável cria ótimas oportunidades de negócio', Sebrae, [online] 27 July, Available from: https://www.sebrae.com.br/sites/ PortalSebrae/artigos/segmento-de-alimentacao-saudavel-apresenta-oportu nidades-de-negocio

Seymour, F. (2017) 'A corporate giant's role in reducing climate change and promoting development: a conversation with Unilever's Paul Polman', Center for Global Development, [online] 15 February, Available from: http://www.cgdev.org/blog/corporate-giants-role-reducing-clim ate-change-and-promoting-development-conversation-unilever

Sexton, A.E. (2016) 'Alternative proteins and the (non)stuff of "meat"', *Gastronomica*, 16(3): 66–78. https://doi.org/10.1525/gfc.2016.16.3.66

Sexton, A.E. (2018) 'Eating for the post-Anthropocene: Alternative proteins and the biopolitics of edibility', *Transactions of the Institute of British Geographers*, 43(4): 586–600. https://doi.org/10.1111/tran.12253

Sexton, A.E. (2020) 'Food as software: Place, protein, and feeding the world Silicon Valley-style', *Economic Geography*, 96(5): 449–69. https://doi.org/ 10.1080/00130095.2020.1834382

Shahbandeh, M. (2022) 'Pork exports worldwide in 2022 by leading country', Statista, [online], Available from: https://statista.com/statistics/ 237619/export-of-pork/

Shapiro, Paul. (2018) *Clean Meat: How Growing Meat Without Animals Will Revolutionize Dinner and the World*, New York: Gallery Books.

SharathKumar, M., Heuvelink, E. and Marcelis, L.F.M. (2020) 'Vertical farming: Moving from genetic to environmental modification', *Trends in Plant Science*, 25(8): 724–7. https://doi.org/10.1016/j.tplants.2020.05.012

Sharma, S. (2014) 'The need for feed: China's demand for industrial meats and its impacts', Minneapolis, MN: IATP.

Sherratt, A. (2005) 'The obsidian trade in the Near East, 14,000 to 6500 BC', ArchAtlas, [online] 23 May, Available from: https://www.archatlas.org/journal/asherratt/obsidianroutes/

Shove, E., Pantzar, M. and Watson, M. (2012) *The Dynamics of Social Practice: Everyday Life and How It Changes*, London: Sage.

Sijtsema, S.J., Dagevos, H., Nassar, G., van Haster de Winter, M. and Snoek, H.M. (2021) 'Capabilities and opportunities of flexitarians to become food innovators for a healthy planet: Two explorative studies', *Sustainability*, 13(20), 11135. https://doi.org/10.3390/su132011135

Silicon Canals. (2020) 'These 10 promising insect-focused food tech startups in Europe aim to redefine the food chain', Silicon Canals, [online] 12 October, Available from: https://siliconcanals.com/news/startups/insect-focused-food-tech-startups-europe/

Silva, B. (2022) 'Unilever quer comprar divisão da GSK, mas tem oferta bilionária recusada: entenda a guerra dos dois gigantes', IstoÉ Dinheiro, [online] 21 January, Available from: https://istoedinheiro.com.br/unilever-compra-uma-batalha/

Silva, S. (1976) *Expansão cafeeira e origens da indústria no Brasil*, São Paulo: Alfa-Ômega.

Sinclair, U. (1906) *The Jungle,* New York: Doubleday.

Singer, P. (1975) *Animal Liberation: A New Ethics for Our Treatment of Animals*, New York: Avon Books.

Sippel, S.R. and Dolinga, M. (2023) 'Constructing agri-food for finance: Startups, venture capital and food future imaginaries', *Agriculture and Human Values*, 40(2): 475–88.

Solidaridad. (2017) 'China's soy crushing industry: Impacts on the global sustainability agenda', Solidaridad, [online] 20 June, Available from: http://www.solidaridadnetwork.org/publications/chinas-soy-crushing-industry-impacts-on-global-sustainability-agenda/

Solis, R.S. (2006) 'America's first city? The case of the Late Archaic Caral', in W.H. Isbel and H. Silverman (eds) *Andean Archaeology III: North and South*, Cham: Springer, pp 28–66. https://doi.org/10.1007/0-387-28940-2_3

Somain, R. and Droulers, M. (2016) 'A seringueira agora é paulista', *Confins*, 27. https://doi.org/10.4000/confins.10906

Sonnino, R. (2009) 'Feeding the city: Towards a new research and planning agenda', *International Planning Studies*, 14(4): 425–35. https://doi.org/10.1080/13563471003642795

Sorj, B. (1980) *Estados e classes sociais no Brasil*, Rio de Janeiro: Zahar.

Southey, F. (2021) 'Has science cracked the world's first animal-free egg through fermentation?', FoodNavigator Europe, [online] 9 February, Available from: https://www.foodnavigator.com/Article/2021/02/09/Clara-Foods-on-cracking-the-world-s-first--animal-free-egg-white.

Souza Martins, J. de. (2003) 'A reforma agrária no segundo mandato de Fernando Henrique Cardoso', *Tempo Social,* 15(2): 141–75. https://doi.org/10.1590/S0103-20702003000200006

Specht, K., Weith, T., Swoboda, K. and Siebert, R. (2016) 'Socially acceptable urban agriculture businesses', *Agronomy for Sustainable Development,* 36, 17. https://doi.org/10.1007/s13593-016-0355-0

Spencer, C. (2016) *Vegetarianism: A History*, London: Grub Street.

Starostinetskaya, A. (2021) 'Perfect Day raises $350 million ahead of IPO, announces dairy-identical cheese label', VegNews, [online] 1 October, Available from: https://vegnews.com/2021/10/perfect-day-cheese-label

State Council, PRC. (2021) 'New protein can lessen reliance on imported soybeans', ENGLISH.GOV.CN, [online] 1 November, Available from: https://english.www.gov.cn/news/topnews/202111/01/content_WS617f3caac6d0df57f98e4596.html

Steele, C. (2013) *Hungry City: How Food Shapes Our Lives*, New York: Vintage.

Steffen, L. (2021) 'Singapore aims to lead the world in lab-grown meat', Intelligent Living, [online] 16 November, Available from: https://www.intelligentliving.co/singapore-lead-world-in-lab-grown-meat/

Stengel, G. (2018) 'How Snow Monkey is to ice cream what Chobani is to Yogurt', Forbes, [online] 25 April, Available from: https://www.forbes.com/sites/geristengel/2018/04/25/how-snow-monkey-is-to-ice-cream-what-chobani-is-to-yogurt/

Stephens, N. and Ruivenkamp, M. (2016) 'Promise and ontological ambiguity in the *in vitro* meat imagescape: From laboratory myotubes to the cultured burger', *Science as Culture*, 25(3): 327–55. https://doi.org/10.1080/09505431.2016.1171836

Stuart, T. (2008) *The Bloodless Revolution: Radical Vegetarianism and the Discovery of India*, New York: W.W. Norton & Co.

Stucchi, A. (2023) 'Startup vegana levanta US$ 3 milhões e expandirá para o Brasil', VeganBusiness, [online] 17 September, Available from: https://veganbusiness.com.br/startup-vegana/

Suescan Pozas, N. (2020) 'Fermentation can help build a more efficient and sustainable food system – here's how', World Economic Forum, [online] 19 November, Available from: https://www.weforum.org/agenda/2020/11/fermentation-can-help-build-a-more-efficient-and-sustainable-food-system-here-s-how/

Sun, L., Ye, L.T. and Reed, M.R. (2020) 'The impact of income growth on quality structure improvement of imported food: Evidence from China's firm-level data', *China Agricultural Economic Review*, 12(4): 647–71. https://doi.org/10.1108/CAER-03-2019-0055

SustainFi. (2022) 'The top 9 vertical farming stocks to buy in 2022', SustainFi, [online] 23 April, Archived at: https://web.archive.org/web/20220517033549/https://sustainfi.com/articles/investing/vertical-farming-stocks/

Tan, A. (2021) 'S'pore high-tech farms seek to export not just produce but their technology too', The Straits Times, [online] 17 March, Available from: https://www.straitstimes.com/singapore/environment/more-than-just-produce-high-tech-farms-in-singapore-seek-to-export-their

Tanga, C.M., Egonyu, J.P., Beesigamukama, D., Niassy, S., Emily, K., Magara, H.J.O., Omuse, E.R., Subramanian, S. and Ekesi, S. (2021) 'Edible insect farming as an emerging and profitable enterprise in East Africa', *Current Opinion in Insect Science*, 48: 64–71. https://doi.org/10.1016/j.cois.2021.09.007

Tantalaki, N., Souravles, S. and Roomeliotis, M. (2019) 'Data-driven decision making in precision agriculture: The rise of big data in agricultural systems', *Journal of Agriculture and Food Information*, 20(4): 344–80. https://doi.org/10.1080/10496505.2019.1638264

Tao, Q., Ding, H., Wang, H. and Cui, X. (2021) 'Application research: Big data in the food industry', *Foods*, 10(9): 2203. https://doi.org/10.3390/foods10092203

Tavares, M.C. (1998) *Acumulação de capital e industrialização no Brasil* (3rd edn), São Paulo: Unicamp.

Temin, P. (2012) *The Roman Market Economy*, Princeton, NJ: Princeton University Press.

Terán, A. and Cessna, J. (2021) 'Farm milk components and their use among dairy products have shifted over time', USDA Economic Research Service, [online] 9 August, Available from: https://www.ers.usda.gov/amber-waves/2021/august/farm-milk-components-and-their-use-among-dairy-products-have-shifted-over-time/

Terazono, E. and Evans, J. (2022) 'Has the appetite for plant-based meat already peaked?', Financial Times, [online] 26 January, Available from: https://www.ft.com/content/996330d5-5ffc-4f35-b5f8-a18848433966

Ter Beek, V. (2020) 'China's pig industry will rise like a phoenix', Pig Progress, [online] 8 April, Available from: https://www.pigprogress.net/health-nutrition/chinas-pig-industry-will-rise-like-a-phoenix/

Teixeira, C.D., Marchioni, D.M., Motta, V.W., Chaves, V.M., Gomes, S.M. and Jacob, M.C.M. (2024) 'Flexitarians in Brazil: Who are they, what do they eat, and why?', *Appetite*, 192, article 107093. https://doi.org/10.1016/j.appet.2023.107093

Testa, V.M., de Nadal, R., Mior, L.C., Baldissera, I.T. and Cortina, N. (1996) *O desenvolvimento sustentável do Oeste Catarinense: proposta para discussão*, Santa Catarina: Epagri.

Thompson, F.M.L. (1968) 'The Second Agricultural Revolution, 1815–1880', *Economic History Review*, 21(1): 62–77.

Thorpe, D.K. (2014) 'How China leads the world in indoor farming', SmartCities Dive, [online] 15 September, Available from: https://www. smartcitiesdive.com/ex/sustainablecitiescollective/chinas-indoor-farm ing-research-feed-cities-leads-world/409606/

TOP. (2022) 'Ranking TOP 100 open corps', TOP Open Startups, [online] Available from: https://www.openstartups.net/site/ranking/rankings-corps.html

Tracxn. (2024) 'AgriTech startups in Singapore', Tracxn, [online] Last modified 17 April 2024, Available from: https://tracxn.com/d/explore/ agritech-startups-in-singapore/__GrUYu_scQ6k05S-MOlUGgNND 2xz_KXLwKgh-gZRyC80/companies

Tubb, C. and Seba, T. (2019) *Rethinking Food and Agriculture 2020–2030: The Second Domestication of Plants and Animals, the Disruption of the Cow, and the Collapse of Industrial Livestock Farming*. London: RethinkX.

Tucker, C. (2020) 'Berlin-based Infarm raises €144 million during pandemic to grow largest urban vertical farming network in the world', EU-Startups, [online] 17 September, Available from: https://www.eu-startups.com/ 2020/09/berlin-based-infarm-raises-e144-million-during-pandemic-to-grow-largest-urban-vertical-farming-network-in-the-world/

Turi, J.B. (2021) 'Lab-grown meat is coming and has billions in VC backing. But will consumers bite?', Crunchbase News, [online] 2 November, Available from: https://news.crunchbase.com/startups/lab-grown-meat-startups-venture-investment/

UNDP. (1996) *Urban Agriculture: Food, Jobs and Sustainable Cities. United Nations Development Program*, Publication Series for Habitat II, Volume One. UNDP, New York.

UNDP. (2021) 'Precision agriculture for smallholder farmers', Singapore: United Nations Development Programme, Available from: https://www.undp.org/sites/g/files/zskgke326/files/2022-01/ UNDP-Precision-Agriculture-for-Smallholder-Farmers-V2.pdf

Unilever. (2022) *Purpose-led, Future-fit: Annual Report and Accounts 2020*. Available from: https://www.unilever.com/files/92ui5egz/production/ 372ab0178e9555aa5010f15aed8295af77149fe3.pdf

USDHHS and USDA. (2016) 'Dietary Guidelines for Americans 2015–2020: Eighth Edition', Dietary Guidelines for Americans, [online] 7 January, Available from: https://www.dietaryguidelines.gov/sites/default/ files/2019-05/2015-2020_Dietary_Guidelines.pdf

Valceschini, E. and Nicolas, F. (eds) (1995) *Agro-alimentaire: Une économie de la qualité*, Paris: INRA.

Van de Weele, C. and Tramper, J. (2014) 'Cultured meat: Every village its own factory?', *Trends in Biotechnology*, 32(6): 294–6. https://doi.org/10.1016/j.tibtech.2014.04.009

Van Gerrewey, T., Boon, N. and Geelen, D. (2022) 'Vertical Farming: The only way is up?', *Agronomy*, 12(2): 2. https://doi.org/10.3390/agronomy12010002

Vegconomist. (2020) 'David Yeung: "This crisis creates a great window of opportunity for the plant-based food industry"', Vegconomist, [online] 24 February, Available from: https://vegeconomist.com/interviews/david-yeung-this-crisis-creates-a-great-window-for-the-plant-based-food-industry/

Vegconomist. (2021a) 'Dao Foods announces second incubator cohort, including cell-cultured lobster startup', Vegconomist, [online] 23 August, Available from: https://vegconomist.com/startups-accelerators-incubators/dao-foods-announces-second-incubator-cohort-including-cell-cultured-lobster-startup/

Vegconomist. (2021b) 'Ingredion: "It is the dawn of a new era, and we are helping our clients lead the way"', Vegconomist, [online] 16 November, Available from: https://vegconomist.com/food-and-beverage/protein/ingredion-it-is-the-dawn-of-a-new-era-and-we-are-helping-our-clients-lead-the-way/

Veiga, J.E. de. (1991) *O desenvolvimento agrícola: Uma visão histórica*, São Paulo: Edusp.

Viegas, C.A.S. (2005) 'Fusões e aquisições na indústria de alimentos e bebidas no Brasil', PhD thesis, São Paulo: USP.

Vigorito, R. (1983) 'Critérios metodológicos para el estúdio de complejos agroindustriales', in *El Desarrollo agroindustrial y la economía internacional*, Mexico City: Dirección General de Desarrollo Agroindustrial, pp 23–42.

Viljoen, A. and Bohn, K. (2014) *Second Nature Urban Agriculture: Designing Productive Cities*, Abingdon: Routledge.

Vogt, M.A.B. (2021) 'Agricultural wilding: Rewilding for agricultural landscapes through an increase in wild productive systems', *Environmental Management*, 284, 112050. https://doi.org/10.1016/j.jenvman.2021.112050

Von Thünen, J.H. (1826) *The Isolated State*, translated by C.M. Wartenberg, reissued 1966, Oxford: Pergamon Press.

Wakabayashi, D. and Fu, C. (2023) 'China's bid to improve food production? Giant towers of pigs', New York Times, [online] 8 February, Available from: https://www.nytimes.com/2023/02/08/business/china-pork-farms.html

Watrous, M. (2017) 'Danone seals the deal with WhiteWave', Food Business News, [online] 14 April, Available from: https://www.foodbusinessnews.net/articles/9197-danone-seals-the-deal-with-whitewave.

Watson, E. (2021) 'Pea-protein fueled Ripple Foods raises $60m in series E, plans move into overseas markets', FoodNavigator USA, [online] 23 September, Available from: https://www.foodnavigator-usa.com/Article/2021/09/23/Pea-protein-fueled-Ripple-Foods-raises-60m-in-series-E-plans-move-into-overseas-markets

Watson, E. (2022) '"Proudly genetically modified..." Moolec "molecular farming" co gears up to launch meat proteins from GM crops', FoodNavigator USA, [online] 25 April, Available from: https://www.foodnavigator-usa.com/Article/2022/04/25/Proudly-genetically-modified-Moolec-molecular-farming-co-gears-up-to-launch-meat-proteins-from-GM-crops

Watson, E. (2023) 'Meatable CEO: "We believe we have the fastest process in the field to make cultivated meat"', AgFunder News, [online] 30 May, Available from: https://agfundernews.com/%F0%9F%8E%A5-meatable-ceo-we-believe-we-have-the-fastest-process-in-the-field-to-make-cultivated-meat

Weber, M. (1958) *The City*, New York: The Free Press.

Wesz Júnior, V.J. (2014) 'O mercado da soja no Brasil e na Argentina: semelhanças, diferenças e interconexões', *Século XXI: Revista das Ciências Sociais*, 4(1): 114–61. dx.doi.org/10.5902/2236672515647

Wesz, V.J., Escher, F. and Fares, T.M. (2023) 'Why and how is China reordering the food regime? The Brazil-China soy-meat complex and COFCO's global strategy in the Southern Cone', The Journal of Peasant Studies, 50(4): 1376–404. https://doi.org/10.1080/03066150.2021.1986012

White, S. (2017) 'Manufacturers to withdraw soft drinks from EU schools from 2018', Euractiv, [online] 6 September, Available from: https://www.euractiv.com/section/agriculture-food/news/manufacturers-to-withdraw-soft-drinks-from-eu-schools-from-2018/

WHO. (2013) 'Global action plan for the prevention and control of noncommunicable diseases 2013–2020', WHO, [online] 14 November, Available from: https://www.who.int/publications/i/item/9789241506236

WHO. (2020) 'Healthy diet', WHO, [online] 29 April, Available from: https://www.who.int/news-room/fact-sheets/detail/healthy-diet

Wild, F., Czerny, M., Janssen, A.M., Žunabović, M., Kole, A.P.W. and Domig, K.J. (2014) 'The evolution of a plant-based alternative to meat: From niche markets to widely accepted meat alternatives', *Agro Food Industry Hi Tech*, 25(1): 45–9.

Wilkinson, J. (1993) 'Adjusting to a demand oriented food system: New directions for biotechnology innovation', *Agriculture & Human Values*, 10: 31–9. https://ageconsearch.umn.edu/record/244104/files/CESR-24-25-131-142.pdf.

Wilkinson, J. (1996) *Estudo da competitividade da indústria brasileira: o complexo agroindustrial*, Rio de Janeiro: Centro Edelstein de Pesquisa Social.

Wilkinson, J. (1997) 'Mercosul e a produção familiar: Abordagens teóricas e estratégias alternativas', *Estudos Sociedade e Agricultura*, 5(1): 25–50.

Wilkinson, J. (1999) 'Perfis emergentes no setor agroalimentar', in R.S. Maluf and J. Wilkinson (eds) *Restruturação do sistema agroalimentar: questões metodológicas e de pesquisa*, Rio de Janeiro: Mauad.

Wilkinson, J. (2000) 'Demandas tecnológicas, competitividade e inovação no sistema agroalimentar do Mercosul: ampliado', Procisur/BID. https://repositorio.iica.int/handle/11324/10074

Wilkinson, J. (2002) 'The final foods industry and the changing face of the global agro-foods system', *Sociologia Ruralis*, 42(4): 329–46.

Wilkinson, J. (2010) 'Recognition and Redistribution in the Renegotiation of Rural Space', in M.K. Goodman, D. Goodman and M. Redclift (eds) *Consuming Space: Placing Consumption in Perspective*, Farnham: Ashgate, pp 97–120.

Wilkinson, J. (2011) 'From fair trade to responsible soy: Social movements and the qualification of agrofood markets', *Environment & Planning A: Economy and Space*, 43(9): 2012–26. https://doi.org/10.1068/a43254

Wilkinson, J. (2021) 'Cidades e as suas estratégias alimentares em uma perspectiva histórica: O caso brasileiro no passado e na atualidade', *Futuribles*, 4(4): 39–59 https://www.cairn-mundo.info/revista-futuribles-2021-PT4-page-39.htm

Wilkinson, J. (2022) 'O sistema agroalimentar global e brasileiro face à nova fronteira tecnológica e às novas dinâmicas geopolíticas e de demanda', Textos para discussão 84, Rio de Janeiro: Saúde Amanhã, Fiocruz.

Wilkinson, J. and Herrera, S. (2010) 'Biofuels in Brazil: Debates and impacts', *Journal of Peasant Studies*, 37(4): 749–68. https://doi.org/10.1080/03066150.2010.512457

Wilkinson, J. and Lopane, A.R.M. (2018) 'From urban agriculture to urban and metropolitan food systems', in P.V. Preiss and S. Schneider (eds) *Proceedings of the Third International Conference on Agriculture and Food in an Urbanizing Society, 17–21 September 2018, Porto Alegre, Brazil*, UFRGS.

Wilkinson, J. and Pereira, P. (2018) 'Soja brasileña: nuevos patrones de inversión, financiamiento y regulación', in M. Ramírez and S. Schmalz (eds) *¿Fin de la bonanza? Entradas, salidos y encrucijadas del extractivismo*, Buenos Aries: Editorial Biblos, pp 201–18.

Wilkinson, J. and Rama, R. (2012) 'Asian agribusiness investment in Latin America with case studies from Brazil', in G. King, J.C. Mattos, N. Mulder and O. Rosales (eds) *The Changing Nature of Asian-Latin American Economic Relations*, Santiago: CEPAL, pp 33–73.

Wilkinson, J. and Wesz Júnior, V.J. (2013) 'Underlying issues in the emergence of China and Brazil as major global players in the South–South trade and investment axis', *International Journal of Technology Management and Sustainable Development*, 12(3): 245–60. https://doi.org/10.1386/tmsd.12.3.245_1

Wilkinson, J., Cerdan, C. and Dorigon, C. (2017) 'Geographical indications and "origin" products in Brazil – The interplay of institutions and networks', *World Development*, 98: 82–92. https://doi.org/10.1016/j.worlddev.2015.05.003

Wilkinson, J., Escher, F. and Garcia, A. (2022) 'The Brazil–China nexus in agrofood: What is at stake in the future of the animal protein sector', *International Quarterly for Asian Studies*, 53(2): 251–77. https://doi.org/10.11588/iqas.2022.2.13950

Wilkinson, J., Niederle, P.A. and Mascarenhas, G.C. (eds) (2016) *O sabor da origem: Produtos territorializados na nova dinâmica dos mercados alimentares*, Rio de Janeiro: Escritos.

Wilkinson, J., Wesz Júnior, V.J. and Lopane, A.R.M. (2016) 'Brazil and China: The agribusiness connection in the Southern Cone context', *Third World Thematics*, 1(5): 726–45. https://doi.org/10.1080/23802014.2016.1259581

Willet, W., Rockström, J., Loken, B., Springmann, M., Lang, T. et al (2019) 'Food in the Anthropocene: The EAT-*Lancet* Commission on healthy diets for a sustainable food system', *Lancet Commissions*, 393(10170): 447–92. https://doi.org/10.1016/S0140-6736(18)31788-4

Williams, R. (1973) *The Country and the City*, Oxford: Oxford University Press.

Williamson, M. (2002) 'UK Supermarkets united in opposition to GM foods ad ingredients', IATP, [online], 6 January, Available from: www.iatp.org/news/uk-supermarkets-united-in-continued-opposition-to-gm-foods-and-ingredients

Wilson, B. (2022) 'The irreplaceable', *London Review of Books*, 44(12), [online] 23 June, Available from: https://www.lrb.co.uk/the-paper/v44/n12/bee-wilson/the-irreplaceable

Winne, M. (2019) *Food Town USA: Seven Unlikely Cities That Are Changing the Way We Eat*, Washington, DC: Island Press.

Wolfert, S., Ge, L., Verdouw, C. and Bogaardt, M.-J. (2017) 'Big Data in Smart Farming – A review', *Agricultural Systems*, 153: 69–80. https://doi.org/10.1016/j.agsy.2017.01.023

World Bank Group. (2021) *Insect and Hydroponic Farming in Africa: The New Circular Food Economy*, Washington, DC: World Bank.

Wunsch, N.-G. (2022) 'Share of consumers who consider themselves vegan or vegetarian in the United States as of June 2018, by age group', Statista, [online] 27 January, Available from: https://www.statista.com/statistics/738851/vegan-vegetarian-consumers-us/

Xiaosheng, G. (2018) 'China's evolving image in international climate negotiation: From Copenhagen to Paris', *China Quarterly of International Strategic Studies*, 4(2): 213–39. https://doi.org/10.1142/S2377740018500112

Xie, J., Yu, J., Chen, B., Feng, Z., Lyu, J., Hu, L., Gan, Y. and Siddique, K.H.M. (2018) 'Gobi agriculture: An innovative farming system that increases energy and water use efficiencies: A review', *Agronomy for Sustainable Development*, 38(62) https://doi.org/10.1007/s13593-018-0540-4

Yakowicz, W. (2021) 'U.S. Cannabis Sales Hit Record $17.5 Billion As Americans Consume More Marijuana Than Ever Before', Forbes, [online] 3 March, Available from: https://www.forbes.com/sites/willyakowicz/2021/03/03/us-cannabis-sales-hit-record-175-billion-as-americans-consume-more-marijuana-than-ever-before/

Yoon, S.J. and Woudstra, J. (2007) 'Advanced horticultural techniques in Korea. The earliest documented greenhouses', *Garden History*, 35(1): 68–84. https://www.jstor.org/stable/25472355

Zaraska, M. (2016) *Meathooked: The History and Science of Our 2.5 Million-Year Obsession with Meat*, New York: Basic Books.

Zelizer, V.A. (1994) *The Social Meaning of Money: Pin Money, Paychecks, Poor Relief, and Other Currencies*, New York: Basic Books

Zhan, S. (2019) *The Land Question in China*, Abingdon: Routledge.

Zhang, H. (2018) *Securing the 'Rice Bowl': China and Global Food Security*, Singapore: Palgrave Macmillan. https://doi.org/10.1007/978-981-13-0236-7

Zhang, T. (2020) 'Xi's remarks are encouraging but alternative protein a long game in China', Just Food Magazine, [online] 23 April, Available from: https://just-food.nridigtal.com/just_food_apr22/china_alternative_protein_market

Zhang, T. (2022) 'What Starfield's $100 million funding round says about China's plant-based market', Vegconomist, [online] 14 February, Available from: https://vegconomist.com/guest-posts/what-starfields-100-million-funding-round-says-about-chinas-plant-based-market/

Zimberoff, L. (2021) *Technically Food: Inside Silicon Valley's Mission to Change What We Eat*, New York: Abrams Press.

Zink, K.D. and Lieberman, D.E. (2016) 'Impact of meat and Lower Paleolithic food processing techniques on chewing in humans', *Nature*, 531: 500–503. https://doi.org/10.1038/nature16990

Zylbersztajn, D. and Scare, R.F. (eds) (2003) *Gestão de Qualidade no Agribusiness: Estudos e Casos*, São Paulo: Atlas.

Index

References in **bold** type refer to tables.